Barbed Wire Kisses

The Jesus and Mary Chain Story

ZOË HOWE

Polygon

First published in Great Britain in 2014 by Polygon, an imprint of Birlinn Ltd.
This paperback edition published in 2015 by Polygon

Birlinn Ltd
West Newington House
10 Newington Road
Edinburgh
EH9 1QS

www.polygonbooks.co.uk

ISBN 978 1 84697 331 4

eBook ISBN 978 0 85790 665 6

British Library Cataloguing-in-Publication Data
A catalogue record for this book is available on
request from the British Library.

Typeset in Sabon by Hewer Text UK Ltd, Edinburgh

Printed and bound by Grafica Veneta

Praise for *Barbed Wire Kisses* and Zoë Howe:

'A great book. Really funny and honest' ALAN McGEE

'Genuinely great' NEIL TAYLOR (formerly NME)

'Howe does a fantastic job at unveiling a band that have been, up until now, shrouded in mystery' THE QUIETUS

'Zoë Howe is one of our favourite music writers – a great writer who is in love with rock'n'roll and one who can make the essence and magic of the dark stuff seem so alive' JOHN ROBB, LOUDER THAN WAR

'Fucking brilliant. Get it read, people'
STUART BRAITHWAITE, MOGWAI

'Suitably candid and diligently researched biography . . . engaging throughout. ▲▲▲▲' RECORD COLLECTOR

'Her interviewees trust her, and so they should'
GLENN AIREY, LOUDER THAN WAR

'A touching story of kids in the music business . . . A cut above the usual' THE SCOTSMAN

'One of the UK's great biographers' DR SIMON WARNER

'One of the best – and funniest – books I've read about music'
SEAT IN THE STALLS

'A stunning reinvention of the rock memoir format. Zoë Howe bottles Wilko's lightning' DAVE COLLINS, *VIVE LE ROCK*, ON *WILKO JOHNSON: LOOKING BACK AT ME*

'Brit-rock book of the year' GAVIN MARTIN ON *TYPICAL GIRLS? THE STORY OF THE SLITS*

A Note on the Author

Zoë Howe's books include *Typical Girls? The Story of the Slits*, *Stevie Nicks – Visions, Dreams and Rumours* and *'How's Your Dad?': Living in the Shadow of a Rock Star Parent*. She co-authored and collated Dr Feelgood guitarist Wilko Johnson's memoir *Looking Back at Me* (Cadiz Music, 2012) and contributed to the Eel Pie Island book *British Beat Explosion: Rock'n'Roll Island* (Aurora Metro, 2013). *Lee Brilleaux – Roadrunner: The Adventures of a Rock'n'Roll Gentleman* will be published by Polygon in autumn 2015.

Zoë's journalism has appeared in *The Quietus*, *Company Magazine*, *Notion*, *BBC Music*, *Holy Moly*, *Classic Rock*, *The Blues Magazine* and *NME*, and she has made music radio series for stations including Resonance FM. Zoë can be heard talking about rock'n'roll from time to time on BBC 6 Music, BBC London, Absolute Radio, E4 and Planet Rock. She lives in Essex with her husband Dylan. She also plays the drums.

Contents

Preface

The Jesus and Mary Chain have always been a contradiction – shy, yet anchored by total belief; gently spoken, yet famous for playing the kind of gigs that would leave you deaf for a week even if they only lasted for twenty minutes (or 'until we got booed', according to William Reid). They created their own genre, born of a cocktail of psychotic noise, Spector rhythms and dark lyrics, delivered via a visual explosion of smoke, leather, big hair, Ray-Bans, silhouettes and searchlights. They took the glittering jewel of pop and casually lifted it up, revealing the darkness underneath. The fractious sound of The Jesus and Mary Chain also reflected a time of significant social tension in the UK, a time of pickets and riots, conflict and change. They were past, present and future rolled into one.

Brothers William and Jim Reid, the core of The Jesus and Mary Chain, seemed to conjure sonic otherworlds inhabited by the ghosts of 1960s pop, swaying beneath layers of powerful feedback and soft, obsessive mutterings. The Mary Chain's debut album *Psychocandy,* is a perfect example of this, and the dreamlike slice of doomed youth, underpinned with fractured sensitivity and subtle black humour, is now hailed as one of the greatest pop LPs of the 1980s While the considerable mystique of The Jesus and Mary Chain has always been a huge part of their appeal, the time is right to hear their story and to reconsider an impressive canon of work.

It has been a genuine pleasure to work with the Mary Chain, and to gather so many memories and perspectives for this long-overdue chronicle of their career. Every contributor has been kinder and more helpful than I could have anticipated, and it's a privilege to present their story. When I was about to start working on this book, one question that kept coming up from various people (including Alan McGee) was: 'Are you sure they can remember anything?' Fortunately for me, and you, they could. Or, at least, they've respectively made up some very convincing anecdotes, some of which even match up with each other.

I first met Jim Reid and Douglas Hart at the Artrocker awards in 2011, where they were collecting an award for the reissue of *Psychocandy*. That was, of course, the main reason I went: to see one of the groups who had sound-tracked my formative years be publicly paid due respect. I already knew Mary Chain/Black Box Recorder guitarist John Moore (who, apropos of nothing, once attempted to teach me to play the musical saw), and through John I had met the Mary Chain's then bass player, and now guitarist, Philip King. But that freezing November day in East London marked my first brief meeting with Jim, who, alongside John, was a touch hungover, speaking in what *Smash Hits* referred to as the famous 'spooky whisper' and concerned largely with the whereabouts of 'drinkies'. Douglas Hart, who towered over me (as most people do), seemed more immediately open to an initial broaching of the book idea under circumstances that were admittedly better suited to . . . well, locating drinkies.

Cut to today and, after an eventful and industrious two years of persuasion, persistence, anecdotes and characters (and alcohol), The Jesus and Mary Chain's biography has finally burst into tangible life, and within these pages is the rich, revealing and absorbing account of the band, thanks to Jim Reid, Douglas Hart, Bobby Gillespie, John Moore, Murray Dalglish, Alan McGee, Geoff Travis and as many former alumni and associates as I could get my hands on. William Reid, unfortunately, chose not to be involved.

On the cusp of the 1980s, before the Mary Chain existed, the Reid brothers found little acceptance in their hometown of East Kilbride, near Glasgow, preferring to stay in, or stroll through town in the middle of the night, rather than risk being targeted by gangs of neds ('non-educated delinquents'). Not unusually for brothers, they didn't even really want to associate with each other until their late teens, when they found common ground in their love of glam-rock and punk. They actively 'hated each other' when they were at school according to William, who was older and didn't want to hang around with his little brother; by the time Jim reached sixteen he still only looked about ten anyway. 'That was quite embarrassing,' admitted Jim. 'Nobody really wanted to talk to me.' But the energy of punk, and particularly proto-punk groups such as The Stooges and The Velvet Underground, would soon unite them, motivating them (despite initial outward appearances) to create their own future, a future of making music with integrity, on their own terms. This would provide their escape and ultimately change their lives. All in good time.

The Reids' shyness was legendary, but they had total faith in what they were doing. It is their sense of being outsiders, never being part of a 'scene', combined with a strong individuality and self-awareness, that really defines the Mary Chain for those who felt and feel similar. It's a lonely but ultimately more rewarding place to be; so many continue to identify with the Mary Chain for this reason. Like the punks who went before them, The Jesus and Mary Chain are the champions of the weird, the poster boys for the misunderstood, and there was no way they were going to remould themselves to suit others. For that alone, they have a special place in my heart. They might have been chaotic onstage, they might have drunk too much, they might have even been thrown out of their own gigs in the early days – but they also knew they were, as they often nonchalantly proclaimed, 'the best'. Once the hip and enthusiastic Bobby Gillespie joined the line-up as their Moe Tucker-style drummer, their confidence could only grow.

With Alan McGee at the management helm in their early years, the Mary Chain knew they had the power to cut through saccharine mainstream pop like a knife, forcing fans to question the culture they were being fed, just as punk had encouraged them to question the same thing. And hits? World tours? Gold records and *Top of the Pops?* It was all on the horizon – and once their music reached the ears of Alan McGee, success would come rapidly. 'It wasn't a rollercoaster,' founding member Douglas Hart remembers. 'It was more like a rocket.'

Acknowledgements

Love and thanks to everyone who agreed to be interviewed for this book: Jim Reid, Douglas Hart, Bobby Gillespie, John Moore, Laurence Verfaillie, Murray Dalglish, Linda Fox, Philip King, Ben Lurie, Steve Monti, Lincoln Fong (who dedicates his contribution to Kyra Rubin, 'the world's biggest JAMC fan'), Alan McGee, Geoff Travis, Jeannette Lee, Chris Morrison, Jerry Jaffe, Neil Taylor, Stephen Pastel, Terry Edwards, Clive 'The Doctor' Jackson, Joe Foster, Alan Moulder, Pat Collier, Mick Houghton, David Evans, Loz Colbert, Mark Crozer, John Robb, James Pinker, David Quantick, Terry Staunton and Kevin Pearce. Gratitude also to Gerry McElhone, Barbara Charone, Karen Ciccone, Gavin Martin, Nick Hasted, Mat Snow, Sigtryggur Baldursson, Tom Seabrook, John Ingham, the essential Mary Chain fan resource that is Niina's April Skies blog, Rock's Back Pages, Mihoko Kimura, Carlos Benavides, Robin Kennedy, Gary Fowles and Filipe Albuquerque.

Finally, thanks to Kevin Pocklington at Jenny Brown Associates and commissioning editors Alison Rae at Polygon Books and Kathy Huck at St Martin's Press. Love and gratitude to friends and family for support and encouragement. Special thanks as always to my husband Dylan.

I

New Town, Punk Rock, Dole Queue

East Kilbride, located close to Glasgow, is a central base for business, a great place to live, shop, work and play . . .
EastKilbride.org, the 'premier community information site for East Kilbride'

East Kilbride was fucking Neolithic. Stonehenge with windows.
Douglas Hart

East Kilbride, Scotland. The 1980s had dawned with little fanfare and, for many, even less opportunity, unless you didn't mind the idea of working in a factory for the rest of your life. Margaret Thatcher (who, oddly enough, died while this paragraph was being written) and her vice-like grip on Britain might have heralded a golden 'me-centric' era for the moneyed entrepreneur, but for most the reign of the Conservative government would be a dark time that, in many areas, destroyed industry and wrecked communities. The post-war new town East Kilbride might not have been as mind-numbingly bleak as it has sometimes been described, but a heady concoction of boredom, inertia and, occasionally, fear – of violent 'neds', mostly – hung in the air. East Kilbride wasn't the worst place in the world to grow up; it was just dull, antiseptic and uninspiring.

There is always, of course, another way; at least, there is for those who have the talent, wherewithal and determination to find and pursue it. The spirit of punk, which lit the creative touch-paper for so many young people in 1976 and in the brief period that followed, was incandescent enough to continue burning in the hearts of many teenagers who found themselves inspired by the music, imagery, strength and sheer can-do/fuck you attitude. This would carry them through, not only to the new decade, but also beyond. Punk also celebrated seminal American acts including The Velvet Underground, The Stooges, Television, Patti Smith and The Ramones, and introduced British youth to transatlantic treasure that they might not otherwise have been exposed to. These influences were essential to unlocking a new life, and as music in the mainstream became more slickly packaged and over-produced they would pass the flame of urgent, raw guitar-based music on to a new generation. The pioneers of this new generation lived here. In East Kilbride.

William and James Reid were actually born in Glasgow, William on 28 October 1958 and Jim on 29 December 1961. The family left the tenement block they once called home after their tiny flat was broken into. Nothing was taken, largely because there was nothing to take. 'They must have been the most disappointed burglars in the world,' Jim later quipped. Still, a life somewhere safer and quieter beckoned. The Reids graduated from what was basically, as Jim puts it, a 'slum' to a small, neat, suburban house in East Kilbride in South Lanarkshire, less than ten miles south-east of Glasgow.

Fast forward to the end of the 1970s, and the two brothers are in their teens, as close as twins and often too close for comfort, skulking in their family home. They barely emerge except to sign on the dole or walk the dog. But, while a shared bedroom in a blustery Scottish new town might not strike one as a potential Petri dish of creativity, the Reid brothers were slowly (very slowly) creating something that would not only offer them an escape route, but ultimately change the course of pop during a time of disinfected chart fodder and anodyne tweeness. This is impressive considering that music was not treated as an important part of life by their parents, who, according to Jim, 'would buy a single once every five years and then play it over and over again.'

'My mum and dad were into music, but very casually. We got our first record player in about 1971, but we had no records, so we went round to our neighbours' house and borrowed one. It was "Chirpy Chirpy Cheep Cheep". We were so amazed we played it about 50 fucking times.'

At least Jim and William had an older cousin, a music fan who lent the Reids his precious Beatles and Bob Dylan albums, but it was glam-rock that first sparked the Reids' serious obsession with pop music. Hard as it may be to believe, Jim Reid remembers getting 'really excited about waiting for a new Slade record to come out, seeing them on *Top of the Pops*, talking about it at school the next day . . .' But exhilarating as the stomping rhythms and dazzling personalities (and trousers) of glam-rock undoubtedly were, punk provided the sea change that ultimately made the idea of forming a band accessible, necessary even.

'Having a band just seemed like something that other people did. It was punk that made you think, you know, what are the alternatives here? We could go and work in a factory, or we could start a punk band,' says Jim. 'But unfortunately me and William were both incredibly lazy. William bought a bass guitar that just sat in the corner for about five years.'

The Reid brothers felt keenly that they were very much alone, culturally, in East Kilbride, which added to their insularity – at the very least they had each other ('we became like weird twins, finishing each other's sentences,' Jim noted). But a young Douglas Hart was another creative spirit adrift in faceless East Kilbride who was kick-started by punk rock. He was more outgoing than the Reid brothers, who were, to be fair, shy to the point of being completely anti-social, but he was still a sensitive outsider who had little in common with his peer group.

For Douglas and the Reids, punk was not just about the music, it was about the DIY culture, dissolving notions of artistic perfectionism and encouraging people to just try things out. You could pick up an instrument, create a fanzine, use a camera or customise your wardrobe – it didn't matter what you chose to do, it didn't matter if you made a mistake, and it wasn't important where you came from, what your gender or social standing was, or what you'd been exposed to (or not) so far. What was crucial was that you were being authentic, autonomous and artistically curious, and expressing your individuality.

This could manifest itself in a joyous way or in a nihilistic way, but the most important thing was that you were being true to yourself. Not a new concept, granted, but one that had for many become buried under concrete layers of conditioning passed down through the generations, particularly if you were working-class or female. For some at least, punk blasted that conditioning into oblivion. It would have been hard for a kid in East Kilbride to take advantage of punk in its live form, and the music might have been boycotted by the mainstream media, with John Peel's BBC Radio 1 show and *The Old Grey Whistle Test* being the most feted exceptions, but when glimmers of this liberating movement shone through the cracks, they didn't go unnoticed.

Douglas Hart says: 'Everyone was starting fanzines. You'd make your own clothes, because you couldn't buy them anywhere, and start bands. That's when I got my first bass. I was in a band called Teenage Vice, but I was only twelve! A lot of people dropped out after a couple of years, but a few of us were totally lit up by punk and that gave us the fuel that drove us creatively up until now.' Douglas also had the benefit of his older brother's record collection, which introduced him to David Bowie, the Velvet Underground and the Stooges. 'So even when I heard punk rock, it was familiar to me from hearing those records,' he explains. 'I guess I was a bit advanced for my age in that sense. I didn't know anyone who had that love and was trying to trace things back.'

It was at this point that Douglas first met the Reids, thanks to his school friend Ivor Wilson. Ivor went to karate classes with the teenage Jim Reid, and on noticing the band names scrawled on Douglas's exercise books, Ivor realised he knew a potential ally for Douglas who would share his musical tastes. Douglas, and subsequently Jim, finally realised they were not alone. This discovery was a lifeline.

'It was, God, there's someone else like that!' says Douglas. 'It was a goldmine for me because both Jim and William had great records, so for a kid like me that was so hungry for things musically, it was incredible.'

Ivor Wilson was a nascent guitarist himself, and shared Douglas and Jim's love of the Sex Pistols, The Slits, The Stooges, Subway Sect and other punk bands not necessarily beginning with 'S'. In fact, the three boys would unite briefly as a band, with a young Edward Connelly (later of the early Creation Records signing Meat Whiplash – another group from East Kilbride) on drums, to play at a local party. It would be Jim and Douglas's first gig together.

'We played to an audience of six in some kid's front room,' Douglas remembers. 'A proper garage band. Me on vocals, Jim on bass, Ivor on guitar, and Eddy on drums. We did "Pretty Vacant" and "Anarchy in the UK" by the Pistols, "New Rose" by The Damned and "Art School" by

The Jam.' It would be Ivor Wilson who also sold William his first guitar – a Gretsch Tennessee that, unbeknownst to Ivor, was a prized possession of his dad's and was also worth rather more than the £20 he sold it to William Reid for. 'I think his dad kicked the shit out of him when he found out,' says Jim. 'But that was how we had at least one decent guitar.' Most of their instruments would come from junk shops or from Woolworths.

Jim was then seventeen to Douglas's fourteen, and William was already twenty. Quite an age gap, admittedly, and Douglas looked young for his age as it was. Not that it bothered Jim, but his dad was more than a little concerned.

'We called him Todd, short for toddler,' says Jim. 'He looked about nine years old. My dad was really worried. I think he thought there was a touch of the Jimmy Saviles or something. He was saying, "Who's that wee boy who keeps coming down to the house?" "It's just my mate!"'

Playing records and getting lost in endless discussions about music and films – *Billy Liar* and the Lindsay Anderson movie *If....* being enduring favourites – provided some respite from the drudgery of everyday life, which for Jim meant working in the local Rolls-Royce Aerospace factory, where Boeing aeroplane engines were being manufactured. William, meanwhile, was a sheet-metal worker. 'A terrible job,' he remembers. 'I was always worried about losing my fingers.'

William, apparently, also worked in a cheese warehouse. This is worth mentioning if only to share this cautionary tale with any lovers of parmesan out there. 'My main task,' William explained to journalist Max Bell, 'was to inspect the parmesans, because cockroaches thrive on them. I had to go through the cheeses, find the cockroaches burrowing inside, pull 'em out and stomp them.' Buon appetito.

Each brother hated his job with a passion. The money at least allowed them to buy records, and would go towards Jim's first guitar, but, as Douglas recalls, 'They were stuck in a rut and maybe got depressed stuck in that small room together, you could tell there were stresses there. Obviously they loved each other and had a lot in common, but they weren't so young any more.'

After a series of dead-end jobs, William finally jacked it in and started signing on, while Jim gritted his teeth at the factory. All of this, coupled with a serious case of stifled creativity, led to a less than comfortable atmosphere at home, and it wouldn't take long for the pressure to become unbearable. By the time he reached the end of his teens, Jim could take no more. However, the idea that Jim was going to just walk out on gainful employment was anathema to his stalwart working-class parents.

'Things were tense with my dad,' Jim remembers. 'I said I was going to chuck my job, and he said, "Well, you're not living in this house . . ." So I went to London. It didn't work out. I stayed there for about six months.'

Jim took the long bus journey from Glasgow and stayed at downbeat Earls Court hotels, trying to find work. He stayed in touch with Douglas by writing messages on the back of customer-comments cards from Burger King, sticking a stamp on the back and sending them off like postcards, but when the prodigal son returned to East Kilbride, the person who had changed most was not Jim but Douglas, who was unrecognisable. Within a matter of months the curly-haired punk-rock 'toddler' had grown up.

Jim recalls: 'When I got back there was this bloke at the door [deep voice], "All right, Jim . . ." "Who the fuck are you?" "It's Douglas!" "What?" I went away for six months and this nine-year-old has turned into a man, stubble and all that. "Do you want to come out?" "Are you sure? You're really Douglas?"'

'I'd literally grown six inches over one summer,' says Douglas. 'It was like in *An American Werewolf in London*. I was racked with agony. It was unbelievable.'

'We kept calling him Todd though,' adds Jim. 'We still call him Todd.'

2

Acid, Paint Factory, Portastudio

Listening to The Velvet Underground And Nico *was like hearing the word of God. The fact that somebody could do 'I'll Be Your Mirror' and 'Heroin' on the same album was exciting. That is, in essence,* Psychocandy. *That's what we were trying to say.*
Jim Reid

Once Jim and Douglas were reunited, their mission to transcend the boredom of their everyday existence intensified. One obvious way to escape at least mentally would be to experiment with mind-altering substances, which wasn't hard to do in East Kilbride. Magic mushrooms were everywhere, dotting the more rural areas that surrounded the town and growing in people's front gardens.

Jim and Douglas would walk for miles into the countryside, or stroll through town in the small hours once the neds had lumbered home for the night. They'd even pitch a tent in Douglas's back garden and stay awake for hours, talking about forming the perfect band and concocting plans for the future. Both Jim and Douglas shared rooms with their brothers, so any sleepovers had to be al-fresco affairs.

'Taking mushrooms was an important part of it, it influenced the music in terms of experimentation,' Douglas remembers. 'It was like a rite of passage. East Kilbride, as much as it marred us, it made us. We were outsiders from an outsider town, so it was good in a way, coming from somewhere with so little to do.'

Another rite of passage, and a vital part of the Mary Chain story, was the discovery of a derelict paint factory languishing on the outskirts of town. It was the perfect place to take pictures, smash things up and let off steam, graffiti the walls and play music as loud as possible. It would be the site of many an interesting scene once Messrs Reid and Hart happened upon it, not least because it was the ideal place to hide out and take acid. Not all of their trips were quite so private, however, and on one occasion the pair had something of an audience.

'One time we got some acid and we planned to take a trip to the seaside, which involved taking a couple of trains," says Douglas. 'Of course we were too greedy to wait, so as soon as I got to Jim's house at about 7.30 a.m. we took it. The station was only twenty minutes away, but it was the most overpowering acid we'd ever had.'

The two teenagers took, it's fair to say, the scenic route to the station, but by the time they'd reached the park across the street from the platform, they could walk no further and collapsed on the grass in full view of the commuters making their outward journey to work.

'We had this utterly out-of-body experience,' Douglas remembers. 'I remember leaving my body and having a transcendental experience. It was like being on this rolling hillside looking towards a city of pure energy.'

As Douglas and Jim slowly came back to reality, however, they realised they had been lying on the grass for eight hours – and they could be seen by the very same bemused commuters, now homeward-bound, who had seen them in the morning. What's more, while they had initially crashed out under the shade of a tree, the glare of the sun had moved throughout the day. Both boys were sunburnt, but only down one half of their bodies, Ziggy Stardust-style. 'It was amazing though,' Douglas says. 'Nothing's ever happened to me like that before or since on acid.'

When not tripping his way around East Kilbride with the not-so-toddleresque Todd, or forming schemes for the future, Jim's nocturnal conversations at home with William would be just as stimulating. The brothers might not have wanted to form a band with each other at this point, feeling, perhaps, that they already spent more than enough time in each other's company, but they were still psychologically inseparable whether they liked it or not. They shared the same ideas, the same mindset, and the same dissatisfaction with the rest of the world.

'We'd sit up all night, jabbering on,' says Jim. 'When I think back now, our ideas seemed rather naïve, but we seemed to think we could subvert things, like . . . if somebody made a film called *Fuck My Dog* or something, and it got a major release, the world would be altered over-night. Now I think, "You idiot. All that would have happened is that people would have laughed at you."'

Musically the brothers had a voracious appetite, listening to bands such as the German industrial group Einstürzende Neubauten, The Beatles, The Birthday Party, The Doors, Dr Mix and the Remix, and 1960s girl groups like the Shangri-Las. But if they had to pick one single group who had the most impact on them, it would have been the Velvet Underground. When they brought home the *The Velvet Underground And Nico* album (famously bearing Andy Warhol's image of a banana on the cover), what ensued was tantamount to a religious experience. It was sweet and bitter, 'psycho and candy', all on one record.

'*The Velvet Underground And Nico*, well, I think I cried when I heard it,' Jim says. 'That record made me feel like I was on drugs. It made me feel happy, warm inside. If I could buy that feeling, I'd pay a fortune for it.'

Einstürzende Neubauten also remained an enduring inspiration to the Reids, who dreamed of creating a band 'exactly as they were, but with a bubblegum song on top of it,' muses Jim. 'Shangri-Las crossed with Neubauten.'

This was the blueprint of what they wanted to set out and achieve. Apart from The Ramones, with their sugar-pop-turned-thrashy-punk schtick, this alchemy of extremes had rarely been managed with great success before. It was a clash of musical cultures, soft and hard, mellif-luous but metallic. Noise pop. Jim and William knew the results could be powerful, and they didn't want to take the sting or the sweetness out of either influence. They wanted to just crash them into each other. The music of the early 1980s said nothing to them, so, like many, they looked back to see what they could draw on to light their own fire. 'Pop' might not be a term that the uninitiated would immediately associate with the Mary Chain – a new term probably should have been invented for them, or maybe we should just dispense with terms altogether and just take them as they were – but to the band themselves, pop not only represented the music they loved and had grown up with, but it was inclusive and would give them the potential to reach as many people as possible. Pop music might not have been in a particularly pleasing state at that time, but that didn't mean the Mary Chain weren't prepared to

a) proclaim their own music 'pop' and b) try to improve the current state of affairs by razing it to the ground and starting again. They were gradually sketching out a sound for themselves, writing songs, creating an image and formulating a plan that would still take several years to come to fruition.

When Jim and William weren't conspiring in their room, they would be downstairs in front of the TV, sometimes for more than twelve hours a day. Their family might have looked on with slight concern as the two brothers sat avidly staring, taping adverts and making video collages from random documentaries and the news, but nothing was wasted from this period, and everything would inform what was to come, no matter how frankly odd it might have seemed at the time. '[Our parents] often used to ask us what was wrong with us,' William told *NME*'s Mat Snow in 1986. 'Whether we needed any help . . .'

'William and I probably started writing songs around 1982, 1983,' reflects Jim. 'Everyone thinks we do nothing but fight, and that is largely true nowadays, but then it wasn't so much like that. We totally trusted each other, as we do now.'

Their parents tried to be understanding of their sons' often insular behaviour – their mother once bought William a key-ring with the inscription 'I'm not weird, I'm gifted' written on it, which cheered him immeasurably. However, a major turning point for the brothers was when their father generously gave them a cut of his 'Mickey Mouse' redundancy pay-out to buy whatever they wanted.

Jim says: 'My dad worked in a factory as a heavy-machinery operator and my mum worked in a chip shop. When my dad got made redundant, he got a couple of grand. He gave me and William £500 and we bought one of the first Portastudios. We made the demos that ended up getting us signed to Creation. Money well spent.'

Jim and William's father was hoping they'd use the cash to buy themselves a car, no doubt to encourage them to chisel themselves out of the family home once in a while. But no, they knew what they needed and it had to be part of their ongoing mission. The Portastudio, a four-track recorder that used a standard cassette to record on, was a new and revolutionary invention at the time, and was perfect for the Reids to lay down their musical ideas and experiments without leaving their bedroom.

Eventually, these hothouse flowers were ready to form a band – just not with each other. The now famous brotherly tensions were clearly surfacing, and although their relationship was still relatively harmonious at this point, they knew that if they were in a band together, there would be sparks. However, as Jim explains: 'The idea of doing two bands just became ridiculous. He was making demos and I was making demos and they just sounded like the same bloody band. We were totally into the same things.'

Jim and Douglas had been talking about the 'perfect band' for months, and it initially seemed to make more sense to Jim to form a group with Douglas. But far from wanting to take the lead and sing his own songs, even though he'd sung them on the demos, Jim would do his damnedest to persuade Douglas to take care of the vocals instead. Jim Reid was clearly immune to the fabled 'lead-singeritis' disease (symptoms include overweening self-confidence and a God complex) that has afflicted so many.

'Jim played me "Never Understand", those demos,' Douglas remembers. 'I was blown away. But then he said, "You sing and I'll play bass or something," and I was like, "That is fucking crazy!" He'd made these demos, he's got an amazing voice and he's a great-looking guy, but he was genuinely shy. He had the same conversation with William later on – "You sing . . ."'

Jim and Douglas decided to head to the local scout hall to rehearse and work up the beginnings of a live set from Jim's songs. Good intentions, but they mainly just used the opportunity to take their favourite cassettes and play the music through their amp at top volume without being disturbed.

Rehearsals (or not) aside, there was also the issue of a band name. One name that was briefly toyed with was The Poppy Seeds, a thinly veiled opiate reference with psychedelic overtones. Then there was The Daisy Chain, which would stick a little longer, gracing the recycled cassette tapes of their demos that were given to indifferent promoters around Glasgow in the hope of getting a gig.

There might have been a thriving music scene in the city, but it was impossible for the Daisy Chain to break into it; Altered Images, Aztec Camera and Josef K seemed to have it sewn up. Groups such as sometime Postcard Records act Orange Juice, with Edwyn Collins on vocals, were gradually relocating to London, but still it appeared these 'hayseeds from

East Kilbride', as Douglas puts it, were apparently not needed to fill the vacuum. Just a couple of years down the line they would be referred to by some as a 'Glasgow' band, but the truth was that there was quite a gulf.

Jim says: 'Nobody would give us the time of day. There was this cliquey white-soul scene and you couldn't get inside it, just couldn't get anywhere. We gave tapes to everybody, tried to get gigs wherever.'

'We were removed from that Glasgow scene,' adds Douglas. 'We didn't live in Glasgow and weren't part of it. Music had lost its way post-punk, and there was a lot of post-Orange Juice crap on the scene. I mean, I love Orange Juice, but what came after . . . people playing guitar with what I call the "wank" rhythm, like George Formby.'

One significant beam of light in Glasgow was the presence of a band called The Pastels, fronted by Stephen McRobbie, better known as Stephen Pastel. The Pastels, formed in 1982, shared the Daisy Chain's independent mindset; they were clearly kindred spirits in what otherwise felt like a rather bleak landscape.

'There weren't many places to go in Glasgow,' Stephen Pastel explains. 'Groups were dropping literary references and trying to play funky, but in a wooden, uptight way. The Pastels' sound was raw and amateur, but we were already starting to make music like "Baby Honey". We didn't feel like we were "the Glasgow scene", we had become our own thing.'

The Pastels also connected with Jill Bryson and Rose McDowall, better known as the goth-pop duo Strawberry Switchblade. They were fellow punky, stylish Glaswegians who routinely caused jaws to drop as they strutted through town festooned in tutus, ribbons and fake flowers, and with huge backcombed hair-dos – one bright red (Jill) and one jet-black (Rose). With The Pastels they created fanzines, put on their own club nights and took the DIY attitude to the nth degree. If what you wanted to see wasn't out there, you didn't just sit back and get depressed, you worked out what was lacking and created it yourself. Possibly while depressed, or at least in an advanced state of frustration. But still, you were doing it yourself, and that was vital. The alternative was wandering through life not really engaging with anything, because there was nothing you wanted to engage with.

The first time Jim, William and Douglas met Stephen was after a Pastels show one freezing winter's night at the Candy Club, a club night that ran for a short time at the Lorne Hotel in Kelvingrove, Glasgow.

The Candy Club would soon play an important part in the destiny of the Daisy Chain, but initially meeting the Pastels was another lifeline for them during a period of knockbacks and isolation.

The Daisy Chain – still just Jim and Douglas at this point – decided to give a tape of demos to the Candy Club promoter, Nick Lowe.* Stephen Pastel helped Nick to run the Candy Club, although the pair had 'very different tastes'. Stephen wasn't aware at the time that Jim and Douglas had sent in a cassette for consideration but destiny works in mysterious ways.

'We couldn't afford a new cassette,' Douglas recalls. 'So we had an old cassette with the demo on one side and just a kind of compilation on the other, like Syd Barrett and things like that.' In his usual unvarnished manner, Jim explains that 'The guy who was running [the Candy Club] thought it was garbage.' Ironically, had Stephen Pastel heard the cassette, the story might have been rather different. 'I was given a copy soon after, and of course I loved it,' says Stephen. 'It had a heavy fuzz sound, but great melodies too.'

As it turned out, this initial rejection would draw a figure into Jim and Douglas's lives who would be pivotal in turning their fate around. 'Nick was mates with Bobby Gillespie,' says Jim. 'He said to Bobby, "You like Syd Barrett, there's a Syd Barrett compilation on the other side of this."' Nick made a note to himself to send the cassette to Bobby. However, by the time he actually got around to it, it would be six months later – and some major changes had taken place within the Daisy Chain by then.

---

* Not the artist of Stiff Records/'I Love The Sound Of Breaking Glass' fame.

3

Gillespie, McGee and a Green Ink Letter

'The whole Scottish scene turns our stomach,' says Jim.
'The Welsh as well,' grins William.
'And the Irish,' shrugs Douglas, dourly.
(from a *Sounds* interview with Sandy Robertson, 1985)

Bobby Gillespie, a skinny, young, politicised Public Image Limited fan, came from the incongruously named Mount Florida area near Glasgow's Hampden Park football stadium. He had already formed his own group, Primal Scream and, like the Daisy Chain, there were just two members at this point: Gillespie and his friend Jim Beattie. Both were dissatisfied with the state of what music had become, describing themselves as 'hateful, angry punk kids'.

'The scene in Glasgow was mostly white-boy funk neds trying to be David Bowie, *Station To Station* era, and failing miserably . . . it was just alien to us,' Bobby explains. 'They wanted to be part of the establishment and we were anti-establishment. For us, punk was a platform for expression, we talked about how we felt and described it in real terms that other people could relate to.'

Even before the Daisy Chain had entered Bobby's consciousness, it was clear that they would, eventually, meet somehow – they were expressing themselves in almost the same way and feeling very much the same confusions, cultural ennui and frustration. They loved the same music – the Velvets, The Doors, The Stooges, The Cramps, The Birthday Party and The Gun Club – and had also found a place to make a lot of noise and burn up some of their rage, transmuting it into something more positive and, dare I say it, fun. It was only a matter of time until their paths crossed.

Bobby says: 'Primal Scream, at the start, were kind of experimental; we used a two-track tape recorder, drum machine, for percussion we used bits of metal, like dustbin lids. Public Image's *Metal Box,* we put that through the echo . . . but it was very primitive. We were just making noise. We didn't know about expressing ourselves because it was beyond our frame of reference, being from a working-class background, but that's what we were doing.'

By the time Candy Club promoter Nick Lowe sent the Daisy Chain's demo tape to Bobby, William had joined his brother's band. It was obvious that the Reids would eventually join forces. Difficult as it could often be, that friction would be as necessary as it is with all of the most interesting artistic partnerships, the grit in the oyster.

The addition of William, of course, meant the addition of William's material. 'Suddenly we had eight songs!' recalls Douglas, who was utterly intrigued by William's demos. They were crammed with surreal imagery and almost Dadaesque lyrics, reminiscent of automatic writing and free association. The Reids have always been keen to retain the mystery around their lyrics, and are rightly reluctant to explain what they mean not least because they feel the listener should be allowed to decide for him or herself. Douglas says: 'I remember reading the words for "In A Hole". *How could something crawl within my rubber holy baked bean tin* . . . amazing! Both Jim and William are really good at creating lyrics.'

One of the most interesting things about so many of the Mary Chain's songs is the contrast between the lyrics and the melodies – a storm of dark, brooding, even threatening words frequently interlace with a sugar-sweet melody; from William's point of view, this is because the melodies and the lyrics come from 'different places'. Lyrics would be written sober, melodies developed while drunk or high.

'Writing lyrics is like tracing the outline of your own soul and it's a mental task,' William would later explain to Japanese magazine *Rockin' On.* 'I'd say melodies are like meeting a girl and finding her pretty, and lyrics are like getting to know her better . . . and maybe you don't like her, or maybe you get irritated because you are not getting to know each other at all . . .'

Jim was still quite keen to slink out of the role of lead vocalist and let someone else do it, and William stepped in briefly, but William admits his 'nasal' voice just didn't sound as strong as Jim's, which was throatier. Even so, persuading Jim to sing was not easy. 'Eventually everybody was like, "Come on, you fucking bastard, you must do it,"' remembers William in an interview with friend Dimitri Coats. 'So he reluctantly became the singer.'

Rehearsals were rare, and relatively unproductive; the group would, according to Jim, 'get there, argue for half an hour and go home'. Which, with the benefit of hindsight and the knowledge of the combative quality that would come to define their live act, sounds about right. Jim would, rather unwillingly, sing; he and William played guitar (Jim's later becoming famous for being deliberately kept out of tune, for 'kicking' purposes) and Douglas would play a bass never burdened with more than three strings. Add to this William's broken Shin Ei fuzz pedal, bought for a tenner, and you had the essential elements of The Jesus and Mary Chain. About that famous pedal: William only realised it was broken when he tried to sell it to someone else, but 'the *noise* it made . . .' he said. 'It was almost as if another member had joined the band.'

The Reids spent hours watching films and reading books, poring over retro pop culture imagery, and they immediately recognised the power of the slightly ravaged style of the Beatles-in-Hamburg look: rock'n'roll era, black leather, big hair, bristling with sleazy energy and an irresistible sense of destroyed innocence. 'Yeah, I was always into The Beatles in Hamburg,' Jim muses. 'But when we dressed in black leather in the mid-1980s, people just assumed we were goths, which was not the case. The big hair, well, everybody had that haircut in the 1980s. You'd go to the doctor and he'd be sitting there with a fucking silly big hairdo.' Echo and the Bunnymen were probably to blame.

As shy as the Reids were, everything they did to further the Mary Chain cause was anchored by a real faith in their own ideas, and this would carry them through. They might not have been self-assured in everyday life, but when it came to their songs, they knew what they had and what they could achieve.

'Jim, deep down, had confidence in it,' says Douglas. 'It wasn't a swaggering confidence though. If a person is just out-and-out confident, those are the people you avoid. You know, the people you fantasise about getting knocked over at school or being killed by some kind of poison . . .' Indeed. But back to the Mary Chain.

Bobby Gillespie, meanwhile, had received that fateful package in the post. He ripped open the envelope and listened to the Syd Barrett compilation. When he turned the cassette over, what he heard sent him into a rapture. The Daisy Chain's demos were confounding and dark, but with a simplicity and extreme energy reminiscent of the first wave of punk.

'"Upside Down" was on there, "Never Understand" and "Taste The Floor",' says Bobby, instantly animated at the memory of it. 'I played it about six times. I thought it was fucking incredible.'

The fact that there were supposedly only two of them excited Bobby beyond measure; his first thought was that he and Jim Beattie could join forces with Jim Reid and Douglas. However, William was firmly ensconced by now, and Bobby's hopes would be dashed – temporarily.

During those early months, for Gillespie and the nascent Jesus and Mary Chain it was often a case of so near and yet so far. A month before Bobby listened to the tape, he and Jim Beattie had sent an advert to be read out on Billy Sloan's show on Radio Clyde. 'It was for Primal Scream,' Bobby explains. 'We were looking for a psychedelic punk-rock vocalist, because at this point I was going to be the guitarist – I wasn't even a guitar player. Jim had heard it and was going to apply.'

After being stunned by the strength of the Daisy Chain's demos, Bobby knew these were people he had to meet. Bobby took out the cardboard insert from the case, found Douglas Hart's phone number and called it. Douglas's mother took a message.

'Apparently,' says Bobby, 'she said "Are you famous?", and I said, "Not yet, but I will be." Yeah, I'm quite pleased with that one. Anyway, I called Douglas again later that night. We spoke for what seemed like three hours. We spoke about The Seeds, the Thirteenth Floor Elevators, films like *If . . .* , the Sex Pistols, Subway Sect, Love, the Velvets, the Banshees, The Slits, Richard Hell and the Voidoids, Johnny Thunders . . . a lot of films, a lot of music.'

The conversation was an important one for both Douglas and Bobby, an 'incredible meeting of minds,' as Douglas put it. 'It was an amazing feeling to find him.' It was only at the end of this telephone conversation that Bobby mentioned a friend called Alan McGee, who was based in London. McGee had gone to school with Bobby in Glasgow, and they shared a love of punk rock, briefly forming a band called The Drains. The line-up included Andrew Innes, now the guitarist in Primal Scream.

McGee and Innes, uninspired by their surroundings and desperate to make their mark on London's seductive, transient music scene, soon left Glasgow and formed the band The Laughing Apple, named after a Cat Stevens song. To support himself and pay the rent on his small Tottenham flat, Alan McGee worked at British Rail as a clerk, which at least meant travel was cheap and easy. This, when he made his first foray into music management, would come in handy. Money was scarce, but McGee and others like him already had a productive DIY, cottage-industry mindset, starting bands, fanzines (such as McGee's own *Communication Blur*) and labels.

By 1983, McGee was at the helm of a label of his own called Creation Records, releasing records ad hoc by artists such as The Legend (alias music writer Everett True), The X-Men and his own band, Biff Bang Pow! He also ran a club night on Conway Street, later moving to Tottenham Court Road, called the Living Room. The Living Room gave vital exposure to artists including The Pastels, the Television Personalities and the Jasmine Minks as well as his own group. McGee was clearly like-minded, and was bound to give Jim, William and Douglas a gig at the Living Room at the very least.

Alan McGee founded and ran Creation, the Living Room and Biff Bang Pow! with two other creative reprobates, Dick Green and the Television Personalities' Joe Foster (alias Slaughter Joe). The operation was ramshackle but it worked, and it snowballed into something that would become well regarded by tuned-in music lovers. McGee says, 'We weren't just accomplishing our dreams, we were accomplishing everybody else's dreams. We were overthrowing the statues.'

'And bizarrely enough,' adds Joe Foster, 'we actually started to make money doing it. After initially putting the whole investment into . . . well, drink, basically, we thought, We should make better use of this. We were still living in that world where, if you wanted to get some shit out there, you just strolled over to Carnaby Street, met people at the *NME* or *Melody Maker*, bought them some drinks, and something would get in. They had to put out a paper every week, so you had a fair chance of something getting in.'

NME took notice of Creation Records, even if it was initially just because McGee would hound them until they did. This was also a powerful era for the music press. A few lines in *NME* meant a lot. If Jim, William and Douglas could tap into this, it had the potential to steer them firmly in the right direction.

A Daisy Chain cassette duly arrived on the doormat of McGee's flat in Tottenham, featuring the same demos Bobby Gillespie had heard. Bobby had already insisted to Alan that they deserved his attention, but after hearing the tape Alan initially had reservations. He was intrigued, but he needed to hear more.

Bobby remembers: 'Alan said, "I'm going to put them on a compilation." I said, "You've got to make a single with them, they're so good. You can't just put them out on a compilation with all these loser bands who play at your club!" And he's going, "Nah, I don't think they're ready."'

McGee clearly heard potential, however, and took the time to write the group a letter – in green ink, no less. 'We'd always read that letters written in green ink were written by psychos,' Douglas laughs. 'He said, "I like the demos, but maybe go into the studio and record something."'

It was certainly encouraging that they were being even tentatively considered by a London-based label – albeit a relatively underground one with no money. The compilation was going to be titled *Are You A Car Or Are You In Love?* (although, as it turned out, it would never materialise). The Mary Chain had to act quickly, and it wasn't easy to find a drummer in East Kilbride. 'Believe me,' says Douglas, 'not only did we not know any musicians there, but cool people who would have fitted in with us? No fucking chance!'

After much racking of brains, Douglas Hart remembered a boy from school called Norman Wilson who had a drum kit. He might not have been on the same wavelength as the Daisy Chain, but not many were. It was something of a desert out there. Douglas paid him a visit. 'We said, "We're recording next week, do you want to come?" I don't even know if we rehearsed. We went to a studio on the edge of East Kilbride (Evenlode) and tried "Upside Down" but it didn't turn out so great; it was rushed and the engineer couldn't get his head round the feedback.* The

---

* There are two versions floating around regarding the Mary Chain's use of feedback. Alan McGee and Joe Foster, who later would go on to produce The Jesus and Mary Chain's first single, 'Upside Down', claim the band's first gig was howling with feedback because they didn't know how to use the equipment and Foster, who was on the sound desk, just turned everything up. But as the Mary Chain remember it, it was deliberate and it was there from the start. Douglas says: 'William was a master of feedback. When we rehearsed in the scout hut, the whole sound was swathed in feedback and William never did anything to stop it. It always sounded . . . well, like the Mary Chain.'
Obviously they weren't the first to use feedback to such electrifying effect, Jimi

song was there, but it was more Ramones-like.' No bad thing, perhaps, but it wasn't the sound they wanted.

Time was running out and they had no choice but to send what they had to McGee. As Jim packaged up the tape, he slipped a note inside explaining that the 'bastard engineer' didn't understand what they were trying to achieve. If nothing else, this provided a neat little preview of the future; the Mary Chain and studio engineers did not always mix well.

McGee's memory of the tape was that it was 'OK', but Bobby had faith in them, and there was clearly something there. Why not invite them down to play at the Living Room? There was nothing to lose. 'That was it,' Jim shrugs. 'Alan wasn't that excited about it, but he gave us the gig anyway.'

Joe Foster remembers: 'We thought, They're totally weird, they're from East Kilbride and they're cut off from the world, let's have them over! Hell, we've given people we don't even really like very much a chance, so why not Bobby's pals? And off we went.'

By this time the group had changed their name, dropping the Daisy Chain for something more dark and controversial. The free-thinking William Reid had come up with the name The Jesus and Mary Chain, which was surreal, confusing and seemed to suit them perfectly. 'It sounded like a psychedelic punk street gang,' says Bobby. 'It conjured up amazing images.'

Rumours abound regarding the name's origin; the band later claimed, and then denied, that it was inspired by a line in a Bing Crosby film. Some believe another story, also propagated by the Reids themselves, that they'd spotted an offer for a 'gold Jesus and Mary chain' on the back of a cereal packet. Both are believable; the Reids are experts at extracting and transforming the mundane and the everyday, Pop Art-style: the afternoon film on TV, the cereal packet on the breakfast table. But in recent years, William announced that the idea just came to him out of thin air. Maybe he was just fed up of being asked about it, but either way the name remains appropriately shrouded in mystery. All that really mattered was that it worked. As Jim said, it 'was like Echo and the Bunnymen . . . only better'.

Hendrix and Pete Townshend being obvious pioneers. (The Beatles, idols of the Mary Chain's, weren't averse to distortion either – the opening moments of 'I Feel Fine' and the spiralling, disorientating 'I Want You (She's So Heavy)' come to mind.) But to have an unholy scream of distortion wrapping itself around what would in many cases be a simple pop melody, sometimes to the point of wilful sonic asphyxiation, was a new and thrilling way to utilise it.

It subverted the concept of religion, a recurrent theme for the group, not that the Reids or Douglas were brought up in such a religious way that they had to rebel against it in their everyday lives; they'd attended the non-denominational Hunter High, albeit regarded as the 'Proddy' (Protestant) school, in the sectarian landscape of the West of Scotland. As a result, they just had to endure 'some half-hearted RE classes', Douglas recalls, 'and a trendy vicar who came to assemblies and who, through his love of Cliff Richard, figured he had some connection with the kids'.

However, despite religion not proving a prominent factor in their early years it was, as Douglas observes, 'William's preoccupation. The themes are universal: love and hatred, revenge. I think William did this very creative rhyming association: Daisy Chain, Mary Chain . . . The name The Jesus and Mary Chain is confounding, but has a real poetry to it.' It was also reminiscent of one of their all-time favourite band names: Teenage Jesus and the Jerks, New York new-waver James Chance's group with Lydia Lunch. All of the ingredients were right for where the group was at that time.

In the not too distant future, the Reids would be called upon quite frequently to defend their band name, but William insisted there was never any intention to try to cause a reaction simply by using a biblical reference. 'I think it's tasteful,' he told *Interview* magazine in later years. 'If you want to use the word Jesus and upset people, you'd call the band Jesus Erected or Jesus On A Stake. I'm always shocked when people say it's blasphemous simply to use the words Jesus and Mary.'

The next step for the band was laden with importance. The combination of their insularity, their supposedly inaccessible music and their location meant that, had they not crossed paths with Bobby when they did, their story might have been very different, not to mention quite a bit shorter. The Mary Chain were serious about what would happen next because it felt, as Douglas recalls, like their last chance. 'It was like, If we don't do this, we will die in East Kilbride by the age of 30.'

Also, as Jim wryly observed, time wasn't the only thing that was running out. Patience, chez Reid, was in short supply. 'My dad was sick of having us about the house, because we'd packed in our jobs and were signing on. It was getting to a point where we were thinking, If we don't get up off our arses, this is never going to happen. And we did it.'

4

The Living Room

*Britain in 1984 was fucking boring. I like ABC, but that was as
exciting as it got: Martin Fry and his gold lamé suit. Then we
found the Mary Chain.*
Alan McGee

The Jesus and Mary Chain were booked to play Alan McGee's Living
Room on 8 June 1984, supporting Microdisney in the upstairs room of
the Roebuck pub on Tottenham Court Road. The Roebuck already had
some significant musical history: it was the site of David Bowie's audition for manager Ralph Horton in the summer of 1965. He was still
Davey Jones at that point, but not for much longer.

There was little danger of the Mary Chain over-rehearsing their set,
which was at this point mainly covers, including Syd Barrett's 'Vegetable
Man' and Subway Sect's 'Ambition', but their overall image and concept
was becoming more honed by the day. However, they were still in need
of a permanent drummer; Norman Wilson might have helped out on
the demo of 'Upside Down', but he wasn't right for the group and, to be
fair, he didn't seem particularly bothered himself.

To say they were cutting it fine would be an understatement, but
during the early summer months of 1984, the Reids scribbled a home-
made advertisement for a drummer on a scrap of paper, slunk into town
and pinned it on the notice-board at Impulse, the record shop in East
Kilbride. Like many record stores, it was something of a hub for young
music fans, but no one ever saw this enigmatic trio in town, or at least a
local goth called Murray Dalglish certainly hadn't – although, as he
observed, they must have gone in at least once to put the notice up.

'They were quite insular,' Murray remembers. 'I would walk about in town for two or three hours at a time, go into Impulse, never saw them. And you definitely would have noticed them.'

Dalglish, a raven-haired sixteen-year-old fresh out of school, was a dedicated drummer who had picked up his skills in the Boys' Brigade. He revered the impressive chops of Rush's Neil Peart over the simple playing of The Velvet Underground's Moe Tucker. However, he also loved The Stooges and the Sex Pistols, and that was enough to make him answer the ad, which was just as well, because no one else did.

A date was set for a try-out at the local scout hut where the Mary Chain occasionally rehearsed, but when the time to audition arrived and William wandered in, he couldn't hide his displeasure at the sight of Murray's kit. It was hardly a 22-piece Neil Peart number, but equally, a minimal Moe Tucker set-up it was not.

Murray recalls: 'I could see William's face kind of . . . you know . . . There's too many drums there! I had the full kit. They just plugged in, played a couple of songs, I just bashed at the kit and that was it.'

It was a big ask for anyone to fit in with The Jesus and Mary Chain. They existed in their own hermetically sealed bubble that rarely allowed anyone else in. But while the age gap was significant and their tastes differed, Murray did his best and he got the job. If the Reids had their reservations about Murray, it wasn't because they found him lacking in competence; if anything, he tended to add nifty little rolls and flourishes where, in the Mary Chain's collective opinion, there should have been none. For them it was more important to have attitude and a direct, no-frills style, and Murray would occasionally get a dirty look (or even a kick to the kit) if he threw in a fill where there shouldn't be one.

On the night of 7 June, the first complete line-up of The Jesus and Mary Chain made their way to the bus station on Churchill Avenue, East Kilbride. So began a sweltering, cramped, ten-hour overnight bus journey to London. 'This bus would show up and everyone piled on it,' remembers Murray. 'Those were the days when people would pile on to go down to their squats, claim a Giro [benefit cheque] down there and then come back and claim a Giro up here.'

The bus finally reached London at around 9 a.m., so the Mary Chain had an entire day during which the increasingly irascible and drunken Reid brothers had to try not to kill each other. It quickly became an unbearably sultry summer's day, and the combination of heat, nerves and Dutch courage* meant the feeling in the Mary Chain camp was far from relaxed. At least they were able to travel relatively light – Microdisney were allowing them to use their equipment, which may or may not have been wise.

The Reids did use some of their time to venture into the NME offices, then in Soho's Carnaby Street, to drum up some music-press support. For any group, let alone one this shy, this was a brave and important move. But they'd loved and read the NME for years, and the opportunity to at least try to attract their attention was too good to miss.

Jim Reid remembers: 'We'd said to McGee that we were going to the NME to give them a tape and invite them to the show, and he was laughing at us, saying, "For Christ's sake, they'll never come." But we went down and said, "Anybody's welcome."'

As it turned out, their leap of faith paid off – David Quantick attended the gig after work, giving the Mary Chain their first few lines in the NME, hailing their sound as reminiscent of a swarm of bees in an elevator shaft. Not bad for their first gig. Quantick remembers: 'They were very tinny, hence the "bee" line, but very intense. I'm still quite proud I was at their first gig, because they turned out to be a great band.'

When the time came to set up at the Roebuck for a sound-check, the Mary Chain's tension – and inebriation – had reached new heights. They were not drinkers in the sense that they would regularly sit in the pub boozing, nor did they drink at home at that point. The alcohol was simply a necessary emboldening elixir, not to mention a vital social lubricant – they were about to meet a whole raft of new people, after all. The only person who steered clear of alcohol that day was Murray. He had to hold it together on the drums. An intoxicated drummer is not generally a recipe for success.

---

* Murray recalls that Douglas, who was working at a bar at the time, had managed to snaffle away 'four beers' for the journey, a rather modest amount of alcohol considering the band's reputation but, as Murray puts it, 'they just couldn't take their drink. They were falling all over the place.'

By 6 p.m., Jim and William were in an extreme state of anxiety, and Douglas was feeling pretty blue himself; apart from anything else, he had a vision of what a cool London club was supposed to be like, and this wasn't it.

'I was imagining something out of *The Avengers*,' admits Douglas. 'Patterned wallpaper, little tables with red lamps on them . . . When we turned up at this pub, I was a bit, "Oh!" Slightly deflated.'

Instead there were two shabby striped beige curtains behind the stage and a bare green light bulb dangling disconsolately above it.

The band waited, bickering all the while, but there was no sign of McGee, whom, up to this point, Jim had only spoken to over the telephone. Finally he arrived, a symphony in paisley. But again, they had visualised a certain type of person at the helm of the Living Room/Creation operation. And again, this wasn't it, although arguably this was better. Jim says: 'We were all looking out of the window wondering who this Alan McGee was. We saw a smart kind of Andrew Loog Oldham type and thought, That's probably him there. Then this maniac with big red hair and a patterned shirt came in. "Jim! Is that you, Jim?"'

To be fair, Alan didn't exactly think the next big thing had just rolled into town. In time, McGee would describe the three key Mary Chain members severally as 'charismatic, a natural rock star' (Jim), 'a genius guitar-player, the original talent' (William) and 'the most striking, like a film star' (Douglas), but his first impressions that day were that, while 'they looked cool', he insisted in his autobiography *Creation Stories*, 'there was something wrong about it, a small-town version of a movement that was dead'. He recalled in an interview for this book that 'Douglas looked about twelve, and Jim and William were screaming abuse . . . I thought they were going to be shit, to be honest. Because I'm Scottish I could pick up what they were saying, basically calling each other a bunch of cunts. They were just swearing away there.'

Jim recalls: 'We were supposed to be doing a sound-check, but in the end we started swinging at each other. McGee's standing there thinking, These guys are fucking mad.'

Actually McGee thought it was 'fucking great', and it was only going to get better. 'We did the sound-check,' Jim continues, 'and I don't think we played any musical notes, but Alan was going, "Genius! We'll do five albums!" We were like, What's going on here?'

There were, by Jim's admission, about six people in the audience by the time they had to play, and William stood resolutely with his back to them while the Mary Chain sound unfurled into a devilish spiral of chaos. Alan McGee remembers: 'They played three cover versions. The first song was "Vegetable Man", the second was Jefferson Airplane's "Somebody To Love". They never recorded it, but what a version.' The third, of course, was Subways Sect's 'Ambition'.

The fact that the band only just avoided outnumbering the audience didn't matter to McGee, who was, in Jim's words, 'frothing at the mouth. Literally, I think.' It was the legendary night that The Jesus and Mary Chain were signed, and the course was set. They would walk away with a one-off deal with Creation Records and a passionate, maverick manager. And tinnitus.

'We had a vocal PA system that Joe Foster was on the controls of,' McGee remembers. 'Now the Joe Foster of today has produced lots of records, but the Joe Foster of 1984 didn't know the backside of a mixing desk, so he just turned everything up to ten, which is logical when you're 22, but basically everything fed back. Most other bands would stop and turn down. Not the Mary Chain. Being insane, they just played on.'

'It was completely chaotic and a total hail of noise,' adds Joe Foster. 'The people immediately around us, our friends, they'd have been amazingly enthusiastic about the Mary Chain sounding like utter chaos. They were loving it. The Mary Chain must have thought, We've obviously come to the right place.'

Douglas's memory, admittedly, is a little different. 'Half the people at the gig hated us. Actually, I'd say less than half liked us.' Which, going by Jim Reid's maths, would leave about two people: Alan McGee and Joe Foster, no doubt.

Douglas continues: 'People were saying, "Alan, you're mad. You're *mad* for wanting to put a record out with them." It was coming out of that twee era. We thought, or certainly I did, that punk changed the world and all the bores and jobsworths had been wiped off the face of the earth, but everywhere you went it was: You can't do that . . .'

On that hot London night, however, McGee felt that the Mary Chain could, and should, continue exactly as they were. The whirlwind of sound that they'd managed to manifest was, by accident or design, startling, scary and magnificent, and it didn't matter that hardly anyone else could see what he saw in them. McGee wanted to be Malcolm McLaren, and in his eyes he'd just found his very own Sex Pistols. The Mary Chain might not have expressed it particularly ebulliently, but they were just as thrilled, relieved even, to find McGee.

'It was straight after that first very short, very extreme thing,' Douglas remembers, 'that he came up to us with a huge smile on his face and said, "Let's make an album." We were like, Fucking hell! Great! We loved McGee's energy, and we loved his love for us. We liked his oddness and, compared to us, he was experienced. To us he was like a saviour.'

McGee says: 'I just went, me being me, "I can sell 20,000 of this." I didn't think, This is a band that will last thirty years. When I went, "Can I sign you?" they looked at me as if I was bonkers. But that was the beginning.'

5

Night Moves, More Acid and Disaster In Wonderland

The reaction to the way we were was instant. People would want to
kill us or throw us off. No one was being two-faced about it, I guess.
Douglas Hart

Two days after their live debut at the Living Room, The Jesus and Mary Chain were booked to play a venue closer to home for the first time. The gig was at Night Moves in Glasgow and the promoter, Tom Coyle, had been persuaded by chief Mary Chain cheerleader Bobby Gillespie to give the band a chance. He agreed to let them play a mid-week show, rather than risk a packed Friday night on the band.

The Reids duly hosed down their insides with alcohol and, within moments of them staggering onto the stage, chaos ensued. It's fair to say it went down quite badly, not least with the group the Mary Chain were supporting, whose gear was in serious jeopardy.

'We were totally pissed. I could hardly stand up,' says Jim. 'I think we played for about fifteen minutes, but it wasn't one of those legendary fifteen-minute shows – we got pulled off after fifteen minutes.'

'Night Moves,' Murray shudders. 'That gig was a disaster waiting to happen. Jim and William were drunk, and we just made this almighty racket. They were falling about on top of the amplifiers. The other band were standing at the side of the stage raging.'

Bobby Gillespie was in attendance that night, with Jim Beattie by his side. Their reaction to what they were witnessing was at odds with the rest of the crowd. It was messy, drunken madness, but it radiated a rock'n'roll spirit that was 100 times more exciting and direct than anything else that was happening at that time. 'I remember them smashing into each other,' says Bobby. 'William, the fuzz pedal, it was just total carnage, really metallic, really sexy. They were all young, skinny guys, good-looking, especially Jim and Doug. I don't remember them playing any songs that related to the tapes that I had, but the first time I saw the Clash, I don't remember the songs sounding like the album, it was just noise and attitude and colour, sound, attack. The Mary Chain were an attack. They were really confused and the sound was confused, but it was really sexy. It was the best thing I'd seen since punk rock.'

The spell was broken when the bouncers physically threw the band not just off stage, but out of the venue. The Jesus and Mary Chain were getting an early taste of how they could provoke a reaction that wasn't just negative, but violent. Douglas recalls: 'One minute we were standing under the warm stage lights and the next we were in the alley in the rain. We'd just played one song the way we always did it, feedback and extreme explosion of energy, and they pulled us off the stage.'

'I remember getting chucked down a flight of stairs,' adds Jim. 'It was the guy who ran it, he was going, "You're useless! That's the last we'll ever hear of *you* fucking losers." We had a few bruises, but it all added to the legend, I suppose.'

To end up being hurled into the rainy night mid-set was something of a shock, but the first thing The Jesus and Mary Chain saw as they dusted themselves off was the beaming face of Bobby Gillespie. 'He was running towards us going, "That was the fucking best thing I've ever seen in my life!"' Douglas laughs.

With the adrenaline still coursing through their systems, it was impossible to just go straight home on the bus, for Douglas and Bobby at least. They headed into the darkness and drizzle of Glasgow's West End and talked all night, further cementing their bond. Both Bobby and the Mary Chain felt very much as if they were on their own, and as a result found it hard to open up to other people for fear of being misunderstood. There was no danger of that here.

Bobby says: 'It was incredible to make a connection with people who felt the same way about things that we did. I was quite closed off; I was waiting for the right people and they were the right people. It was a major moment in my life, meeting them.'

★

Fired up by their landmark Night Moves experience and Bobby's enthusiasm, Douglas, Jim and William knew they could turn the whole debacle to their advantage if they acted quickly and creatively. In true Sex Pistols style, they sat down and feverishly wrote a stack of fake letters to their local radio DJ, some praising the Mary Chain's first Glasgow foray and some expressing utter hatred for the racket that had offended their precious lugholes. It was an inspired publicity move that McGee himself, or even McLaren, would have applauded.

'We wrote maybe twenty letters between us,' says Douglas. 'Half of them said, "I saw the most terrible band last night, they made me sick!", and then asked him for a crappy record by someone like Lloyd Cole and the Commotions, and then the other half said, "I saw the best band ever!", and asked him for The Birthday Party or Subway Sect. And the guy read them all out!'

Back in London, Alan McGee was making plans for the Mary Chain. After their volcanic appearance at the Living Room, Alan wanted to record a single with the group as soon as possible, and while he might not have predicted how they would soar once their first record was released, it was time to prepare for their first national assault. First off, they needed to organise some press photos. 'We said, "Well, describe a press photo,"' says Jim. 'So he said, "Well, it could be live . . ." So I thought, Ah, OK.'

Again nothing if not creative, The Jesus and Mary Chain set up their own photo shoot in Jim and William's heavily disguised bedroom. They didn't need anyone to show them what was required, and they were already very much in control of how they wanted to be presented. Jim says: 'We put a big plastic sheet on the wall – this is pathetic, I shouldn't be admitting this – we got microphone stands and we'd all stand on the bed, and we had this big spotlight shining up. We took these photos as if this was us playing live. And bloody hell, it worked!'

'Jim and I both took photographs and made little collages,' says Douglas, 'so when we first had to do artwork for the band, we took all the photographs ourselves. If you look at the inner sleeve of *Psychocandy*, it's a kind of ripped collage of photographs that we had. All of our early artwork was done with great joy.'

In addition to photographs and collages, the Mary Chain also expressed their creativity by customising their clothes – a nod to their early love of punk. At one point Jim had a T-shirt with the words *Fuck Fuck Fuck* emblazoned on the front, while William's bore the stencilled message *Fuck Cunt Candy Cunt*. Plans to market these T-shirts quickly went adrift, as did a later idea to open The Jesus Fuck Café, where the Mary Chain themselves would bring you whatever they felt like serving regardless of whether you wanted it or not, and, as they put it themselves, 'you'd better bloody well like it.' Still a viable idea, no doubt, although the scenes in the kitchen might get a bit heavy.

While East Kilbride – the Reids' bedroom excluded – might have seemed to the untrained eye to be bereft of potential photoshoot locations, the Mary Chain had another ace up their sleeves. It was time to return to the derelict paint factory, armed with their cassette recorder, a camera, The Jesus and Mary Chain fan club (that is, Primal Scream) and some acid. Jim Reid recalls: 'We basically did our first ever proper photo session. We took all the Primals, we all dropped acid. A memorable day . . .'

Acid had a psychedelic lustre that pot-smoking lacked. As far as the Mary Chain and Primal Scream were concerned at that time, pot was a hippie drug. Unlike the Mary Chain, Bobby also avoided alcohol – 'I'd seen a lot of damage due to alcoholism in my family, I was kind of put off by that.' LSD didn't have any of those associations. The associations it did have were cool and poetic. 'Syd Barrett, Jim Morrison, Roky Erickson and Lux Interior from The Cramps,' Bobby muses.[*] 'The acid thing seemed glamorous, and also it seemed like, if you took LSD . . . there's got to be something in it. Maybe it helped these guys get some kind of vision or insight. I remember saying to Alan McGee that I was going to go and take acid with the Mary Chain, and his quote was: "Meeting of minds . . ."'

---

[*] Bobby Gillespie remained a devoted fan of the late Lux Interior, drawing inspiration from him as a frontman in Primal Scream's later years and also naming his son after him.

It was a hot day, 12 July, the day the Orange Order was marching through town. But inside the safety of the paint factory, the tape recorder was switched on with one of the Mary Chain's compilation tapes inside it, photos were taken, and acid was dropped. The factory practically pulsated with heat, sound and energy. The UK charts were dominated that summer by Wham!, Phil Collins and Nik Kershaw, pop stars whose music would obviously never trouble the Mary Chain's ears, at least not deliberately, anyway. Garage rock, punk and psych provided the soundtrack for them.

'I remember listening to The Stooges' "I Wanna Be Your Dog" and smashing things up with bits of metal,' says Bobby. 'We were trying to make a psychedelic connection. The connection was listening to The Stooges on acid and smashing up the factory. We weren't violent people, but there was a lot of anger and violence there. I remember playing "Primitive" by the Cramps and using branches as drumsticks on the hot ground. I wasn't in the band yet, but I might as well have been, in a way.'

The first hour was sheer euphoria. 'We were all coming up together,' Douglas remembers. But for some, things took a turn for the worse. 'Bobby and I were having a great time, but a few people had freak-outs. Jim and William had to go and there were all these other strangers.' It didn't help that some had spotted the Orange Order stumbling up the road towards them after a hard day's marching and drinking. 'Not what you wanted to see,' says Bobby.

Because Douglas was the only one left who knew the area well, he took the lead and, like a psychedelic Pied Piper, led his charges out of the glaring sunshine to a quiet glade in a nearby wood where they were less exposed. Or so they thought. 'Suddenly I heard this "Pyow, pyow!", the weirdest noise I'd ever heard,' he says. 'I looked up and there was the biggest ned from school, with an air gun, shooting at us! I was like, "Ah, no!" I don't know why I did this, but I just walked up the hill towards him and said, "Me and all my friends are on acid, can you stop doing that please?", and he goes, "All right," and just walked away. I thought he was going to kill me.'

Occasions such as this naturally strengthened the friendship between Bobby Gillespie and the Mary Chain. Drummer Murray Dalglish was significantly younger than the rest of the band, and had his own set of friends with whom he preferred to spend time. 'It wasn't like there was any friction, he's a nice guy,' says Douglas. 'But he was younger, you know? It was just different.'

Alan McGee wasted no time in organising more gigs for The Jesus and Mary Chain down south. The group might have viewed the English as an obnoxious bunch who did little other than 'watch *Terry and June* and say 'Crikey!' a lot, but London was where they had to make their mark if they wanted to get anywhere; so roll on more cramped Stagecoach journeys, more nights sleeping on McGee's floor, more drinking to oblivion to numb the nerves. 'They did a bizarre set of gigs,' McGee remembers. 'There was a gig in Mayfair where the audience was literally me and Joe Foster, and we ended up just playing our favourite records. It wasn't like "the next big thing". Nobody out there could give a fuck.'

Another occasion saw them supporting Five Go Down to the Sea at the Thames Polytechnic. Music journalist Kevin Pearce recalls the gig, which was slightly unusual as Jim was suffering from a sore throat, and vocal duties were taken care of – sort of – by William. 'It was lovely,' remembers Kevin. 'William read the words from a notebook, but if I remember rightly he gave up and just screamed ad libs.'

One of the most memorable gigs of that period was at a club night called Alice in Wonderland at Gossip at 69 Dean Street, Soho. The club night was a psychedelic 1980s extravaganza if ever there was one. It was run by Christian Paris and Clive Jackson, better known as the Doctor from Doctor and the Medics. McGee had persuaded Jackson to have the Mary Chain on one Monday night, and the Doctor gave them a slot on 17 September 1984, supporting Green On Red, a tough country-punk band from Tucson, Arizona. Once again, they would be using the headlining band's gear.

Unlike their stage debut at the Living Room in June, the Reid brothers managed to keep it together during the soundcheck. The problem was that while the soundcheck was at 7 p.m., stage time was closer to midnight, by which time, unsurprisingly, many a tincture had been imbibed. To make matters worse, Jim's sore throat showed no sign of abating, and McGee, clearly a man with excellent contacts, managed to find a doctor willing to give him an injection to dull the pain. The combination of a local anaesthetic and five hours of dedicated boozing promised an interesting result. The band staggered onstage and proceeded to wreak musical havoc. It was impossible to hear what they really sounded like, and Jackson was not happy.

Clive 'The Doctor' Jackson casts his mind back to that fateful night: 'It was absolutely . . . well, it wasn't even music, it was such a shambles. Green On Red had a lot of gear, and one of the concerns was that the Mary Chain were tottering about on stage and we were thinking, Some of the gear's going to go any minute. Murray was trying to hold it together, but Jim was just kicking his guitar around on the floor. People were complaining.'

Jim Reid admits: 'I was just out of my brain again, steaming. We didn't do set-lists back then. I would just shout out a song and we'd play it. We usually started with "In A Hole", so we played it, and then I was like, "Er . . . 'In A Hole!'" – "We've just played that, you idiot . . ." "Oh no . . ."'

Clive Jackson was unable to watch either the chaos onstage or the mass exodus of punters any longer. Not that that would have bothered the Mary Chain. As Jim said some months later, 'People who walk out of our concerts don't deserve to be there. They're stupid.'

Clive recalls: 'I just looked at Joe, Christian's brother, and said, "Shall we get them off?" I just picked Jim up and carried him off. He's not a particularly big bloke. Joe grabbed another one. You'd normally expect bouncers or crew to do that but, "Hang on, the DJ's carrying me off!"'

Murray kicked at the drum kit in frustration, knocking a cymbal to the floor. Then he remembered whose gear he'd just kicked – Green On Red's. A bunch of 'six-foot-six brick shithouses', as Murray puts it. While his bandmates were being hoisted off-stage, Murray was frozen to the spot, anticipating the rearrangement of his face at the hands of someone rather larger than him. 'This guy walked up to me. I'm preparing for it and I'm preparing for it, I thought he was going to thump me right in the face, and he just said, "Hey man! You were just like the goddamn fucking Sex Pistols!" I really thought I was going to get my arse kicked.'

'So that was that,' Jim sighs. 'We got chucked into the dressing-room. Christian, the guy who used to run it, I threw up on him. "You've let me down!" "Oh, fuck off. Bleurgh." I remember puking on his purple velvet trousers. I think that's what made me puke, actually.'

While the rest of the group came to in the sleazy, neon-lit murk of

Monday-night Soho, Murray managed to wheedle his way back inside, and he was glad he did. One of the people who had stuck around for the gig was none other than Murray's goth-punk drum hero Rat Scabies from The Damned. 'He came up and said I'd played well, and I was like, "Rat Scabies!" I was only sixteen and I thought this guy was a god on the drums. I also met Razzle from Hanoi Rocks. About six months later he was in a car with Vince Neil from Mötley Crüe and died in a car crash.'

The Jesus and Mary Chain might not have had the best gig of their lives that night, but Alan McGee was rubbing his hands together – he knew how to get the best out of any situation, and the more controversial or downright disastrous the better, in publicity terms at least. Months before 'riots' at Mary Chain gigs were reported, this was an early seed planted in the consciousness of any avid reader of the music papers, a seed that would ensure that as it grew, the Mary Chain's name would soon be inseparably linked with trouble, unpredictability and general bad behaviour, even if they did only get drunk to drown their stage fright. The readers of *Sounds* didn't need to know that.

'Alan just jumped on this,' Jackson grins. 'The next week in *Sounds* it was "Band Thrown Off Stage", all of that. When I saw that I thought, Oh Alan, you cute little so-and-so! Alan didn't care if they got chucked off stage. It added to the whole story, it became part of it – it was edgy. Alan created a legend within about six months.'

6

Upside Down

*Everything hasn't been done. No one has ever made a record
remotely like 'Upside Down'.*
Jim Reid to *The Face*, June 1985

Soon after their brief but memorable appearance at Alice In Wonderland in September 1984, The Jesus and Mary Chain prepared to cut their first disc. Alan McGee booked two midnight sessions at Alaska Studios in Alaska Street, Waterloo. Studio owner Pat Collier's least favourite time to record was through the night, but it was cheaper for McGee, who estimates the Mary Chain's sessions, funded by the Living Room club night, cost 'about £172'. There were also fewer distractions, and the idea of the Mary Chain recording 'Upside Down' and 'Vegetable Man' in a studio under a grimy railway arch at the dead of night does seem somehow fitting.

The day before the first session McGee and Joe Foster listened to a very specific clutch of records for inspiration and to be 'surrounded by the right kind of noise,' Foster recalls. '"Be My Baby", "Nag, Nag, Nag" and all that kind of thing, to get into the right atmosphere.' They also attempted to get some rest in during the day, which wasn't easy. 'Upside Down' couldn't have been a more appropriately titled debut.

'I was at my mum's place,' says Joe. 'I said, "Tomorrow I've got this recording at twelve and I've got to get up for that, so don't wake me up early." But she dutifully woke me up at 10 a.m. to start work at midnight. Right, OK, thank you . . . She was like, "I can't believe Alan would make you work at midnight. He's a good boy, he doesn't do weird stuff like that," and I was thinking, For God's sake, you don't know the half of it.'

Come the witching hour, some rather conspicuous characters with guitars could be seen loping into Alaska Studios, once again with minimal gear. Studio manager Pat Collier was already semi-prepared for this. 'I'm going, "OK, what are we going to use for amps and drums?" And they said, "We're going to use the Pastels' gear." This was par for the course. All the Creation bands would turn up and say, "We're using the Pastels' gear."'

It hadn't occurred to anyone, however, to contact The Pastels in advance to make sure they could get into their equipment cage in order to actually use it. It was now past midnight and no one was picking up the phone. The solution? Good old brute force.

Joe Foster says: 'We just had to break into their cage and borrow their gear, which they were quite baffled by when they found out. They were like, "If you're going to break into someone's equipment cage and steal something, aren't you supposed to, like, keep it and not give it back?" And we were like, "Yeah, but we were only borrowing it." We just had to buy them a new padlock.'

Pat Collier hauled the gear out of the cage only to find that the bass drum skin was, as he remembers it, 'pretty much ripped in half. At midnight there's not much you can do, but we got around it. I gaffer-taped a bit of plywood to the skin, so there was no drum sound but it went "click", and I used that to trigger a Linn drum, which would just give you a sampled bass-drum sound.'

The Jesus and Mary Chain's idea for 'Upside Down' and Syd Barrett's 'Vegetable Man', the planned B-side, was that the recordings would sound as close as possible to their original Portastudio demos. However, McGee, hooked on the band's gut-wrenching live sound, was keen to bring out the noisier, dirtier side of the Mary Chain. For the band, this, their debut recording, was all-important. Douglas Hart remembers there was 'a debate about how extreme to make it, not that we were anti that, but we were starting out with making a record'. There was always going to be a healthy amount of distortion on the tracks, however.

'They played guitar through a rack-mount digital delay,' says Collier. 'Quite a cheap and cheerful thing. I said, "What are you going to do with that?" And they plugged into it and cranked up the input so it distorted, like a transistorised distortion. Actually sounded pretty cool.

That was the guitar sound. I was thinking, This is ridiculous, you can't do that, you've got to have an amplifier! But of course, it worked fine.'

The session might have felt like a 'fraught disaster' as it was happening, to quote Pat Collier, but it was coming together exactly as it should, and by the end they had the proof. The sound was already huge, even before extra feedback was added during the mixing stage, and the octave-apart vocals and stark lyrics, detailing the Reids' very real and almost claustrophobic sense of isolation and disconnection, were by contrast mumbled quietly by Jim over the Mary Chain's own Wall of Sound.

Pat Collier says: 'By the time we got to the end, it was like, Blimey! It sounds really good. When you added it all up it was more than the sum of the parts.' Collier engineered and mixed the track, and McGee and Foster were present to encourage, oversee and generally 'produce' – or, as Collier remembers it, they 'sat in the producer's chair and went, "Yeah, right. Hmm . . . OK." It was just banging it down as fast as we could and that was it.' The Jesus and Mary Chain themselves needed no one to tell them what to do. The Reids had already made great demos on their own, after all.

Jim Reid says: 'Having other people there was more of a hindrance in some ways. We knew how the Mary Chain were supposed to sound, we didn't need a producer.' 'Alan encouraged us to make it louder,' Douglas adds. 'But no one pushed us to record it or to sound that way. William knew his way around the Portastudio, he's a smart guy and he's an intuitive musician, he's no slouch in the studio. If anyone produced it, it was Pat Collier and William, maybe. But even then it was a Mary Chain production.'

Once the basic tracks had been recorded, the Mary Chain added squeals of feedback using one of Alaska Studios' rehearsal amps. When Pat Collier finally handed them a copy of the rough mix, which the Mary Chain themselves had been closely involved with (each mainly to turn up his own part when the others weren't looking), they took it away, fatigued but euphoric. However, when they took it back to Alan's and listened to it on a ghetto-blaster, it sounded rather different to how they remembered it.

Jim says: 'We mixed it on these big Tannoy speakers that were bigger than my first flat. It sounded immense. That's pretty good, we thought. You can't do better than that. Then we took the tape home, put it on and it just sounded dreadful. It sounded like FM American rock or something. How did that happen?'

Alan and William went back to the studio the following day to remix the track and crank up the feedback. As Pat Collier remembers it, it took some time to get the required sound. 'We had four or five tracks of feedback on the 24-track tape, so I pushed the feedback up and they went, "OK, we need more." I pushed it up a bit more. "No, we need more." I pushed it up and we reached the top of the fader. "No, we need more."

'I pulled all of the faders down, cranked all the input gains in the top and off we went again. We reached the top of the fader again and I said, "Whoa, hang on a minute, you sit in front of the desk." I went round the back of the desk and they kept pushing the fader up and reaching the top, and we kept going until we basically had that well-known record that, when everyone heard it, thought their radio had gone wrong.'

It took time to get the mix right, and, as McGee remembers it, the band still weren't entirely happy with the result, but Alan was seriously excited and called Bobby Gillespie as soon as he could. Bobby: 'McGee calls me up and says, "This is the best thing I've ever released. It's going to blow the fucking scene wide open. People are waiting for this." You can never underestimate the enthusiasm this guy had for pushing that band.'

McGee was so enthusiastic, in fact, that he decided he couldn't wait to post Bobby a tape of the mixes; he bought a £10 Stagecoach ticket from London to Glasgow and travelled overnight to play it to him in person. Bobby had been printing record sleeves for Creation, as he'd previously worked in a print factory and knew someone who had a printing machine in his garage. Said machine would normally churn out wedding invitations and Christmas cards, but, as Bobby explains, 'All the early Creation sleeves were printed in this guy's garage. Alan would give me the artwork, this guy would do a lithograph and we would do 500 of them.' Had Bobby had any record sleeves ready for Alan to collect, so much the better, but either way, McGee was just bursting to play Bobby the tracks.

McGee arrived in Glasgow at around 7 a.m. and made his way straight to Bobby's house, brandishing the tape like a man possessed. As soon as that now well-known screech of feedback kicked in, Bobby was as smitten as McGee. 'He played me the Joe Foster mix, which had no feedback,' Bobby says, 'and then the William Reid/McGee mix. He said, "What do you think?" And I said, "Yours and William's."'*

The Mary Chain themselves still weren't satisfied, but McGee was confident that once both he and Bobby got behind it, they'd soon persuade them they had an underground hit on their hands. 'Common sense over-ruled,' says McGee. 'They went with it and it fucking exploded.'

Another ally of Creation who was given a preview of the release was the writer, musician and then Membranes frontman John Robb, he of the Mohawk haircut and husky, rapid-fire northwest delivery. 'The single was really fantastic,' he says. 'I liked "Vegetable Man" better, actually. It was such a cool idea to cover that track. Stuff like Syd Barrett at that time was very cult, you had to be kind of a student type to be into it, so it was like, Wow, these scruffy kids . . . We *thought* they were kids, we didn't realise they were older than we were. Quite funny.' The Reids in particular were always cagey or downright dishonest about their ages in interviews. For all of their radicalism and punk insouci-ance, they were keenly aware of the pop world's love of 'bright young things' – William was already pushing twenty-seven at this stage. The Mary Chain were ambitious but, it's fair to say, were never known for rushing into anything. However, when challenged on this point, Jim airily delivered the following statement: 'Sometimes I lie about my age, sometimes I don't. Sometimes I lie about what I had for my dinner as well. I'm a bit of a lying bastard.' Which may also be a lie.

John Robb was writing for the music magazine *ZigZag*, a publica-tion started by *Rock Family Trees* creator Pete Frame. It was hailed as less mainstream than the competition and had strong punk affili-ations, thanks to its years under the editorship of Kris Needs. It received a fresh injection of energy when it was relaunched in 1984 with the introduction of new editor and goth aficionado Mick Mercer. The Jesus and Mary Chain, as they have long found them-selves having to insist, were never goths (black clothes and big hair do not necessarily a goth make) but they would fit into the new *ZigZag* neatly.

---

* The 'Upside Down' that was released was William and Alan's mix, and the mix of 'Vegetable Man' credited to Joe Foster was used for the B-side.

McGee swiftly arranged for John Robb to conduct the Mary Chain's first interview for an established music magazine,* which took place at John's flat in The Membranes' band house in Didsbury, Manchester. It isn't remembered as a particularly comfortable afternoon. 'Alan used to work for British Rail before he went full-time with his label, so he'd get free passes,' says John. 'He brought the band to Manchester on the train, the two brothers and Douglas. McGee had a bag with about eight cans of lager in it, and the interview was basically McGee ranting and the band just moping in the corner. The Reids were so insular it was like the world hardly existed for them.'

*

London 1984/5. Everything is dead, everyone's waiting for something. Too many false starts have made people cynical, though a beacons [sic] remain. 'Mad' Alan McGee, Creation supremo, needs an exciting group: is this another false start? Who needs starts anyway? . . . Jesus and The Mary Chain [sic] huddle together on the bed, protected only by their cynicism . . .

'Any careerists in the room? What'll you be doing in five years' time?'
'We're only seventeen, we don't care what happens next.'
And what's more folks, they don't!

John Robb/ZigZag

---

* The band's first ever interview was conducted by Chris Davidson and featured in his cult fanzine *Slow Dazzle*.

7

Murray Leaves, Bobby Joins, Germany Beckons

They were real outsider, loner guys. Weirdos. Like I'm a weirdo.
Rock'n'roll kids, basically.
Bobby Gillespie on The Jesus and Mary Chain

Just weeks after the recording of 'Upside Down', McGee had an announcement to make: Creation Records would be going on a tour of Germany, and The Jesus and Mary Chain were on the bill, alongside Alan's own band Biff Bang Pow! and the Jasmine Minks. For the Mary Chain, it would be the first time they'd ever left Britain. Home was still East Kilbride for the band, but life was accelerating and the Mary Chain's confidence and power were increasing by the day. However, a temporary disaster was about to strike.

Murray Dalglish was uncertain of what the future held with The Jesus and Mary Chain, and when he was offered an apprenticeship in East Kilbride he decided to take it. It was 1984, unemployment was high, and there were no guarantees in the music business. Murray, encouraged by his family, wanted to earn a living.

Murray says: 'It was decision time for me. I'd been offered a job to build buses. Getting offered an apprenticeship was a massive thing, you couldn't get them for love nor money. We were on the Tube going somewhere and I just came out with it. I don't think there was any trying to change my mind.'

Certainly Murray didn't think there was any danger of 'Upside Down' doing particularly well. 'I wouldn't have been thinking it would have done anything near what it did do,' he says. 'Even when it did go to number 1, number 2 in the indie charts, by that time I was out of the band. But even that, it wasn't like that's a massive thing to have done. If you weren't on *Top of the Pops* then you were nobody. A few years later they were on *Top of the Pops*, of course.'

While the news sent Alan McGee temporarily into a tailspin, the rest of the band were philosophical. They liked Murray, but for a while they hadn't been sure whether he fitted in – which, admittedly, would have been a tall order for most people. He was also just sixteen years old, and the rest of the group, despite what they might have told John Robb, were not seventeen.

'We – Jim, William and I – had been around together for ages, so it must have been difficult for Murray,' says Douglas. 'But he's a well-adjusted guy, I don't think it fucked him up to any degree. When there were arguments about style, musically, then that was upsetting for him. "Other drummers are laughing at me . . ." For us it was like, Uh-uh. I guess when it came to it, the most important thing was the music.'

Jim Reid's stand-out memory is that Murray was also concerned about the money – or lack of it – that they were making as a band. 'We just wanted to make a hell of a racket and grab people by the throat,' says Jim. 'But Murray would be saying, "My dad said we should be making more money." – "Well, Murray, we will, but we have to go through this." He would say things like, "If I joined a country and western band and toured Canada, I'd make £500 a week." There's nothing you can say to that, really. He was just a kid. You kind of knew it wasn't going to work. He left before he was pushed, if you know what I mean.'

After returning to East Kilbride, the Reids and Douglas bade Murray farewell and left the teenage drummer to venture forth in his new life. He would still play drums, but the difference was that he would soon join a band with people he knew and fitted in with. Murray explains: 'I went on to play in a band called Baby's Got A Gun, named after the Only Ones song. I'd gone to school with some of these guys. I probably had more enjoyment with what I was doing then. I would have still been an outsider even if I'd been in the Mary Chain today, I think.'

Once again, the Mary Chain needed to find a drummer quickly, and the solution was already under their noses. Alan McGee knew Bobby Gillespie had been drafted in the past to drum for Altered Images, the Scottish pop act of 'Happy Birthday' fame, fronted by the elfin

Gregory's Girl starlet Clare Grogan. Gillespie would be the ideal replacement: he was already part of the Mary Chain family anyway.

Bobby recalls: 'I used to roadie for Altered Images because we were friends. I was eighteen and they were fifteen, they were at school, they were punks in Glasgow. I used to go up to town on a Saturday and buy records, and these kids were always in the same record stores. Eventually I'm checking them, they're checking me, I could see they were buying cool records, and they could see I was buying cool records. So it was like, "Are you going to see Siouxsie and the Banshees this week?" – "Yeah." Turns out they've got a band, and that band became Altered Images.

'One time they were supporting Spizz Energi at the Rock Garden and the drummer, I don't know what happened, he just disappeared. So I played drums in front of all these crazy skinheads. I mean, it was just filling in. Pretty primitive drumming.'

'I don't even think we auditioned Bobby,' Jim Reid admits. 'We just said, "Can you drum?" "Yeah, a wee bit." "Right, OK."'

The Creation package tour of Germany was just weeks away, but The Jesus and Mary Chain had some pre-tour gigs in the book that could act as a warm up for their new drummer. This called for something that marked a break in Mary Chain tradition: a rehearsal.

The Mary Chain booked some time in the crypt of a church off Sauchiehall Street in Glasgow, where Fire Engines guitarist Davy Henderson had a studio. It was a hub for bands such as Orange Juice and Strawberry Switchblade, 'and we all kind of fancied Strawberry Switchblade,' Bobby admits. Once the band had set up, Bobby walked over to the drums, ignored the drum stool and started to play standing up, simply but powerfully, Moe Tucker-style. Floor tom and snare. No danger of any unnecessary fills here. He'd stripped the drum sound back, perhaps because he wasn't really a drummer and couldn't throw in an extravagant drum-fill even if he wanted to, but for the Mary Chain he was ideal.

Douglas Hart says: 'I remember when we rehearsed in Glasgow with him. The energy . . . it had been good before, but it was just, "This is it". The difference was quite marked. Not just in the simplification of the drums, but his personality, the energy that he brought just completed it. We got the bus back to East Kilbride, and we were all thinking, Well, this is going to be great. It had always been great; it wasn't like Murray was letting it down, but when Bobby joined it was a band.'

'I thought about this a few years later,' Bobby muses. 'They had the image sorted out, and when I joined it made it better. Everything about me joining was better for them musically, psychically, image-wise. I can say that without sounding big-headed. It just felt like a unit.'

This was a thrilling watershed for the Mary Chain – they didn't just have a new drummer, they had a close friend in the line-up, infusing their live show with an electrifying new vitality, confidence and visual impact. Bobby was on his feet, dressed in black, often wearing dark glasses like his new bandmates, playing with furious energy on just two drums, a look and sound that would be emulated by later groups such as fellow Scots Glasvegas. The Jesus and Mary Chain would also be going abroad for the first time in their lives in just a few weeks' time.

Bobby Gillespie says: 'Me and Douglas went to get our passports on the same day. We went for a coffee or an ice-cream afterwards and Douglas said, "We're all going to get leather trousers in Germany, it's going to be like The Beatles in Hamburg. We're going to be rock'n'roll stars." I was like, "I'm not getting leather trousers!" And he went, "You are. We'll be like Generation X!"'

8

Peel Session, The Three Johns,
NME *Falls in Love*

We want success, but we want to do it on our own terms.
Jim Reid to *Picture Disc,* 1985

McGee had secured a session for The Jesus and Mary Chain on John Peel's Radio 1 show, the only broadcast outlet that was simpatico to what they and others like them were doing. They also had two gigs to play before they boarded their ferry to Germany – one in Glasgow with Primal Scream and the other, the night before they left, at the Three Johns pub in Islington, North London.

Although Primal Scream and the Mary Chain had wanted to put their own gig on together for months, Bobby had felt his own group weren't ready. But the time had come, and in a reaction to the Mary Chain being rejected so vehemently by Glasgow so far, they found their own venue and did everything themselves, from the booking of the PA to the publicity. The gig took place on 11 October 1984 at the Venue in Glasgow, and Bobby, of course, would be playing in both groups. He also designed the poster, which took inspiration from the film *If....*, printed a stack in his friend's garage and went around town with the Mary Chain, pasting them up on every available wall space.

Bobby says: 'It was the poster from the film *If....* with the hand-grenade, "Which side are you on?"

'I met them in town, and I think my girlfriend at the time worked in a bank, she was eighteen but looked younger, and the Reid brothers were quite impressed. They thought I had a schoolgirl girlfriend. "You've got a schoolie, yer dirty bastard!" And I was going, "She's not, she works in the bank!" "Nah, she's at school!" I don't think they had girl-friends, you know. Douglas did.'

The Mary Chain and Primal Scream were noticeable at the best of times, but they attracted even more attention when they started wallpapering Glasgow with Bobby's arresting posters. 'We were putting them up in broad daylight,' Bobby laughs. 'You're supposed to do it at night-time when nobody's looking . . .'

'At one point we were at the entrance of this cinema, down some steps by the fire door,' recalls Douglas. 'We were pasting these things up, and we looked round and there was this big gang of neds hanging around, real rough-looking guys. We were like, "Oh fuck. We're never going to get out of here alive." We carried on putting the posters up with wallpaper-paste and there was this long, silent pause. We didn't want to look round. Eventually one of them punched his mate on the shoulder and said, "Ah Willy, look what they're doing! They're using that see-through paint." See-through paint! Then they just went away.'

The eleventh of October swung around, and after minimal rehearsal, and with East Kilbride groups Meat Whiplash and Ochre 5 in support, the Mary Chain and Primal Scream were ready to launch a full-scale musical attack on Glasgow. This would also be the first time that the Reids would have really seen Bobby performing live. 'Jim watched us [Primal Scream] do "Nobody's Scared" by Subway Sect at the sound-check,' Bobby recalls, 'and he came up to me and said, "You're the best band in the world." That was amazing. It was real validation because I didn't know if we were any good.'

Bobby played guitar in Primal Scream, and then, as he remembers it, 'went off for ten minutes and then came back to play drums with the Mary Chain'. The sets were short and fierce, with Primal Scream and the Mary Chain each slipping in a Subway Sect cover ('Ambition', in the Mary Chain's case). The Reids' set was growing all the time; they still played Syd Barrett's 'Vegetable Man' but they were becoming more assured in terms of performing their own material. Their progress was evident: the first Living Room gig had consisted of mostly covers but just four months later more originals were working their way in – 'Taste The Floor', 'Inside Me', 'The Living End' and 'Barracuda', as well as their regular opener 'In A Hole'. Bobby's presence also gave them confidence on stage, not just because he was so enthusiastic but because his drumming was just right.

The Mary Chain had shifted into a new and powerful gear, and as the feedback howled around the waspish Jim Reid's dark incantations, the audience were, whether they realised it or not, staring at a band whose debut single alone would soon crash into the pop and indie world like a well-aimed missile, ushering in change and burning up the dross. This was the future.

Nearly two weeks later, The Jesus and Mary Chain were on their way back to London to stay with Alan McGee. They'd packed their bags for the Creation package tour, which was almost upon them, and were ready to record their first session for John Peel on 23 October, two nights before the tour. Trips to London meant, unfortunately, freezing nights trying to sleep, fully clothed, under one sleeping bag on the floor of Alan's draughty Tottenham flat. There was no money for hotels – and besides, Alan could also take the opportunity to put the boys to work for the common cause of Creation. Many an evening would be spent folding record sleeves and putting them in plastic bags. Readers who own some of Creation's early output on the original vinyl may well have a record that was packaged by hand by The Jesus and Mary Chain.

The Jesus and Mary Chain's Peel Session was due for transmission on 31 October, while the band would be away. They could have had no sense of what the combined effect of this broadcast, their pre-tour London gig and the release of their debut single, 'Upside Down' would be – not least because their session for Radio 1 was, the group felt, something of a disappointment.

They weren't allowed to play as they wished, and there was a distinct but not untypical lack of respect radiating from the jobsworth engineers (Peel was not present) at London's iconic BBC Maida Vale Studios. This was the case, they would find, with all of their Peel Sessions to come; and of course the groups they had listened to themselves on Peel's show had had similar experiences. (The Slits, for example, had to put up with the patronising 'can't-do' attitude of various engineers, who tried to retune the band's guitars and questioned their sound.)

As William Reid put it in an interview with *NME* at the time, 'It's as if there's a secret bible written just for sound men, saying what they can and cannot do.' The irony was that the reason Peel featured certain

bands on his show was that they were subversive, exciting and glee-
fully broke the rules. But then they had to abide by the rules once they
reached Maida Vale to record for the man himself. Much of what Peel
had heard and loved in the first place would be absent from the ultimate recording. Fortunately, though, enough of the group's essence
would shine through.

Bobby Gillespie says: 'Those sessions were a big thing for us. We'd
listen to the programmes in 1978, 1979, 1980, maybe less so in 1981
because music was somewhere else then. But you'd hear bands like
Subway Sect and the Psychedelic Furs, PiL, the early Banshees and The
Slits, bands that didn't necessarily have record deals but were buzz
bands. You'd read about them in the music press and you'd think, "If I
lived in London I'd go and see that band, they look cool." You could
hear them doing Peel sessions and tape them. So to do a Peel Session
ourselves was like, Fuck, this is a real test, you know. Our heroes had
done this and done it right, we had to do it right.'

Despite the Mary Chain's misgivings about the results, every session
recorded by them for Peel would still be memorable, electrifying and
unique. They just weren't, to the Reids' minds, as they might have been.
Peel might have loved them, but life was not made easy for The Jesus
and Mary Chain in those hallowed studios, and it didn't help that they
already had a reputation for drunkenness and having a blithe disregard
for equipment.

'John Peel was supportive right from the beginning,' says Douglas. 'It
was a real thrill for us, going to Maida Vale. But it was difficult with the
engineers. Our reputation would precede us and we'd go to places where
people would be expecting these psychos, and we'd just be like, "Can I
have a cup of tea, please?" Later on we might go mental when we'd had
a few drinks, but, you know, outside of night-time when we were a bit
drunk, we were nice people, we're not really that bad. On the other
hand, having a reputation like that gets you a long way. You don't even
have to do anything, just look at someone in a certain way.'

The Jesus and Mary Chain's sessions for Peel would differ from their
trademark sound partly because William would usually record layers of
feedback and, as Douglas puts it, 'mix it like a symphony – you can't do
that on a Peel session.' At least the engineers made a concession when,
as a tribute to the Fire Engines, those godfathers of angular Scottish

post-punk, the Mary Chain requested that one of their songs, which had a false start, should be left as it was.

One producer working at Maida Vale was Dale 'Buffin' Griffin, former drummer with Mott The Hoople. 'I think he had loads of kids like us coming in who didn't know how to tune the drums or the guitars,' Bobby admits. 'It was very amateur, and I think that's what John Peel liked about these bands. I don't remember Dale Griffin being very encouraging. The Mary Chain obviously did not give a fuck.'

Jim Reid says: 'The Peel Sessions were the worst. You knew exactly what you wanted to do, but you've got these guys who don't want you to do it. They actually don't want you to do what you're trying to do. It would be incredibly childish things like, we'd say, "Can we have the guitars up a bit?" And they'd go, "Yeah", and they'd put them up, and you'd look over there and you could see out of the corner of your eye that he's putting it back down again. Or he'd slide it up here but be turning it back down with the thing at the top. Ridiculous.

'That was always the way when you did any TV or radio. They'd be looking at us like, "Is your guitar broken?" You'd be explaining, "Look, I know this isn't what you're used to, but this is what we sound like, so just whack those guitars up as loud as you can." "Right, squire." Then you'd do your rehearsal and there'd be no guitars in it.'

Their first Peel session, which consisted of the songs 'In A Hole', 'You Trip Me Up', future single 'Never Understand' and 'Taste The Floor', would have a far-reaching effect, however, as would their gig at the Three Johns the following night, on 24 October 1984, just hours before the band set off for Germany.

Alan McGee had just mailed out press copies of 'Upside Down', packaged by hand by the Mary Chain in Alan's spare room. The image of the Pollock-style, paint-splashed guitar on the cover would soon be capturing imaginations all over the country, including that of John Squire, later of the Stone Roses. 'John Squire's got this paint-spattered guitar because, to him, this paint-spattered guitar, that was the sound of the Mary Chain,' Bobby explains.

'Upside Down', a veritable psychotic breakdown on vinyl, was landing on desks across London on the very day of the Three Johns gig. Timing was everything, and Alan's aim was to ensure that as many eminent members of the music press as possible were present at the

Three Johns while the single was fresh in their minds. *NME* writer Neil Taylor was just about to leave Carnaby Street for the night when the then Live Pages editor, Mat Snow, approached, 'Upside Down' in hand.

'I was covering new bands at the time,' says Neil, 'the June Brides, the Wedding Present, Big Flame and Tools You Can Trust, who would go on and become part of a C86 tape which I compiled for *NME* – obviously that was a year and a bit off. I was doing a lot of work for Mat Snow, and he said he'd got this single from Alan McGee at Creation. It was literally out of the mailer, and he said, "They're playing tonight at the Three Johns pub." It was about six o'clock, and he said, "Do you want to go?" I played the single and it sounded great. So off I went.'

The back room of the Three Johns, filling up slowly, was tense with anticipation. The Mary Chain never mixed with the audience before or after the gigs, developing a mystique that also suited their personalities perfectly. As soon as Neil Taylor arrived at the pub, Alan McGee spotted him. 'He was straight on to me,' remembers Taylor, 'pushing, pushing, pushing the music. Very willing ears, open to what he had to say.' McGee wouldn't have to push too hard with the Mary Chain, however. By the time they were on stage, Taylor was already mentally forming a review so positive it would cement their position as the agitative saviours of rock'n'roll. *NME* writers do this from time to time and sometimes, inevitably, they're wrong, so they save face by later snatching back the golden words they briefly bestowed upon yet another new indie-pop hope. That wasn't the case on this occasion. 'It was a revelation,' confirms Taylor.

'The gig was out of control,' McGee recalls. 'I don't even know how to describe it. Every single one of them bar Gillespie was sort of having a nervous breakdown as they played. Douglas Hart was . . . well, I don't know what drug he was on, but he was, like, pinned to the wall. Jim was having an epileptic fit, William was on his knees, and then they proceeded to smash their instruments up. Gillespie – the guy barely drank, but he was drunk, manically drumming away.'

In an era of often twee, anodyne music, these intoxicated misfits and their earth-juddering sound had a quality that went straight to the heart, brain and nerves and, as always, prompted a totally divided reaction. The sound and atmosphere created was actually frightening, and it was certainly unnerving for the support band, who were standing in the wings watching the gear they'd reluctantly lent the Mary Chain get trashed.

'We borrowed an amp off the support,' Jim remembers. 'The guy said, "Please take care of it." "You've got my word, I'll treat that like I treat my own." Even though ours was in the repair shop because I'd kicked it over. I wasn't trying to upset the guy, I was just falling all over the place. I bumped against his amp and it just went flying. There's a photograph in the paper of him getting ready to punch me.'

The gig was typically short, and there's an argument that, with this level of intensity, any longer would have been overkill. From the band's point of view, they poured so much raw energy into their live appearances that they were often just too exhausted to continue any longer.

'The Fire Engines only played for twenty minutes and we used to love them,' concludes William Reid. 'I don't remember anyone wanting their money back or rioting at a Fire Engines show.'

As soon as they'd finished their brief, provocative set the Mary Chain were off, out of the venue without meeting any of the press, wisely keeping the spell unbroken as Alan McGee worked the room. It was all theatre, and the Mary Chain knew that the show continued after they had left the stage. This worked for them – they were generally uneasy in company, and this enigmatic closed-door policy would last for much of their career. 'If people burst into our dressing-room expecting a wild party, they would be frozen out within about ten seconds,' says Douglas. 'I always thought it was funny. It was never like, Hey! What a great show! We'd sit in silence and then go home and watch the telly.'

Meanwhile Neil Taylor was already filing his review. 'We got the live review into the paper quickly,' says Neil. 'It became the lead review because it was so enthusiastic and it made these ridiculous comments about them being the best band since God knows who, the Sex Pistols or Joy Division.'

Oblivious to the effect they had had on the NME, and how their world was soon to change as a result, the Mary Chain made the short journey back to Tottenham for another attempt to sleep on McGee's floor. They also had to prepare for the trip ahead, now just hours away. It might not have been easy to sleep that night, although the amount of alcohol that had been imbibed at the Three Johns probably helped at least a couple of them to pass out. But they were all full of fevered expectation about what was to come; Bobby in particular still couldn't quite believe he was in his favourite band, let alone embarking on their first tour as their drummer – and he wasn't even a drummer, anyway. Life was taking some interesting turns.

'It was really exciting,' says Bobby. 'At that point in my life it was such a big deal to me. I was on the dole and I was kind of a bit depressed. But suddenly I'm going away with The Jesus and Mary Chain.'

Planet Mary Chain didn't know what was about to hit it. Neither did Germany. It was, as McGee remembers, 'insane'.

'We were all there together,' says Joe Foster. 'Us against the world, or at least normal German people. Maybe that was a bit delusional, because they weren't really normal German people, they were rock'n'roll German people. But it was fun. We felt immune to everything.'

9

Brothels, Barbed Wire, Blanco Y Negro

*All their songs are very noisy and sound a bit like fingernails being
scraped down a blackboard. (False)*

*Some of their songs are very noisy and sound a bit like fingernails
being scraped down a blackboard. (True)*

William Shaw, *Smash Hits*

The Creation package tour of Germany was, to put it mildly, something
of a lo-fi affair. Alan and Joe's band, Biff Bang Pow!, had only released
two singles, and as Alan remembers it, 'sold about fifty to a hundred
copies. The Jasmines had done about the same.' The Jesus and Mary
Chain still didn't technically have a record out at all. The groups travelled in two dodgy-looking vans, freezing air blasting through the
broken windows, and stopped off at small rock venues around the
country to play to a handful of people curious to see who had just rolled
into town. 'We were roughing it pretty badly,' Jim says.

This was the Mary Chain's first experience of being on the road, and
it was an early taste of how they would cope crammed inside a van for
significant periods of time. They were used to sharing rooms and sometimes even beds, but any hopes they might have had for anything beyond
the basics were swiftly trounced. 'McGee had promised a certain level
of comfort and style,' says Jim Reid wryly. 'One of the places we were
staying in was a doss-house. A pretty good one, I have to say. We probably lowered the tone a bit, but there you have it. That's McGee's idea
of the Hilton. It was a good time though. We'd been signing on the dole,

and suddenly we were riding around Germany and Switzerland, playing in front of an audience.'

As McGee remembers, anything that could happen really did on that fateful tour. 'We nearly crashed in the van when the person behind the wheel went to sleep,' he says. 'There was inter-band arguing with every band, although funnily enough not so much with the Mary Chain. We nearly got beaten up by a bunch of skinheads, there was fighting, bottles thrown . . . Nobody had any money. Nothing against brothels, but we slept in one.'

A particularly memorable gig on this tour was at the Loft in Berlin, the first show of the tour and one that counted My Bloody Valentine among the audience, although they didn't make themselves known to the Mary Chain at the time. Berlin was eventful for various reasons, not least because Bobby broke his self-imposed alcohol ban.

'When we went to Berlin I remember Douglas getting off with an older woman,' remembers Bobby Gillespie. 'She seemed like a real woman, not like a girl. I remember drinking vodka and jumping over the drums. Generally I didn't get smashed – I had to play the drums.

'One night I remember sitting on the floor and just looking at the others and thinking, I belong. I never said this to any of them, I just felt a really deep connection with those guys. It was special. You don't get that every day of the week.'

'It had become something really special,' agrees Douglas Hart. 'The energy you got from that can see you through anything, and I guess that tour was the first real load of gigs with Bobby. The beauty and energy of it is hard to describe, we were a powerful force when we were all together in that way.'

There wasn't a huge amount of camaraderie between the Mary Chain and the other groups, however. Bobby initially felt that the other groups didn't take them very seriously, but the feeling toward the Mary Chain, from some individuals at least, soon graduated to irritation as they watched the new boys inadvertently steal the show.

The Jesus and Mary Chain started off at the bottom of the bill, but it quickly became clear that this would have to change. 'About mid-way through, me and the Jasmines just put our hands up,' says Alan. 'The Mary Chain were just blowing every other fucker off the stage. They headlined most of the rest of the dates. There were a couple of dates where the Mary Chain insisted one of us went on last, because they're nice people, but they were just killing every show.'

Douglas Hart says: 'I think a lot of the guys in the other bands were . . . not jealous, but couldn't get it. Not McGee, he was always excited by us, but I think we felt a slight resentment from some of the others.'

Band rivalry aside, the travel arrangements alone were enough to ramp up the tension. 'At first we were all kind of together,' Douglas continues, 'but after less than a week it had become quite fraught. The tour was quite hard, you know, none of us had travelled before. And the guy driving only had one cassette tape and he was just playing it over and over. It was like a psychedelic garage compilation, but not a good one. There were two good songs on it, but by the 700th time you'd heard it . . .'

As the tour rumbled to a close and the Creation bands boarded the ferry home, the Mary Chain felt a little deflated. The idea of travelling around Europe had been a romantic one but the reality was tough. Little did they know that everything had already changed for them back in the UK. The single had reached the ears of everyone who was anyone in the music press, and Neil Taylor's exultant *NME* review put the buzz around the band into overdrive. But they didn't know any of that yet. All they knew now was that, if this was how life was going to be for the next few years in their bid to succeed, well, as Douglas says, they would 'probably kill each other'.

Douglas continues: 'On the ferry back, all of us were going, "Fucking hell, man!" It wasn't a disappointment, because we were so excited to play, but we weren't really enamoured of the rock'n'roll life. We were all thinking, God, with our kinds of personalities . . .'

'The bottom line was that it was a fucking rough tour,' McGee concludes flatly. The mood changed, in the Mary Chain camp at least, when they were back on dry land. In this pre-internet age, being out of the country for a couple of weeks would leave you feeling relatively out of touch, so as soon as possible Bobby bought the music papers, including, naturally, a copy of the *NME*. He hurriedly leafed through the pages, his eyes scanning for their name. This time they would have more than the usual cursory mention about being turfed off stage in an advanced stage of refreshment.

Bobby found the reviews and read them aloud to the rest of the Mary Chain who were, as Jim Reid recalls, 'Just pissing ourselves laughing. We said, "That's it." And it was. We were beating them off with sticks after that.'

'The headline was something like "Hark the Herald Angels Sing", Neil Taylor remembers. 'Around that time, the *NME* still had a large sales base, so the right thing said in the *NME*, you still had the power to create an effect, which is what happened when that review went in.'

Bobby says: 'It was like Douglas said, "We're going to go to Germany and come back and be rock'n'roll stars." It was all coming true. And it was like, "Yeah, that's right. Because we should be rock'n'roll stars. We're the best."'

Jim, as always with his feet firmly on the ground, remembers the glowing review well. He also remembers the terrible review. '*Sounds* said it was the worst gig by the worst band they'd ever seen, and the *NME* said it was like the Sex Pistols crossed with Joy Division or something. So somewhere between those two . . .' Both write-ups were more than welcome, however. 'Those are basically the only kind of reviews you want,' said William. 'The best and the worst.' There was nothing vanilla about The Jesus and Mary Chain, and there was nothing vanilla about the reaction they prompted. Indifference would have been the ultimate insult. Meanwhile, 'Upside Down', which had entered the indie chart at number 34, was steadily rising, and would be in the top ten in a matter of weeks (and at number one by February 1985).

To be compared to Joy Division or the Sex Pistols must have meant they were doing something right but, always contrary, Jim would later casually claim in an interview on Belgian television that the comparison with the Pistols was way off the mark, and that he 'didn't even like them'. He also declared that 'Joy Division were rubbish', a statement that drew a gasp from the journalist interviewing him. It made for a memorable interview that was already guaranteed to stick in the mind because, on the couch next to Jim and Douglas, was Bobby, energetically making out with his girlfriend.

The reality of the situation was that Jim had been pre-warned not to say anything against Joy Division during the interview because the journalist was a major fan of the group. This was a red rag to a bull, naturally: Jim was as big a fan of Joy Division as the interviewer, he just couldn't resist temptation. Unfortunately, whenever he praises Joy Division now, fans reliably remind Jim of the Belgian TV interview. 'I didn't expect to be apologising for it twenty years later,' he grumbles.

This was all to come, although it wasn't far off. The idea of undergoing interview after interview was never something the Mary Chain would relish, especially as, more than once, they were greeted jovially by unfamiliar journalists trying to lighten the mood with the opening gambit: 'So! Which one's Jesus and which one's Mary?'

All the same, Jim would display a natural talent when it came to delivering acidic soundbites and sometimes shocking statements, especially on the subject of rock'n'roll's sacred cows. On one occasion, Jim declared he was 'embarrassed to tell people what I do with my life, to think that what I do is the same as what Eric Clapton does. He's raping it, he's puking on it, he's pissing on it. For that reason I don't want to be a part of it.'

The Rolling Stones, while the Reids loved their 'scruffy degeneracy', would also come in for a verbal pasting back in the day. This from William: 'The best thing that could have happened to The Stones was if they'd have met Charles Manson in 1969 and he could have hacked their heads off with a chainsaw.' Pithy.

While they were at it, they also archly dismissed their enduring hero David Bowie as a 'fucking scumbag who should have been shot in 1972' and, while William graciously hailed the genius of both John Lennon and Paul McCartney, the latter's mistake was apparently that he 'never got murdered before he wrote "Mull Of Kintyre".'

Respect was always reserved for the Velvets (the perfect pop song, according to Jim, would have 'Maureen Tucker playing drums and Eric Clapton's severed head hanging from the drum kit . . .') and of course The Stooges, although even the latter didn't get away without a few jabs. William once said that: 'After us, the perfect record is "I Wanna Be Your Dog" by The Stooges. But the horrible guitar solo fucks it up.' Despite the obvious shock value of some of their statements, however, there is also the feeling that rock'n'roll means so much to the Reids that they take offence at anyone who dares ruin it by being over-indulgent, embarrassing or just downright naff. The Reids' interview technique drew much from the punk tradition, and their quotes are often reminiscent of Public Image Limited's confrontational interviews during this period. And on the subject of PiL, John Lydon would be branded a 'sad comedian' by the Reids at the time, long before that infamous butter advertisement was a mere twinkle in an ad exec's eye.

In terms of the press the Mary Chain were getting at this early stage, Neil Taylor would observe with interest how diametrically opposed *Sounds* and *NME* were in their opinion. But not only is all publicity valuable ('Don't read your press, weigh it,' as one wise soul once said), the *NME*, he asserts, 'would always have had the upper hand because the circulation figures were far higher.'

★

The next gig in the Mary Chain diary was on 25 November at the Ambulance Station in Old Kent Road, Deptford, a notorious squat/ venue known for being so lawless that bands would frequently take to the stage (which was surrounded by barbed wire) tooled up in case of trouble. 'It was skinhead, NF territory,' remembers Neil Taylor. 'Some of the bands who played at the Ambulance Station would regularly go on with a claw-hammer or a baseball bat.'

Between the Mary Chain's return to the UK and their appearance at the Ambulance Station, they were, understandably, suddenly required to do a lot of press. The buzz around the band was escalating daily; they were fascinating and mysterious and the music papers were gripped. It was an exciting, if not disorientating, time to be in The Jesus and Mary Chain. (Or 'Jesus and The Mary Chain' as they were accidentally called on occasion.)

'It seemed to have come from nowhere, which pissed a lot of people off,' admits Douglas. 'Just by being, we polarised people. We would say, when anyone interviewed us after the first few gigs, that we wanted to be on *Top of the Pops* and in *Smash Hits*. They would look at us and burst out laughing, but we were like, "We're not fucking kidding." In a year and a half we'd done it, and people couldn't believe it.'

Generally, the kind of artists who hankered after a cover feature in *Smash Hits* weren't normally the types you would expect to see braving a crowd at the crumbling Ambulance Station, but the Mary Chain were nothing if not perverse. But they also wanted to be stars, something most indie artists were not ready to admit.

Neil Taylor was in attendance that night. 'The problem was,' he recalls, 'that following the review in the *NME* and the word-of-mouth excitement, masses of people turned up, far too many. I seem to remember you had to climb through a hole in a door that someone had bashed open to get in, and you took your own alcohol and whatever. There were quite a few drunk people there. The June Brides played first, and played very well.'

Bobby Gillespie says: 'I think Morrissey and Johnny Marr were at that gig. I remember being upstairs in the squat and someone giving us some speed. I don't remember that gig being that musical, but that was the one where you felt like, Right, this is going to take off.' The tension levels at the gig were high from the start, but the audience's expectations, extreme inebriation on the part of the band, and the general air of violence that pervaded the Ambulance Station all added to the thrilling sense of unpredictability around the Mary Chain.

'They were incredibly drunk,' says Neil Taylor. 'I don't know how feasible it was for them to actually play. There were sporadic moments of unrest, not aided by the fact that halfway through the set, Jim decided to harangue the audience in quite an aggressive way; basically, "Where the fuck were you six months ago? You're all wankers, I despise you." Along those lines. Otherwise there was no engaging with the audience, it was more straight down to business with the music.

'So: music, harangue, music, off. Many enjoyed it, but some were thinking, This could all kick off and I'm going to enjoy that as well, and some of them are feeling slightly cheated. There are a couple of shouts of "Best live band for seven years? You must be joking." So there's a combustible atmosphere there. The police were called.'

As well as Morrissey and Johnny Marr, Lindy Morrison and Robert Forster from the Go-Betweens were in attendance, because Geoff Travis, founder of Rough Trade Records (who distributed for Creation) and Warners imprint Blanco Y Negro, had invited them down. This was the first time Travis had seen The Jesus and Mary Chain play live, and this exhilarating, amphetamine-fuelled appearance cemented his decision to sign them himself. 'It was incredible,' he says. 'A mind-blowing gig. It was a bit heavy, though. When I came out, all the windows on my car were smashed.'

There's a picture that certainly portrays the scene inside the makeshift venue as utter mayhem, with punters seemingly falling face-first onto the stage at the Mary Chain's feet, and Bobby, standing at his snare, with a look of disbelief mingled with mischievous hilarity on his face.

The sight of four musicians on their feet, as opposed to having a seated drummer, had a certain assertive power in itself too. But while Jim is quick to credit Bobby for bolstering him onstage by radiating sheer positivity, Bobby and Douglas knew the main reason they could feel sure of themselves as a band was the Reids' powerful songwriting. No matter how extreme the gigs became, the songs were the core of what they were doing, and their strength was indisputable.

'Jim and William's songs were the secret weapon, not the feedback,' insists Douglas. 'We knew that the songs could take us further than anything anyone termed as a gimmick. Those songs are not a fucking gimmick.'

10

Tea and Cakes with Travis

I want them to be everywhere, to be like Coronation Street.
Alan McGee in *The Face,* June 1985

The Ambulance Station gig in November 1984 was the latest milestone in the Mary Chain's trajectory, yet again polarising the audience and, crucially, attracting the attention of Geoff Travis. The Jesus and Mary Chain were already Creation's biggest-selling artists at this point, but now they had an opportunity to move to a bigger label and fulfil further ambitions beyond the so-called indie scene. As Jim Reid admits, 'I wanted to be Marc Bolan. I wanted to be Johnny Rotten. I didn't want to be this little oik in a Fair Isle jumper playing in some indie club with just my friends in the audience.

'We all wanted to shake things up quite a bit. The worst thing I can imagine is just being another band that gets ignored. We were into the whole rock star thing, Bowie, T. Rex. That was nowhere in the picture at that time, and that's what we wanted to bring back to the table.'

McGee, who would continue to be the group's manager, was philosophical about the next necessary step. 'We couldn't really carry on,' he admits. 'We had no money with Creation, it was such a little label. We were used to doing 7,000 copies and suddenly we're doing 45,000 copies, and Geoff . . . you know, it looked like the best deal. We'd done well to press up 40,000 records, never mind pay everybody, so to think we were going to hang on to The Jesus and Mary Chain against the weight of Warner Bros, that was never going to happen.'

The chance to go with a major label, but with Geoff Travis at the helm, seemed ideal at the time. The Mary Chain knew Travis was serious about his music. He also had indie integrity, but they would be getting major-label support. Blanco Y Negro had already released records by the Monochrome Set, Marine Girls, Everything But The Girl and Subway Sect's Vic Godard, and had worked with Lawrence from Felt. It seemed like a good home for the Mary Chain.

'The Mary Chain knew they were good,' says Travis. 'They didn't know how they would fare in the commercial world, but they definitely knew they were good. So they probably thought, Indie, schmindie, what's that got to do with us? Fair enough. Jim and William had bigger ambitions. If we didn't have that hybrid with the major label, maybe they would have signed to someone else.'

Jim Reid says: 'Had Creation Records been what it later became, there would have been nothing to think about, but you have to remember that at that time Alan was still working for British Rail. We got "Upside Down" out, we physically bagged all of those records. That's what it was; you were never going to get on *Top of the Pops,* or if you were, it was going to take some time.

'We were like, "Just show us the fucking money!"' adds Alan McGee. 'Everybody else was being really indie; we couldn't give a fuck about indie. We were influenced by punk.'

'Our big thing was that Geoff had released a couple of Subway Sect singles,' says Bobby Gillespie, 'and we thought, He works with Vic Godard, that's cool. That's as far as our business acumen went. Rough Trade was like a Marxist, right-on record label, but really Geoff was signing us on behalf of Rob Dickins at Warner.

'I love Rob Dickins, he's great, but he was a bit more flash. His wife was Cherry Gillespie from Pan's People, so that was pretty glam, right? We were four not-very-well-educated – not stupid – working-class kids from Glasgow and Glasgow suburbs. So it was a classic music-business thing, Oxbridge-educated record company guy . . .'

A meeting was arranged between Travis and the Mary Chain at Alan McGee's parents' house in the Glasgow suburb of Mount Florida ('Something of a misnomer,' observes Douglas Hart), complete with cups of tea and French Fancies. The path to rock'n'roll stardom is lined with cake. And coke, of course, but mainly, at this stage, cake. Despite the chintzy surroundings, for Travis this was 'the most difficult meeting with a group I've ever had in my life.

'They were all sitting on the sofa, all in a line. They sat staring at the floor for about an hour and a half. Didn't say a word. It was really insane.' (Alan McGee remembers it well, although he 'thought it was just normal Mary Chain madness, to be honest.')

The idea was that Geoff would sign The Jesus and Mary Chain on behalf of Blanco Y Negro on a one-single deal for the song 'Never Understand'. The Mary Chain might not have piped up much, or indeed at all, but their minds were whirring with the possibilities. 'He said he was going to sign us and gave us £1,000 each,' says Douglas Hart. 'We were like, Wow! Just for one record. It just seemed surreal, like a film. And we were all in Alan's very prim and proper mum's house, dressed like beatniks, all sitting there on our best behaviour with our little china cups and French Fancies.'

Geoff Travis left the McGee residence in a state of vague confusion. He had no idea what the band members were feeling and no clue as to how they thought it went. He wasn't even sure how he thought it went. To add to the slight surrealism of the day, Alan McGee then took him for a walk to the run-down Hampden Park football stadium, close to his family home. They had to climb in through a hole in the fence. 'It was really shocking because it was all overgrown with weeds and shrubs,' Geoff remembers. 'It just seemed like this archaic place which had gone to seed.'

And regarding The Jesus and Mary Chain's first major record deal? 'They hadn't said a word to me,' says Geoff, 'but Alan said, "Oh, don't worry," and they loved Subway Sect, and I think that was enough. So we negotiated the deal, which was pretty straightforward, and we signed them.

'Our relationship with them was always quite odd, though. They were always distant. They're very insular, very Scottish, they were fiercely proud of what they were doing. They didn't want to join in with the outside world that much.'

Not long after the weirdest meeting in Geoff Travis's history, The Jesus and Mary Chain had to fly down to the Warners office in London to sign the deal. It was a time of new experiences – apart from anything else, they'd never been on a plane before. Douglas Hart recalls: 'When we came into land we got that pressure thing in our ears. No one had told us about it and we thought we were going to die.'

To quell the inevitable nerves, the Reids and Douglas decided to down a few beers before the meeting. By the time they reached Soho they were, as Douglas breezily recalls, 'pretty drunk.'

The Mary Chain stumbled into the Warners building and were instantly 'horrified at all the Dave Lee Travis types,' says Douglas, with a note of disgust. Rob Dickins, then chairman of Warners, was an exception to the rule. He might not have loved the band in the same way that Travis and McGee did, but he believed in them. The Mary Chain, however, sensed immediately that most people at Warners, including those who would be promoting their records and supposedly fighting their corner, were repelled by the band. It was a culture clash, and the two sides would never have met in the middle without Travis as the bridge between them.

Jim Reid says: 'It's like, if you could go back and do it again, this is something you'd change. The thing was, Warners or Rough Trade. Geoff was obviously trying to get us onto Rough Trade at first, but at the time it was like, you've got to be "indie", and we were thinking, Why? To me at that time, the indie scene represented failure. The Sex Pistols were on Virgin Records, The Doors were on Warners . . . everybody that made me want to make music was on a major label, so I sort of thought, Well, we need a bankroll.

'The joke is that *Psychocandy* and everything that went around it came to £17,000, and I'm thinking we needed a bankroll! We didn't. We also hadn't anticipated that the people at Warners would utterly despise us. The only one that seemed interested was Rob Dickins, but that didn't filter through to the people doing the plugging. We should have grabbed Rough Trade, but Geoff was going to be involved no matter what, and thank God he was.' The instant and overwhelming feeling of antipathy was not merely Mary Chain paranoia at work. Soon after their ill-fated visit to the WEA office, one of the Warners marketing executives told journalist Max Bell they were 'the most revolting and disgusting group ever'. (With PR like this . . .)

'He didn't mean it as a compliment,' said Bell at the time. 'I couldn't be bothered to point out that he was right, The Jesus And Mary Chain are guilty on all counts. That's why they're so welcome.' Not everywhere, evidently.

Perhaps it was because they were drunk and awkward; perhaps it was because, when you feel nervous and defensive you do things you normally wouldn't. But the fact that most of the Warners collective weren't too keen on the Mary Chain was not helped by a couple of small accidents that occurred during the band's brief visit and a touch of mischievous graffiti on a poster of Rod Stewart.

'On the stairs there was a poster for his latest record,' says Douglas. 'We drew on it. People did go mad, they genuinely were complaining. We were banned from Warners. "Never come here again," you know. "You can't do that to Rod Stewart."'

'It was embarrassingly juvenile,' Jim cringes. 'We drew a moustache on him. A bit of graffiti on gold discs. But it caused such a hoo-hah they were never going to let us in the building after that. Christ almighty . . .'

To conclude this eventful afternoon, there was an incident on the staircase that, thanks to the Mary Chain's reputation as rock'n'roll's new bad boys, was seen as a deliberate act of violence. It wasn't, but, as far as Alan McGee was concerned, the press didn't need to know that. Cash from chaos.

'Only the Mary Chain, specifically Douglas Hart, could do this,' Alan says. 'They had all the gold records on the wall, and on the first floor, Douglas, because he's basically nuts, was . . . well, he was walking down the side of the wall. He managed to take down about three or four gold, silver and platinum discs. And because he was just a clumsy guy, he also managed to kind of smash the wall up.

'It looked to the world as if we'd smashed the place up. The truth was that Douglas Hart didn't know how to walk down a flight of stairs. Of course we went and said, "Yeah, not only did we smash the place up, we stole Rob Dickins' wallet." That made the national newspapers. I thought, We're going to get hung anyway. Everyone played along and *The Sun* printed it.'

'We were drunk,' says Douglas with a shrug. 'There was a bit of elaboration, but that's the way of the world. Up in East Kilbride we'd read *NME* and the gossip columns and we thought it was all gospel, but then you realise it's not quite . . .'

Alan McGee was living the dream, teasing the music papers with stories about the Mary Chain being arrested for possession of speed, 'destroying a radio station' (William and Jim were having a spat in the foyer of Capital Radio in Leicester Square) and building on their troublesome aura. It worked from the point of view of attracting attention and remaining in the press – even the tabloid press, where bands at the time, especially alternative ones, rarely featured. On the other hand, it was also magnetising the kind of trouble the Mary Chain themselves never wanted to be involved with. Still, McGee was in his element, and he freely admits that part of the thrill of what was unfolding was that he was closer than ever to emulating his idol, Malcolm McLaren. 'All I wanted to be was Malcolm,' he admits. 'I'm not in denial of that. If you're going to have a hero, you might as well have the best one.'

McGee had to take some stick for his obsession with his fellow flame-haired Svengali, particularly because he had seemingly assimilated the entire script of Julien Temple's Sex Pistols film *The Great Rock'n'Roll Swindle*, regurgitating lines from it as if they were his own words. Jim Reid says: 'We used to take the piss out of him mercilessly. He would say things and we would say, "Alan, that is actually in *The Great Rock'n'Roll Swindle*." I remember him saying, "Jim, we're not going to play any of those rock'n'roll houses . . .", and I thought, I've heard that before.'

After a quiet Christmas in Scotland, The Jesus and Mary Chain would have to return to London again before the old year was through, and it was clear that, fairly soon, it would make more sense to leave East Kilbride and move down to London for the foreseeable future. They emerged from the post-Christmas ennui to play ICA Rock Week on the Mall, near Buckingham Palace, on 29 December 1984.

It was also Jim's twenty-third birthday, and it was on this afternoon that he bought his prized (but later pinched) Vox Phantom guitar from Alan McGee for £150. 'It was,' Jim recalls, 'quite an eventful day.' And that's not even including the gig. The Jesus and Mary Chain might have played it down but they were the band to see, and their show at the ICA, supported by These Tender Virtues and Shelleyan Orphan, had been fully booked for months.

Meanwhile, a young French music fanatic called Laurence Verfaillie was making her way over to England on the ferry to see this very gig. Laurence had made the crossing the previous month to see the Mary Chain at the Ambulance Station, but, due to stormy weather, her ferry was kept just outside Dover for hours while the Mary Chain took to the makeshift stage some 75 miles away. She was not going to miss them this time.

Laurence Verfaillie was first captivated by The Jesus and Mary Chain's music after hearing their first Peel session with her friend

Aline, who ran a fanzine called *Agent Orange*. Both friends were serious about their music, and when they first heard the Mary Chain it was like an epiphany. The fact that there wasn't as much deliberate distortion or feedback on the Radio 1 session wasn't a problem for those tuning in from abroad, who were listening on crackly medium-wave. Laurence says: 'The reception was so bad we didn't know what was actually part of the sound or not. But we really thought there was something interesting there, we were hearing the song as opposed to the production.'

After her previous experience of missing the band, Laurence made sure she reached the ICA, in cold, grey central London, in plenty of time. There was just one problem: oblivious to the group's surging popularity, Laurence Verfaillie hadn't booked a ticket in advance.

'I turned up innocently and the guy looked at me and laughed and said, "Darling, it's been sold out for God knows how long." I started causing an absolute commotion, saying: "I came all the way from France to see them! Let me in!"'

Laurence would not be placated, and out of desperation a member of the ICA's front-of-house staff rushed inside the venue to find Alan McGee. 'Never to be forgotten,' says McGee. 'Someone demanded that I come to the front desk because some French woman who I'd never met in my life was kicking off that she wanted to get in.' Little did he realise that the woman causing a righteous scene at the entrance of the ICA would, in years to come, work closely with him at Creation Records, and be a lifelong friend. She certainly made an impression, however. 'I was pretty feisty back then, but she just shouted at me until I let her in,' he says, still incredulous.

★

Laurence went up to the bar, squeezing through hordes of people, all of whom were talking feverishly about The Jesus and Mary Chain. What amused Laurence was that at least three members of the band were lurking in the bar themselves but either no one had spotted them or no one had the confidence to approach them. As Laurence puts it, the likelihood was that it was still so early in their legend that not many people really knew what they looked like.

The Jesus and Mary Chain's appearance at the ICA was a landmark, and it pointed the way forward for the band. But as always, it elicited mixed feelings. 'It was short and pretty non-musical, as I recall,' says Jim. 'We'd do too much drugs or drink too much and just get into the noise aspect of it. It was good.'

Bobby Gillespie says: 'It felt like we were the Pistols, there was a feeling that everybody wanted to see this band. It was a really exciting thing to be part of. I knew we were great and there was no compromise. And you never knew what was going to happen.'

Geoff Travis was in the audience, accompanied by Rob Dickins. Dickins might not have entirely got the group, but 'he was nodding away,' Geoff remembers. 'He realised something was happening. They were brilliant in those days, like molten lead pouring off the stage.'

Alan McGee is less romantic in his memory of that night. 'They went on for fifteen minutes, made a noise, I don't know if they even completed a song. Jim called the entire audience cunts. They all got upset. People were shouting abuse at me, going, "You're a rip-off bastard." I just went, "Go fuck yourself."' William Reid's take on the band's early exodus from the stage was that, quite simply, 'We just got bored. I think it's fairly honest.'

The feedback howled as the group left the stage, leaving a lot of people 'extremely puzzled,' as Laurence puts it. Within a noisy, anarchic quarter of an hour, they left a divided audience – some in raptures, some outraged, most wondering whether they'd ever hear again. 'It went into chaos, but there was so much energy,' Laurence says. 'You know when you hear live recordings, everyone goes mad at the end, and there's all the feedback in the encore – but this gig was that, the gig *was* the encore. They completely let go from the first moment. It was mind-blowing.'

> *At the volume Jesus and sons play at, anything is enervating and*
> *psychologically disorienting; I felt quite violent and didn't like it at all.*
> Ralph Traitor's review of The Jesus and Mary Chain
> at ICA Rock Week, *Sounds*

11

Escape From EK

I don't lose sleep thinking about Wham!
Jim Reid, 1985

The band's star was rising and the time had finally come to move on from East Kilbride, although Bobby Gillespie would stay in Glasgow as he was still developing Primal Scream. There was no pressure on Bobby to choose between bands at this point, but even though Primal Scream was his own group, he still felt more connected to the Mary Chain.

'I was just happy to be part of it,' he says. 'I didn't really feel part of Primal Scream at that point. The Mary Chain's thing was more fully formed. And they had better songs.'

Because Jim had lived in London in pre-Mary Chain days, staying in cheap, down-at-heel hotels in Earls Court, in January 1985 Jim, William and Douglas checked in at one of the hotels Jim had stayed at before, a shabby bed and breakfast then known as the Hunters Hotel on Trebovir Road. The hotel boasted such benefits as 'hot and cold running water', and it was just a few moments from Earls Court underground station. The Mary Chain crammed themselves into a family room to save money, and paid for it between themselves. It was one of the strangest places they had ever lived, replete with seedy Pinteresque intrigue and assorted maniacs. Memories of living on Trebovir Road are still etched on the Mary Chain's respective memories.

'We'd never seen prostitutes or junkies before,' says Douglas, 'and suddenly we were in this insane place. We were broke, but it was a real adventure. There was a block of hotels in Earls Court and William

Burroughs had lived in one in the 1960s two doors down. It was like something out of a Harold Pinter play, total *Birthday Party*. People in their pyjamas wandering about, you could hear people fucking, fighting . . .'

'Weird place,' says Jim. 'There was a Polish immigrant that lived in a cupboard under the stairs. He was a wee bit not right upstairs. They let him live there just to do maintenance work. He was nuts. We had these big brothel-creepers and we'd stomp downstairs to go out and he'd jump out and shout at us. He'd be waiting for us.'

Tempting as it must have been to stick around at the Hunters Hotel – which sounds like a real-life version of the dilapidated Happiness Hotel in *The Great Muppet Caper*, only with a bit less happiness and presumably fewer musical numbers – it wasn't long until the Reids and Douglas found some cheap bedsits in nearby Fulham. The flats might have been fleapits, but it was an exciting time, filled with possibility, and with no parents or hotel receptionists to slink past. For the first time in their lives William and Jim would be living separately, and Douglas would also be in his own place after years of sharing not just a bedroom but a bed with his older brother back in East Kilbride.

The advance had come through from Blanco Y Negro, which meant that finally they were able to sign off the dole. For William, this was partially a disappointment, as he was a whisker away from his fifth anniversary of signing on. 'He was going to celebrate it,' McGee says. 'He was pissed off that he never got to do that. That's not even a joke.' Still, independence was theirs for the first time.

'We were all living round the corner from each other,' says Jim. 'But Douglas's flat was horribly damp, so he moved in with me for about six weeks. We slept in the same bed like Morecambe and Wise, reading the paper with our pyjamas on. Not very rock'n'roll.'

Despite the Fulham years being a happy time, some of the neighbours were a little offbeat, to say the least. 'There was this nutter woman,' Jim says. 'We used to hear her having arguments with herself at 3 a.m. She'd be screaming, and then there'd be a pause where you knew that she was hearing voices, and then she'd scream, "You fucking . . ." Then there was this toff called Adrian who lived next door to me. He used to have friends over to play charades on a Friday night.

'To top it off, there was this psychotic Scottish drug dealer called

Archie, and he was bad news. I was always terrified he would figure out that we were in a band. He'd have broken into my shabby little room.'

On one occasion, William came over to use the communal bathroom. Just as he was getting out of the bath, the door was unceremoniously kicked in by the drug dealer, his face covered in blood. 'He needed to wash it off,' explains Jim. 'You'd get out of there quick. Having said that, I lived there for years.'

★

All the while, the Reids had been working on new material. They were and always have been prolific songwriters, and the future months were already being mapped – there were more gigs, more sessions for John Peel and, first things first, it was time to record 'Never Understand', the band's first single release on Blanco Y Negro.

'We'd made "Upside Down" in the studio Alan used to use,' Douglas says. 'But obviously Geoff knew everyone, and he suggested we do it with Stephen Street at Island Studios.'

Island was based in Ladbroke Grove, West London, a stone's throw from Rough Trade. The studio was imposing and sterile, and the Mary Chain were not keen on where Stephen Street was trying to go with their song. Street, who had already worked with Rough Trade signings The Smiths among others, was pretty nonplussed himself. It probably didn't help matters that the proposed title of the B-side they were recording was 'Jesus Fuck'.

'He was disgusted,' Douglas recalls. 'He was quite . . . well, it didn't go well. He was shocked that I only had two strings on my bass and we couldn't really tune up by ear; it was a bit of a clash. We stopped after a day. He's a good producer, but not to do us at that point. No.'

'It was quite problematic making that record,' Jim adds. 'We just couldn't get it right. We knew what the record should sound like, and there'd be this guy in the middle trying to take it somewhere else. What's the point in that?'

Geoff has no memory of recommending Stephen Street at all, however. 'That wouldn't make any sense,' he says. 'They did try to work with Stephen Hague, and they spent three days trying to get the drum sound, and William just said, "This is a waste of time." Conventional producers bored them. Later on, Daniel Lanois wanted to produce them. He had a house in New Orleans and all the gear in there. William said, "I'm not leaving Archway."'

However, Geoff Travis's subsequent suggestion of recording at the late John Loder's Southern Studios in Wood Green, North London, was, as Douglas puts it, 'genius'. 'Geoff told us about this guy who had a studio in his garden,' says Jim. "He said, "I think you're going to like this guy." I thought, Here we go again . . .'

Loder was like no engineer they'd worked with before, and Southern, set up with the anarcho-punk group Crass, reflected his relaxed attitude. It had an atmosphere that was conducive to lateral thinking, freedom and creativity. McGee says: 'Crass have now become incredibly hip, but in 1985 they were about as hip as the UK Subs. We knew deep down it was cool. It just wasn't *hip*. It was smelly. But Loder was a nice guy.'

Far from trying to impose his ideas or try to patronise the relatively inexperienced group, Loder would set everything up, head back to the main house where he ran Southern Records, light a spliff and simply be on call in case anything got blown up.

'We immediately hit it off with John,' says Jim. 'He was exactly what we were looking for. He just set all the faders up and left us to our own devices. Obviously we didn't know what we were doing and we fucked up a lot, but it was great. We'd sit there and press buttons. "This is pretty good! I think I broke something but it sounded good!"'

The band were learning as they went, and, as they recorded, certain elements of the song evolved, particularly the lyrics. 'Never Understand' would end up featuring an homage to American garage rock band The Seeds, of 'Stranded' fame. Bobby explains:

'If you listen to "Never Understand", on the original, Jim sings "Looking too hard and you just can't see me . . .", and I said, "Change it to 'pushing too hard' as a tribute to The Seeds." And he did.' The song ends with a tangle of noise; the Reids wanted to make it sound as if everything was descending into a violent maelstrom. William provided 'most of the yelling,' Jim recalls. 'He was good at shouting.'

The pairing of the Mary Chain and Loder evidently worked, and it would be at Southern Studios that the band would record their first album, *Psychocandy*. 'Never Understand', meanwhile, was released in February 1985, the first of their records to chart. The finished product was the ideal next step from 'Upside Down', another major-key vocal melody murmuring through a screech of feedback and relentless snare cracks. Lyrically, the song echoes 'Upside Down's sense of alienation, but a wasted confidence and carelessness pushes 'Never Understand' somewhere else. 'The sun comes up, another day begins/And I don't even worry about the state I'm in./Head so heavy and I'm looking thin/but when the sun goes down I wanna start again . . .'

A video was made to accompany the track by the late Tim Broad, who took the group to a disused warehouse in Wapping to film them playing along with the song. There was no high concept here; the Mary Chain didn't need one. Watching the video to 'Never Understand' is basically as close as you can get to seeing how the group manoeuvred live at that time – hunched over guitars, swearing, physically clashing, knocking over drums – only a little more self-conscious than they would have ordinarily been.

'If you see the videos, you can see the connection between the four boys,' explains Bobby. 'It's emotional. Crashing into each other, it's quite homoerotic. It's interesting. We were young, not sexually experienced. It's just a need for connection, it's not that you fancy the other guys.'

'Jesus Fuck' was still the track that the Mary Chain wanted on the B-side, but this was not to be. Geoff Travis insists there was never a problem at Blanco, but 'they might have been a bit disturbed at the pressing plant'.

Alan McGee says: 'The old-age pensioners who put the records in the sleeves at Warners, they were a staff of 67-year-olds and they all went to church. I'm not even taking the piss. Of course somebody took offence. It had to be changed.' The alternative? The still relatively salacious 'Suck'.

Jim Reid told the *NME*'s Mat Snow: '"Jesus Fuck" was downright repulsion at how sacred the name Jesus was. People seriously think this little group making an obscure little record called "Jesus Fuck" is going to do any harm?'

The song 'Jesus Fuck' really was just Jim screaming 'Jesus! Fuck!', and was born of his usual sound-check routine. McGee recalls: 'He'd go, "Fuck! Fuck! Fuck! Fuck! Jesus! Fuck!" It was kind of catchy.' The rejected B-side would eventually see the light of day (after being forgotten by the Reids themselves for years) when *Psychocandy* was reissued in 2011.

In true lo-fi Mary Chain style, the single was promoted with a poster created by Jim Reid and Douglas, scribbled vigorously in crayon. The original is still on the wall of Geoff Travis's office. Douglas says: 'I remember Geoff saying, "We need a poster for 'Never Understand'," so we were like, "Give us a bit of paper . . ."'

★

McGee had organised a UK tour around the release of 'Never Understand', but when the group played Brighton Pavilion on 2 February 1985, the sense of turmoil in the audience always simmering at Mary Chain gigs was now manifesting in a more sinister way. 'The first real signs of trouble coming were in Brighton,' says Jim. 'We got bottled off.'

Up to a point, the Mary Chain would often feel as if they were surrounded by such a strong psychological force-field that they were invincible even as missiles whistled past their heads, but this was the first gig that saw the audience turn. Who knows whether discord was sparked simply because the Mary Chain seemed to have a gift for inadvertently inciting a collective experience of exhilaration, frustration and confusion with their music – emotions that the band themselves often felt? All we do know is that the concert quickly spiralled into a very angry situation, and the Mary Chain were under siege. Bobby tells the story: 'We were playing, then suddenly we looked up and there was a guy on top of the PA, throwing stuff at us. I stopped playing. Jim was singing, but I was like, "This guy . . ." At this point I got smacked in the face with a plastic glass, then I started throwing stuff back at the audience, then more stuff came.

'My girlfriend Karen was at the side of the stage and she got smacked in the head with a bottle. She had a lump like a tennis ball coming out of her skull. That was four songs in.'

Jim Reid says: 'Not taking any of this, I got back on stage with our fee and waved it at the audience, Loadsamoney-style. They were lobbing glasses at us.'

'This was before the internet,' adds Bobby. 'If you'd had the internet then it would have been even worse. Everywhere you went would have been riots. It became the norm, see the Mary Chain, start a riot.'

★

The day after the Brighton gig, The Jesus and Mary Chain would have to shake off the insanity of the night before and head up to Maida Vale to record their second session for John Peel, to be broadcast ten days later. If they thought their first Peel Session was fraught between themselves and the engineers, this one would be worse. Their name and reputation had grown overnight, literally, and the studio hands were taking no chances.

Jim Reid: 'We wanted to break glass. There was an oil drum there so we said, "We'll stick a bottle in there, put a mic in and record it." The engineer said, "No way." "We've been asked to do what we do here, and you're saying we can't?" And he said, "Not in my studio, sonny boy."'

'I don't know why we didn't think of using a fucking sound effect,' adds Douglas.

The tracks recorded were 'The Living End', conjuring visions of the doomed biker in the Shangri-Las' 'Leader Of The Pack', the Stooges-esque 'In A Hole' and 'Just Like Honey', which featured Bobby's girlfriend Karen Parker on backing vocals. This was the latter song's debut: it was so fresh that the Reid brothers were still writing the lyrics during the session.

John Peel loved the Mary Chain, as did his listeners, and he would be inviting them back again soon. But in the meantime the band had a tour to do, although after the Brighton fiasco, in true Pistols-style repetition of history, some local authorities were quick to cancel gigs. The problem wasn't so much the band as the fans who were attracted to them, but, as frustrating as this was for the Mary Chain, Alan McGee was rubbing his hands together.

'I understood the media,' he says. 'Doing the gig or not doing the gig, it was almost as if it didn't matter. We had so much publicity from being banned, more than if we actually played a good gig. The Mary Chain would be pissed off to have driven all the way to wherever to find they'd been banned, though. We got banned from half of the gigs we were booked to play, and of course, every time I'd be phoning the newspapers and they'd print it.'

As an electric wind of tension crackled around the Mary Chain, the group must have been glad to cross the Channel for a night or two. A gig was booked at Les Baines Douches, a small but significant club in Paris, for 6 March 1985.

McGee contacted Laurence Verfaillie, the Parisian Mary Chain fan who had made such an impression at the ICA, and she organised an interview with Bobby for her friend's fanzine before the gig. After the interview was complete and night had fallen, Laurence took her place in Les Baines Douches as the room filled up.

The club was just the size of an average pub back room, which made the energy of the show all the more concentrated. 'It was as if the place was going to blow up. And it was packed, there were about 60 or 70 people. Of course,' Laurence adds, 'three months later about 500 people pretended they were there.'

12

Smashing up Pop

*For Alan McGee, the Mary Chain was a way that he could say
'Fuck you' to the world.*
Bobby Gillespie

The twelfth of March 1985 was the date of The Jesus and Mary Chain's appearance on the BBC's legendary *The Old Grey Whistle Test*. It was their television debut, and although it wasn't live, the producers were anxious about what might happen with The Jesus and Mary Chain on set. The main concern, perhaps unsurprisingly, was that they would turn up drunk and unruly, so it was arranged that they would be at the studio by 6 a.m. By their own admission it was rare for them to get up before 11 a.m. They got themselves through the ordeal in the most sensible way possible: not going to bed at all.

'We thought, Six in the morning? Fuck that.' Jim says. 'We got wasted, then turned up with a big crate of booze.'

Bobby Gillespie was panicking. Visions of a successful appearance on the *Whistle Test* were dissolving rapidly. 'They were just knocking it back,' he remembers. 'I'm going, "What are you doing? We're going to be on fucking TV!" and they're going, "We're shitting it, we're totally nervous!", I was thinking, You're going to be too wasted to play! You can't blow this.'

'All of us would get nervous,' Douglas says. 'Bobby not so much, but Jim particularly, being the frontman. We'd have to drink, we needed it.'

At least their inebriated thrash through 'In A Hole' would bring stunned TV audiences a taste of the live Mary Chain experience. The sound was fierce and atmospheric, by TV standards at least, and they looked impressive: Bobby in a checked shirt, mallets bouncing off the drums, the beat thudding rapidly like a heart about to burst, the Reids and Douglas stalking the stage in black leather and Ray-Bans. The song eventually seemed to wilfully dismantle itself, and by the end Jim sat down next to a half-collapsed Bobby, whacking the floor tom petulantly as William, on his knees, provided a constant scream of free, distortion-drenched guitar. Jim describes their appearance with his usual *sang-froid*: 'It was all right. Nothing bad happened.' But when the show was broadcast and the Mary Chain themselves watched it, huddled around the electric fire, within a moment a great swathe of the country was hooked.

Future Mary Chain drummer and guitarist John Moore remembers seeing them on TV for the first time and realising that 'it was "game over". No point in starting a band. *That's* the band . . . fuck, how *could* they? They're doing what you should be doing! 'I thought Douglas looked marvellous, Douglas Hart . . . my mother fancied him. God, she really did. Dirty old goat! "Ooh, that Douglas Hart, he looks like an Adonis!" With his hair and his big semi-acoustic bass and cheekbones. Yeah, iconic.'

Jim's main memory was not of how especially splendid Douglas's bone structure looked under the lights, but rather a needless fracas between himself and the show's producers. Just before going on set, Jim had spotted the *Whistle Test* mannequin on the studio floor, whipped off the dummy's sunglasses and wore them for 'In A Hole'. Then he broke them. Accidentally, of course, but 'there was just such a big hoo-hah about it,' he sighs. 'For fuck's sake, they cost a fiver, I'll buy you a new pair. Do we need to have this big drama?'

*

From this point forth, opportunities for further TV exposure came thick and fast. As well as the live appearances, the video for 'Never Understand' was everywhere, and the music papers they had been so obsessed with as teenagers were now, in turn, obsessed with them. Bobby says: 'It was so fast. Bang! But we definitely felt entitled to it. We felt, Yeah, we are the best band going. There's nothing happening. We've got the spirit of punk and we're going to rip a hole in the fabric of reality. It definitely felt like we were righteous. Whether we were, I don't know.'

If you were to ask Mick Houghton, press officer for Warners and Blanco Y Negro, he would assure you that they certainly were. Part of what enhanced their appeal was that magical James Dean blend of trouble, angst and, most importantly, unattainability – a quality that was becoming rarer by the day in the chirpy pop world of the mid-1980s.

'Journalists were always apprehensive about meeting them,' remembers Mick Houghton. 'Interviews always took a while to get going. Neither side felt comfortable. We did interviews in a pub on Old Compton Street, the one that got blown up by a nail-bomb in 1999 [the Admiral Duncan].' Alternatively, interviews would be conducted in a greasy spoon over cod and chips, a welcome change from that other culinary staple of the Mary Chain's diet: the Pot Noodle.

Beers, however, were always necessary for both Mary Chain and journalist. The band found it hard to relax in company at the best of times, and this, often interpreted as chilly indifference, meant it would take time for any kind of fruitful exchange to develop. But still, this helped to stoke their reputation for being enigmatic. Paradoxically, they seemed more in control as a result, no matter how nervous they actually were.

'What they had,' says former *NME* writer Neil Taylor, 'and what all great groups tend to have, was a distinct air of being a sealed unit against the world, and you're not always allowed into the inner sanctum. It was a similar thing with Morrissey and Marr from the Smiths.'

*

Tickets for their next gig, at the North London Polytechnic, sold quickly. The show was to take place on 15 March, the famous 'ides of March' of which the soothsayer in *Julius Caesar* bade the doomed emperor beware. It wouldn't be quite as dramatic a situation for the Mary Chain, but there was quite a night in store. The band's fan base had been growing daily, and by the time Neil Taylor walked through the doors at the North London Polytechnic on Holloway Road, the overriding feeling was that, in his words, 'the beast is getting too big'.

That night the Mary Chain would be supported by fellow Creation artists the Jasmine Minks and Meat Whiplash. Jasmines' frontman Adam Sanderson was evidently anticipating trouble, much to the bemusement of the headline act. Bobby Gillespie says: 'At the soundcheck Adam was saying, "Look at that." He opens his Crombie and he's got a hammer. I said, "Why have you got that?" And he said, "It's gonna kick off tonight . . ."'

'He lived in a squat in King's Cross, he must have heard people talking. He was going, "Aye, I'm ready for it. Any cunt comes near me, I'm gonna fucking brain them!" I was just like, That's a bit much. Bit presumptuous.'

The venue was already at capacity, but as the Mary Chain languished in the dressing room drinking determinedly, the door burst open. 'Someone said, "There's hundreds of people in the street who can't get in,"' says Gillespie. 'Me and Douglas opened the fire doors. It was a punk gesture. Get everybody in!'

Meat Whiplash, young lads from East Kilbride playing their first London gig, went on stage and were promptly hit by a missile. When the Jasmine Minks came on, the lead singer hurled a wine bottle into the audience. 'Probably not a good way of starting,' Neil Taylor observes.

By the time the Mary Chain made their way onstage the atmosphere was seriously charged. For a while the anarchic rumble in the crowd was drowned out by sheer noise, as the Mary Chain's live sound engineer David Evans, a former member of Biff Bang Pow!, remembers. 'They never addressed the audience, but created this loud ad hoc feedback that stoked you into a state of excitement but also left you frustrated, hanging, waiting for the next song as false starts and messing around delayed it yet again. It really was something special, though.' Fans were electrified by the North London Poly performance. One punter, asked by a TV journalist why he liked the Mary Chain, simply bellowed: 'They're noisy.'

Bobby Gillespie says: 'Every night would be different, free-form. William is a virtuoso guitar player. I always just had his guitar in my monitor. He'd start with these riffs and then he would go somewhere else, and that would inspire me to play harder. I'd take my cues from him and be sensitive to what he was playing. Then Jim told me that when he saw me go mad, then he would go mad as well.'

'Bobby was like the engine back then,' says Jim. 'I could be thinking,

Well, I don't know about this, how's this going? And I'd turn around and look at Bobby and there'd be a big beaming smile on his face, and I'd think, It's all right.'

The audience was a mixture of Mary Chain devotees, people curious about the phenomenon and a significant injection of troublemakers. 'And sure enough,' says Neil Taylor, 'what happened was: short set, garrulousness, the usual drunkenness, falling over, off the stage, and people either demanded more or thought, Right, this is the signal for us to have a good old knees-up and a fight.'

Alan McGee and David Evans insist they genuinely didn't expect things to kick off to the extent that they did. They certainly didn't think their safety would be in jeopardy. Equipment was fair game, of course, at a Mary Chain show. Speaker stacks were being kicked over, gear was getting damaged – but the difference was that this time the fans were attacking it, not Jim Reid. This was not part of the show, although for those involved, no doubt it was simply a continuation of the violent energy and noise that had been conjured by the band.

Bobby Gillespie viewed the escalating turbulence, which started before they had left the stage, with characteristic glee. 'People were throwing stuff at us, I was the one picking up the drums and throwing them at people. I didn't have any fear. North London Poly, hey, I was loving it!'

Joe Foster, who was teaching at the Poly at that time, was horrified at what was unfolding, particularly when one of the burlier students managed to pull Jim off the stage. 'It was bizarre, chaos, it was dreadful,' Joe remembers. 'Being – how can I put it? – an idiot, I dived into the audience and grabbed Jim. We tried to push ourselves back on to the stage, and that was when one of the student bouncers decided that was a good time to stop us. It was like, "Right, you are going to push us back so your rugby-playing buddies can give us a good kicking? That's not going to happen."'

McGee was aghast, and within moments he'd hurled himself into the fray as well. The following day, Joe Foster would be fired from the college due to his involvement with the Mary Chain.

As more police officers arrived, serving largely to inflame the situation even further, the Mary Chain escaped to the safety of the dressing room, barricading themselves in because, sure enough, a handful of marauding punters had come looking for them. 'There were people smashing the door with fire extinguishers,' says Douglas. 'It was beyond funny, it was brutal.'

Bobby Gillespie's memory of it is slightly different; he was thrilled by the danger their presence seemed to have provoked. 'When McGee came in and said, "They're trying to get into the dressing room!" I was like, "Amazing!" I just wanted to wind as many people up as possible. I'd been waiting for my whole life to be at the eye of the storm, fucking right.'

Once the situation calmed down and the hall was cleared, the group eventually emerged for an interview, seeming very much in control. Whether or not they were just masters of disguising their apprehension we can only guess, but their whispery nonchalance is certainly convincing.

During the interview, Jim spikily defended an accusation that the guitars were out of tune by explaining that William's was perfectly tuned, but his own was not because 'mine is for kicking'. Douglas responded to an inevitable query about his two-stringed Gibson bass by telling the interviewer softly, but not without swear words, that they were the only strings he used, so what was the point in buying the other two? Jim followed this by quipping that 'any more would confuse the guy'. The journalist asked how they felt about being described variously as both the best and worst group in the western hemisphere. William replied, after a contemplative pause, 'My favourite colour is gold.' For a supposedly 'sociopathic' group of young men, they knew how to give good quote.

'I watched some of that footage recently,' says Gillespie. 'We were just trying to look cool. At the end I'm sitting on the stage saying, "I just want people to listen to the music. Listen to yourself! Who do you think you are?" We don't look too scared in that film, do we? We look quite arrogant.'

While the interview was underway, Neil Taylor was already on the phone to the *NME*, and the legend of the North London Poly gig was set in stone. 'There were probably two days to go for press, and they pulled whatever story they had on page three and ran this. I always get cross about this because the sub-editor put the headline in that said "Jesus And Mary Chain Riot". I didn't refer to it as a riot, although it was pretty close; there were violent scenes. Then the band started going around saying, "It wasn't a riot, it was that guy from the *NME*" or whatever, which is why I always raise it.'

William often insisted there were never really any real 'riots' at all, just 'the odd clown who thinks he's Rambo, tap-dancing on the mixing desk'. Still, no amount of playing it down could change the fact that the increasing number of disturbances at their shows were becoming a concern, not just from the point of view of personal safety, but because violence was totally at odds with who the Mary Chain really were. 'I hate it,' said William at the time. 'We're trying to present ourselves as serious, not a Cockney Rejects, Oi! type of group.'

The day after the North London Poly fiasco, the Mary Chain and McGee were on their way to Germany for a TV appearance. 'It was fine, bit of sanity,' says McGee. Naturally the press had already been in touch about the previous night's madness, but McGee had put his real feelings on ice in a bid to release a dispassionate, Malcolm McLaren-esque statement: 'The audience were not smashing up the hall, they were smashing up pop music . . . this is truly art as terrorism.' The Situationists would have loved it.

'It wasn't cool though,' he says now. 'It went a bit weird, and after that point it was a little bit Cinderella going to the ball. I thought everybody knew we were taking the piss, and suddenly people were actually smashing things up and it wasn't that funny. Even though we made the most of it, "art as terrorism" and all that, the truth of the matter was that we were going, "What the fuck happened there?"'

13

New York, *Innocence Lost*, Psychocandy

It was happening really fast: from the time we got rejected from
that Candy Club to making Psychocandy, it was one year.
Douglas Hart

When the Mary Chain played gigs outside of London, the response
from the audience was never quite as physical. It was mainly in the capital that opportunists would appear just for the chance for a fight. The
band might have sneered that they didn't care, that the idiots fighting,
and in many cases causing the gig to be curtailed, were just ruining it for
themselves, but the violence was odious and, at times, frightening.
Occasionally the promoter would have to pull the power in a desperate
bid to pour cold water on a brewing skirmish. Meanwhile, the Reids
just wanted people to pay attention to the songs they were trying to
perform. Something had to change.

*

'People would be throwing bottles at us and just missing us,' says
Douglas. 'That's not what we were about. We hated and avoided
violence: we're not neds, we didn't get off on fights. We were the kind
of guys who'd be chased around town by people like that, we didn't
want them coming to our gigs. I'm sure Alan saw that, but I think he got
caught up in it.'

It was agreed that the Mary Chain would have a break from playing
shows in London to allow things to cool off, and this would give them
the perfect opportunity to work on their debut album at John Loder's

studio. But first they had a trip to New York to look forward to, organised by the late US promoter Ruth Polsky.

Polsky was well known; she had brought The Smiths to the US and was the promoter who had organised the US Joy Division tour that never happened, due to the tragic suicide of singer Ian Curtis on the eve of the trip. This would be the first time the Mary Chain had ever been to the US, and though they were playing just two shows they were booked to stay in New York for a week.

'Ruth Polsky was a wonderful lady, and that trip was magical to me,' says Jim. 'I mean, the idea of going to New York is pretty cool anyway, but we had only signed off the dole in January. By April 1985 we're playing in front of an audience in New York City.'

They had to get there first, though, and McGee admits this was the first time he'd ever had to think about getting a band over to the US. He was a one-man operation with ambition, a telephone and a lot to learn. 'I was just 23 when I found them, and 24 when they started getting big,' he says. 'I didn't know about getting visas, because I'd never had a band that anybody in America had wanted to put on. We didn't even know anybody who had done it. I basically had to find out – I know it sounds mental – how to do the forms and send the equipment over, get the visas. Now you'd just hire a tour manager, but we were so young and naïve.'

Thankfully, Alan managed to organise everything in time, and soon they were wandering Times Square, sightseeing and enjoying springtime in New York (which was, as Douglas remembers, 'just like an episode of *Kojak*'). It was quite a contrast to the gloom of London and the wide-eyed Mary Chain were dazzled by the experience of simply being there.

The general innocence in the Mary Chain camp would inevitably be eroded but during this first trip to New York it was still relatively intact. However, the Warners executive sent to meet them didn't know that. Assuming this rock'n'roll band would be requiring some entertainment, he turned up with a pair of prostitutes.

'He was a real old-school music guy,' Douglas remembers. 'I think he was thinking back to the 1970s. We were just like: "Hi! Do you come from round here then? What school did you go to? Do you like Subway Sect?" I was going, "Do you like *If* . . . ?", and they were like, "F?" "No, the film *If . . .*" They eventually just said, "Don't you wanna fuck us?" We were innocents abroad. We were corrupted over the next few years, though.'

For many young men, the whole point of being in a rock band is the ego trip: the praise, the parties, the legitimate wearing of leather trousers and, most importantly, the guaranteed no-strings sex with nubile women. However, groupies were, comparatively speaking, not the Mary Chain's scene by all accounts. This attitude was quite punk – many UK punk and post-punk groups proclaimed groupies to be just another sleazy element of the priapic excess associated with faintly embarrassing rock dinosaurs.

'I think some of the American promoters assumed they were gay,' says Laurence Verfaillie, by now Jim's girlfriend. Apart from anything else, as William himself put it – albeit evidently speaking from some experience – 'there's nothing worse than waking up next to someone you don't even know or like'. Some of the reluctance to indulge at the time might also have been down to sheer familial awkwardness. 'Imagine trying to pick up girls in front of your little brother,' William cringed in an interview with sometime bandmate John Moore.

This isn't to say the Mary Chain were unaware of the effect they had on their audiences. They knew sex was an intrinsic part of rock'n'roll. As soon as you put anyone on a stage, they are instantly more desirable. Give them a guitar, sexier still. The Mary Chain had the advantage of being cool, stylish and toothsome in the first place. There were no illusions as to why there were a large number of girls at their gigs.

'On stage we're one of the sexiest groups you can imagine,' Jim deadpanned at the time. 'Three or four guys in leather, rolling around showing their backsides to the audience. All I know is that we get tons of screaming young girls. If a gig doesn't have sex, there's something wrong.'

The trip to New York would be a baptism of fire as far as drugs were concerned. The Mary Chain were no strangers to mind-altering substances but they were now being inducted into a new league of showbiz drug-taking. Alan McGee says he'd 'never seen so much cocaine in my life. Ruth Polsky fancied Douglas, and Lord knows what went on in that room but he was in there for a long time. There was a mountain of cocaine on the table. I don't even know if I took any, but I do know I started wearing shades around that time. I've stopped now. It was one of my phases. Now I'm trying to look like a Welsh farmer.'

The Mary Chain were booked to play two nights at the Danceteria, a hip four-floor nightclub frequented by the likes of Madonna. There they would play to their biggest crowds yet, though the audiences were largely made up of curious punters and regulars – no-one knew who they were, with the exception of the handful of people from the record company.

The first night had an alternative, indie feel, and inevitably drew in people who 'looked a bit like us,' according to Jim. However, the second night was not aimed at the usual Mary Chain crowd. 'There were people break-dancing,' Jim recalls with amusement. 'We were playing away there, doing what we do, and there were these guys who seemed to be digging it but it was all baseball caps on backwards and spinning about on the floor. It was surreal!'

'There were 200 Anglophiles and then about 1,000 people who were just roller-skating,' adds McGee. 'Quite a bit of roller-skating going on there.' Roller-skating to the sound of the Mary Chain: there's an image. This certainly made a change from being attacked by morons who weren't even listening.

Stimulated by the welcome culture shock, after the gig McGee and Jim headed out into the New York night to another club, eventually returning to their hotel via Times Square. They were on a high, undoubtedly in more ways than one, and as they walked, Jim and Alan found themselves surrounded by such glorious, almost clichéd sleaze that it was hard not to feel as though they were on a movie set. Their education continued.

McGee says: 'We walked past all the prostitutes, and – this was not one of my better moments – I was shouting out, "Hey darlin'!" They threatened to stab us! They knew we were out of our depth. I think they were probably men.'

The Mary Chain spent the week in an overstimulated daze. They'd grown up with American culture and were obsessed with American film and style. Douglas remembers that New York stint with the band as 'the best week of my life' (even if he often had to be left behind when the others headed into nightclubs – unlike the others, he really was still a teenager and the bouncers were strict). Returning to England, having survived, thrived indeed, in New York City, the Mary Chain and Alan McGee would view their situation with a fresh perspective.

The thrill of New York and first-time transatlantic travel had barely worn off, and suitcases were still half-unpacked on the floors of the Mary Chain's bedsits, but they had to get back into studio mode to work on their album, *Psychocandy*. They were welcomed back to Southern by John Loder, who was as generous as always – and being trusted by someone like John meant they rose to the occasion even more. That's not to say they were ever going to slack off; this was their first album, after all, and they took the whole process very seriously. There would be no alcohol in the studio. 'Occasionally we'd take a line of speed,' says Jim, 'but we wouldn't get out of it.' Speed was useful, enabling more to be done in a shorter space of time, but William 'hated it. I just couldn't stand it,' he recalled. 'Then I met a girl who turned me on to marijuana, and that was that.' Still, it would be some time before the Mary Chain allowed themselves to get stoned in the studio.

An average day was, as Jim recalls, 'quite civilised'. They would get up, sling on some clothes and catch a cab from Fulham, arriving at Wood Green for midday. After a fry-up at the local Wimpy Bar, they were ready to work. 'Later, we'd have dinner, stop at about 9 p.m. and then go home,' says Jim.

'We made the album during the day, totally straight,' Douglas adds. 'Go to the Wimpy for tea . . . it was a really happy time because we knew we were making something that would stand the test of time. It's not like we discussed it, but we knew. There was a quiet confidence.'

Before they'd even entered the studio, William in particular had a clear idea of how he wanted the album to sound. As with every other element of the Mary Chain, what would often look effortless or accidental was considered and decided upon. 'William had thought about how they were going to mix the record,' says Bobby. "They had the image sorted, how they were going to record, even what you should and shouldn't say in interviews. Very rigorous.'

A song that was recorded relatively early on at Southern was 'You Trip Me Up', a melodic paean to troubled love and abused feelings, turning from melancholy (*I walk sideways to avoid you, when I've annoyed you*) to the sly, teasing: *I'd like to trip you up*. The lyrical contrasts were echoed by musical contrasts, sweet simplicity crashing into distorted dissonance. Geoff invited Pat Collier, who had engineered the first single 'Upside Down', to mix the track.

By this time, the Reids had, as Alan McGee observes, 'started to gain control of making the album. They didn't need babysitting. I would just go up once a week, they'd play me something, and then I'd go home.'

Tim Broad was commissioned to make the video for 'You Trip Me Up', but while the mood and setting would be quite different from the promo for 'Never Understand', the glum wariness of the Reids and the slightly cockier attitudes of Bobby and Douglas were still present and correct on the finished result. Location-wise, they were a long way from an abandoned warehouse in Wapping; this time Tim wanted guaranteed sunshine. It was decided that the Algarve would be ideal; Tim had checked the weather reports and was satisfied that the conditions would be typically sunny and bright. When the Mary Chain arrived it rained non-stop for four days. There was a heatwave in London, naturally.

Jim and William were keen to emulate the kind of music videos The Monkees used to make, 'where it's not necessarily about the playback of a song and a band performing,' Jim explains. 'It was more the band walking along a beach in a sunny location.' Or that was the idea. Fortunately there was half a day of good weather, and the group rushed to the beach and shot the video as quickly as they could. The sight of such (temporarily) beautiful weather and the black-clad, squinting Mary Chain provided just the juxtaposition that Tim wanted.

'It was a great trip,' says Jim. 'It was special. We were in this little village, completely untouched by tourism. Of course, we were like aliens who had landed in this little town. Nobody knew what we were about. Everybody thought we were some kind of freakshow that had rolled into town. Which, of course, we were.'

'You Trip Me Up', released in May 1985, peaked at number 55, but the *NME* hailed it as a 'brilliant two-minute-odd gobbet of pop' and declared it their Single of the Week on 1 June, affectionately praising the Mary Chain's 'usual sound of civilisations collapsing, small Scotsmen falling over, rose bushes being stuffed into human ears . . .'

★

Laurence Verfaillie visited London for the *Psychocandy* sessions, either spending time in the studio or meeting up with Jim afterwards. At Jim's encouragement, she also reluctantly provided backing vocals on the track 'Cut Dead', although they were never used. 'I'm not the best singer on the planet,' admits Laurence. 'John Loder always threatened he would release the tapes of me singing as blackmail! But Karen Parker, Bobby's girlfriend, did backing vocals on "Just Like Honey", and she had such a beautiful voice. "Just Like Honey" has the dream backing vocal, as far as I'm concerned.' Interestingly, the seductive 'Just Like Honey' was originally going to be a fast-paced song, hard as it may be to imagine – or it would have been had William had his way. 'I'm thinking, "Yeah, it's gonna be really fast,"' William recalled in an interview with *Goldmine* magazine. 'Jim's like, "No, bring that down a bit," and I was like, "No, Jim. No, Jim. You don't know." He was like, "Please, please, please, just bring it down a bit." He was right. He was totally right.'

Both Jim and William were keen to have their girlfriends present at the studio – having them around no doubt helped break up the inevitable tension – but if you were in attendance at the sessions, or even in the wings at a gig, you were likely to be invited to get involved at some point. While Laurence's contribution was not used on the record, she (not Lawrence from Felt, as some sources state) is credited on *Psychocandy* for backing vocals on 'Taste Of Cindy', 'which I never did,' she corrects. William's then girlfriend Rona McIntosh, an artistic young goth, also had her name included in the credits for photography. Various curious artists also visited the studio while the Mary Chain were recording, including Public Image Limited's Keith Levene and Jah Wobble, the Mary Chain's heroes and post-punk noise forefathers. 'A good omen,' says Douglas.

The Reid brothers were generally getting on at this point, and most of the arguments that kicked off were constructive discussions that needed to be had. That said, Jim and William's disagreements would still get physical from time to time, and the studio itself wouldn't get away unscathed. 'I threw William against a door and knocked it off its hinges,' Jim recalls. 'Can't remember why. But back then it was all about the music. Ten minutes later we'd be fine with each other.'

Staying with Jim in Fulham, Laurence was granted a unique insight into the workings of the group, and specifically how pressured the Reids felt when it came to recording. Making the record was – had to be – an obsession. However, rather perversely, there would be some elements that were left to the last minute – which, as Laurence observes, is testament to their skill as songwriters. 'I saw how they wrote lyrics, and sometimes it felt like, Quick, I've got to go and record, what do you think we should say? But how good is that? Subconsciously you still come up with something that says who you are. But it cracked me up, it was like kids going to an exam.'

'I don't like recording,' Jim admits. 'You're very aware of the fact that this is make or break. You know that if you just go on to auto-pilot for a moment, the whole thing could sink. You have to think, "I'm going to look back on this ten years from now, and I might think I fucked that up and I didn't have to." It's stressful. It might not be for other people, but that's the way I felt about it. I'm sure William did as well.'

Was it more comfortable for the Reids to express themselves on stage than work on a new release in the studio? Apparently not. 'Really they just wanted to be at home, surrounded by gadgets and playing music and having nothing to do with the outside world,' explains Laurence. 'They were completely asocial, not anti-social. If only it could have been just about music and none of the obligations around it, the guys would have been the happiest pop stars on the planet.' William had already bought a flat with his girlfriend Rona, and there was nowhere he'd rather be than there, holed up with their cats (whose nicknames were, incidentally, 'Jim' and 'William').*

Part of what piled extra stress onto the Reids' shoulders from the point of view of recording was the level of expectation from the outside world, and the sense that critics felt there might be little beyond their initial impact, which had been considerable. The word 'hype' had been used too many times in connection with The Jesus and Mary Chain, and both brothers felt keenly that they had much to

---

* William described his cats in an interview thus: 'Jim's a moaning bastard and William is the nice one. I chose the names after I'd had them a couple of days so I could work out which was the cutest. Jim is very, very unfriendly . . . I love to torment him the way I used to torment Jim when he was a kid. Jim makes a brilliant squealing noise. I'm thinking of making a tape loop of it.'

prove with their debut LP. Every track had to be as good as it could possibly be, and, as confident as the Reids were when it came to their output, they knew they were in a fickle industry. This was a chance they could not afford to blow.

Jim Reid says: 'If it had just been the singles surrounded by B-sides the Mary Chain would have gone down the toilet. Pressure is the name of the game. You always think, "This could end tomorrow." You have this mental image of yourself wearing a McDonald's hat, going "Would you like cheese with that? I used to be in a band, you know . . ." If someone could have told me in 1985 that I'd be talking about it now, and I'm doing all right, I would have relaxed a lot more.'

Psychocandy would, in its initial form, consist of fourteen cuts, including 'Never Understand', 'You Trip Me Up', 'Just Like Honey', live favourites 'In A Hole' and 'Taste The Floor', and early songs such as 'The Living End'. It came in at just over 38 minutes long. Brevity was still a significant element in the Mary Chain formula.

While mixing is a key part of any record's success, it's a step in the process that many artists don't involve themselves with directly. However, the Mary Chain knew it was vital that they all had a say, and their sound depended particularly upon William really getting to work on the desk, layering shroud upon shroud of feedback. The guitar sound on the record is metallic and spacious, slicing across Jim's brooding whispers like razors, while the drums thud against the warmth of the bass, relatively low in the mix.

The result was an intense, at times fantastical album that has the unfailing capability to ensnare the listener into a hypnotic state. You can get lost inside *Psychocandy*, and it bears the Mary Chain's unique musical stamp, psychotic and sweet, at once powerfully anchored and oddly fragile. Yes, the layers of noise could be intense and disorientating, but, in William's words, 'it was also the most beautiful tenderness'. As Douglas describes it, the album is 'psychedelic in the true sense of the word', and that sound and feeling come very much from the Mary Chain's experimentation with drugs back in East Kilbride during their formative years.

'Nobody really talks about it, but it really is a psychedelic record,' he explains. 'There are no sharp sounds. It's aggressive at times, but also ethereal. Those layers of guitars on *Psychocandy* where you don't really know where you are, it's like being in a kind of womb of reverb and noise.'

And how did William and Jim feel about the album? 'We were very happy with it,' says Jim. 'We could have tinkered with it until doomsday, but really it wasn't going to get any better than this.'

14

Rants, Reality and Trouble in the Ballroom

An immaculate conception of love songs, and one of the finest
debut albums ever . . . The kids from East Kilbride should now
split up before they have a chance to ruin the bliss.
Jack Barron reviews *Psychocandy* for *Sounds*, 2 November 1985

The period spent making *Psychocandy* was productive, concentrated and exciting, and there was a genuine sense even as they worked that history was being made. Alan McGee loved the album, as did Geoff Travis, although when it was duly delivered to Warners, Geoff chuckles, 'dear Rob Dickins, he thought there was something wrong with it.'

The next release would be the dreamily erotic 'Just Like Honey' in September, a still of the group huddled on the beach from the 'You Trip Me Up' video on the cover. This was a motif the Mary Chain would regularly repeat: the cover of *Psychocandy* would be an image of Jim and William Reid on the white, box-like set of the 'Just Like Honey' video, the word 'CANDY' emblazoned twice behind the group in black and red. This was the single that many new fans would really fall in love with, and it would reach number 45 in the UK singles charts. The album itself was due for release in November.

In the meantime, there was still a pervading feeling amid the press and public that the Mary Chain's time was already over. Jim explains: 'We had the singles, but I think everybody thought that that was all we had in us.' The critics would be in for a surprise just a few months down the line.

The Mary Chain were booked to play a handful of live dates over the summer, and this included the group's first visit to Scandinavia – a memorable if not especially enjoyable stint, largely because William had already started to dislike touring considerably. He was disillusioned with the music business – 'business' being the operative word – and, after entering it with hopes of a magical future, the scales were falling from his eyes, revealing to him the grubby reality. It wouldn't take long before he started to view much of his life as a pop star through a glass darkly.

'It must have been really hard,' muses Alan McGee. 'To suddenly be told, not just by me but by the *NME*, that "You're fucking amazing and Warners have given you a publishing deal, and loads of girls now fancy you," when you might not have had a girlfriend in five years . . . they just rolled up like a hedgehog, they didn't trust anybody. They were the most unready people for that experience.'

At times much of what was spewing out of William onstage would be simple drunken ire. The crowd in Denmark would be subjected to one of William's now famous onstage tirades, and this one was culturally customised to the Mary Chain's Copenhagen fans. Douglas Hart remembers: 'He went into this mad rant and he was going, "You bacon-eating bastards!" Where did that come from? Kind of great. Yeah, there've been a few of those.'

The band's visit to Finland also ended in a well-lubricated sulk. Laurence, who was backstage at the gig, relates her memories of Helsinki: 'William was paralytic even before the gig. He was almost falling off his chair. I could see out of the corner of my eye that William was starting to go. When he actually fell off the chair, everyone was like, "What the hell are we going to do?" At the time they had two guitars on stage, and the sound engineer was given instructions, if William was completely losing the plot on the guitar, to put him down in the mix and the other guy would have to pick up.

'They managed to salvage the gig. William was all over the place, but we couldn't hear him too much. At the end, there were these flowerpots on the edge of the stage and William went and kicked them all over into the mosh pit. Bless him!'

'He's a complicated guy,' says Douglas with a shrug. 'He's one of the funniest people, but you just have to look at the lyrics, there's a darkness to him – which we all have to some degree, but maybe he's just more honest about it. It's like that with the both of them. Maybe it sometimes comes out the wrong way, but you know what? Fuck it.'

After returning home, a trail of offended Danes and broken flowerpots in their wake, the Mary Chain played Manchester's now iconic Hacienda club with Meat Whiplash, The Pastels and Primal Scream, taking the stage at around two o'clock in the morning. This, incidentally, was when Karen Parker famously joined the band onstage, not just to sing backing vocals on 'Just Like Honey' but to play drums. According to Jim, the story that Bobby had hurt his hand and thus couldn't play is not true. It was just typically mischievous Mary Chain spontaneity at work.

'Our attitude was punk in its purest form,' says Jim. 'We just said, "Karen, do you want to play drums tonight?" She was like, "I cannae play!" We were like, "Oh, it sounds all right." She knew all the songs. So she played Bobby's set, and she was bloody good. And I still got the Bobby grin that I was always looking for. He was standing at the side of the stage going "Yeah!"'

While for some members of the Mary Chain touring was a necessary evil, Douglas generally loved the experience. 'It was always a thrill to go somewhere new. Even later on I enjoyed touring,' he reflects. 'Some people thrive on every part of touring, staying up all night every night. We, being slightly more sensitive, would get comedowns. But I'm not going to moan, we loved it.

'McGee would come on a lot of those tours as a tour manager – he wasn't just our manager. Especially on the early ones he would be with us, so it really was like a gang, in the best way.'

'There were camps within camps,' McGee remembers. 'Obviously there were the Reid brothers, who confided in each other. Bobby and Douglas were close, but then you had other twists in it: Bobby and I were close, we went way back. Jim and I were close, and I got on well with Douglas. William and I never really connected. I thought he was an incredible talent; we just didn't connect as human beings.'

What would often make the touring experience more enjoyable was travelling with people they liked, such as Felt and of course The Pastels, who would reconvene with the Mary Chain in early September for a gig at Preston's Clouds venue.

'We did OK,' Stephen Pastel recalls. 'My main memory is that William was quite drunk and he told me he loved our music. He was really unguarded and it was a sweet moment.'

Douglas Hart says: 'I loved playing places like that because they were a bit like the places we grew up in. I remember in Preston this kid came up to me, really young, strange-looking guy, and he said, "I'd like to start a band." I was like, "You should, you should!" And he said, "But I've got no friends." God, what a thing to say. Kind of beautiful. It haunted me. I always wondered what happened to him.' This poignant exchange must have accessed a part of Douglas that would surely have felt similarly isolated – another outsider from an outsider town – had he and the Reids not found each other in East Kilbride when they did.

Violence at Mary Chain gigs was not such a problem in the regions, although if you weren't keen on spitting, that rarely welcomed hangover from the punk years, a Mary Chain gig was probably not the place for you. 'Those first few tours we did of Britain, people would spit all the way through,' Douglas recalls. 'Someone's mum came to see us and she said, "What were those bits of paper people were throwing at you?" We were like, "Those were not bits of paper . . ."'

The general feeling was that, even after a hiatus, London was still the main problem in audience terms. It was where the most dangerous scenes had been sparked, and care would be needed when the band played there again. It might have seemed over the top, but Alan McGee was nervous enough to employ two Scottish ex-SAS bodyguards. Even they wouldn't last the course; the last straw for them was the Mary Chain's show at Camden's Electric Ballroom on 9 September 1985.

A good proportion of the crowd that piled into the venue that night was keyed up and ready to fight. They weren't 'smashing up pop', they were kicking the living daylights out of each other. Unlike North London Poly, McGee 'expected it to be heavy, and it was. Very heavy.'

'It happened straight away,' adds Douglas. 'There were big, thuggish guys there, throwing bottles from the back, like at the football – that used to make me sick – so that people down the front would get hit.'

Jim Reid, who felt largely immune to what was happening thanks to being utterly plastered, admits the Mary Chain didn't help matters by coming on to play a good 90 minutes later than they were expected. 'I know why the riots happened at the North London Poly, and I know why it happened at the Electric Ballroom,' he says. 'They kept coming into the dressing-room and saying, "It's time to go on," and we were going, "No, we're just chilling out, playing some music, we'll be on in fifteen minutes." That went on for about an hour and a half.

'Looking back on it, it was idiotic, but at the time I thought, We're the band, we should go on whenever we feel like it. Was that a smart thing to do? Probably not, but there you go.'

They didn't want to just listen to music and relax, of course – they wanted to knock the edges off their nerves by getting as obliterated as possible while still being able to function. 'The drinking was always there,' Jim admits. 'Me and William, we're not really at ease socially, to say the very least. It's a social lubricant. At the beginning we'd go on tour and we'd get shit-faced every night for ten weeks, and then you'd get back home and be kind of glad not to drink any more. I never used to drink at home, though, and couldn't understand why anybody would. That changed. I can't remember when or why.'

Laurence Verfaillie was backstage that night and she knew from experience there was no way they'd be going on stage until they had reached a satisfactory level of drunkenness. That, plus adrenaline and the jolt of hearing the menacing shouts of the crowd, would create a combustible chemical reaction in terms of their own stage presence. 'They had to have a serious amount of alcohol before going on stage. But the gigs would be fabulous. It wasn't like Amy Winehouse slurring her words, it was getting them into the mood.'

No matter how fabulous they were, this crowd, despite having paid to get in, was in no mood to listen to them. The Jesus and Mary Chain walked on stage 'expecting to be worshipped,' Jim chuckles. What greeted them was an angry mob.

The band warily regarded the broiling darkness in front of them for a few silent moments. Then Jim pushed the neck of Douglas's bass out of his way, Douglas and William turned their backs, and they started to play, lit by three pale spotlights beaming over them and on to the crowd like ghostly searchlights. Jim, leaning forward malevolently, thrashed the floor with his mic stand, William struck his guitar like an anvil, notes ringing and sputtering out like sparks – it was as much a show of strength, a roar of defiance to shout down the crowd, as a gig. There was something of a rumble about it, band versus audience.

This would be one of the first times the Mary Chain played 'Just Like Honey' live, and it was utterly lost on the majority of the audience. 'I was thinking, You fucking idiots, just shut up and listen to this song,' says Jim.

Alan McGee was standing at the side of the stage with Laurence, who was hit on the back of the head by a flying bottle. Before eventually giving in and rushing backstage for safety, they watched their friends trying to play under increasingly hostile conditions. 'Football hoolies had suddenly got involved with it,' McGee says. 'One of the bouncers got his head cut open. I remember a quarter-bottle of whisky going flying between Jim's head and Bobby's. I just thought, If that had hit either of them, they could have lost an eye. That's when you realise it's starting to get out of hand.'

Bobby Gillespie remembers that very whisky bottle – it's not the kind of thing you forget – although the person who forcibly delivered it, he insists, was a friend of his from Glasgow, who had travelled down on the Stagecoach and was now showing the advanced effects of a day's worth of dedicated boozing. 'He shouted, "Gillespie!" and threw a bottle at me . . . but, you know, as an act of love.' Heart-warming indeed.

'The security did face off the crowd,' McGee continues. 'But it was pretty unpleasant. And we were just kids. That's the thing that people don't talk about enough with the Mary Chain. With Oasis, they had a manager who'd managed Johnny Marr, Noel was 27, I was 33, 34. If we needed security it was a phone call away. The Mary Chain thing was ten years before. Yes, maybe I was out of my depth, but I'd got them to that point as well, so there was some degree of talent. But there was also a degree of complete inexperience.'

Jim Reid says: 'We just played fifteen minutes and left; you know, if you don't want to hear it then we won't play it. On a normal night we would just be locked into each other, it was almost as if the audience didn't matter.' The crowd became enraged when the band decided to leave the stage, but the way William saw it was that they were simply sticking to his quite sensible ethos: play until you get jeered by the crowd, that's your cue to leave.

Meanwhile, David Evans, the Mary Chain's live sound technician, was desperately trying to protect the mixing and lighting desks from being destroyed but in doing so he could only watch as, post-gig, the 'fans' started to help themselves to equipment from the stage.

By the end of the night the ex-SAS man-mountains hired by McGee had had enough, both of the violence (one bodyguard was knocked out with a scaffolding pole) and of the people they were meant to be looking after. Jim Reid says: 'At first they were like, "Wait! I'll check this door," but by the end of it they were saying, "If I ever see you little fuckers again I'm going to rip your heads off. Give me one good reason why I shouldn't beat the shit out of you?" "Er . . . because it would hurt?" We were probably winding them up.'

When the coast was clear, team Mary Chain decamped to recover at McGee's flat in Tottenham. They'd managed to escape unscathed, but feeling grateful that they were still in one piece was not how they wanted to end every London show. It had become, as Alan McGee admits, 'a circus'. The group's surly attitude and explosive music was part theatre, part expression, part defence mechanism, but it was being taken too seriously by too many.

'There was a lot of talk about this,' says Douglas. 'We were like, "Alan, we want to go down and play, we don't want to witness fights, we don't want people to get their heads smashed in." I think he saw that, but it was out of control. Alan was a young guy as well.'

Events like this, as Mary Chain press officer Mick Houghton observes, would ironically launch the Mary Chain into the public consciousness, but the fact people associated the band with riots would be a millstone for the band for years to come. 'It overshadowed their career throughout,' Mick admits. 'It was very hard for them to escape that initial impression that people have of the Mary Chain.

'I always felt that a lot of their attitude, which the press loved, was more born out of a lack of confidence. I never thought they had this intent to cause trouble – it was more like trouble followed them.'

15

Milestones/Millstones

*Our mum's terribly proud. The black sheep of the family have
become ... hopeful.*
Jim Reid to Mat Snow, *NME*

When *Psychocandy* was released in November 1985 a nation, or at
least many of its hipper inhabitants, fell in love. The album went to
number 31 in the otherwise Spandau Ballet and Elaine Paige-domi-
nated charts and was loved, revered and included in best-of lists the
world over. The element of surprise didn't hurt; as Jim observed, the
Mary Chain were previously suspected by some of being a one-trick
pony, with little substance beneath the noise, image and stories to
sustain their career. *Psychocandy* put paid to all that. This release
cemented the Reid brothers' position as serious craftsmen of delicate,
beautiful pop songs. 'It sounds big-headed,' says Jim, 'but we knew we
had a record that wasn't run-of-the-mill, and we knew that almost
every track could have been an A-side in itself.' They had peaked
quickly, some might say too early. There would be no resting on laurels
– the Reids now had to sustain their success and, as a result, 'could
never entirely enjoy it,' as Jim recalls. The Reids' sense of anxiety
would at least mean they rarely took their privileged position for
granted – for years they could never shake off the feeling that their
success was 'just temporary'.

The other prevailing feeling, one that would ultimately become a
source of pride, was the fact that, although *Psychocandy* was a hit, The
Jesus and Mary Chain would always be outsiders in the pop world. This
wasn't necessarily a bad thing; as Jim put it: 'if there was a place in the

pop market for The Jesus and Mary Chain, The Jesus and Mary Chain wouldn't exist. We're the misfits of the pop music world.'

This quality of never quite fitting in would ensure that other people were already starting bands because of the Mary Chain, just as punk had inspired likeminded outsiders to do the same less than a decade earlier. And as far as charting was concerned, they might have loved the idea of being 'pop-stars', but Jim Reid certainly deemed it a 'sin' to treat music as if the most important thing was who was highest in the chart. To someone with such a fierce, pure love of music, this kind of attitude didn't exactly seem to be in the right spirit. 'It shouldn't be a competition,' he chided at the time. This was not necessarily a feeling shared by Warner Brothers.

After some promotional dates in the UK and Germany, the Mary Chain flew back to the US for their first full American tour that winter. What was strange for the Mary Chain was the fact that they'd travel to far-flung parts of the US and there would be people there who had not only heard of them, they were fans.

The tour was a success, but the mood was fractured and low. The band were tired and road-weary and Christmas Day, which they spent together after flying back from New York, did not feel particularly festive. After New Year the band was back on the road, going back to America in March – and it was around this point, by all accounts, that the first real cracks started to appear. William now hated touring with a passion and the more he understood the machinations of the music industry, the unhappier he became. That year William would, as he recalled, suffer the 'first of many breakdowns because of that'.

'At that time,' says Jim, 'I don't know what it was, but William was having a hard time with touring, which is weird because now it's the opposite: I'm quite happy to be at home and he's desperate to get out on the road. For whatever reason, around 1985, 1986, he'd just had enough. We had to stop for a time while he got his head together.'

On the road William would avoid sight-seeing, preferring to stay in his hotel room. The booze was flowing, magnifying every problem, and the relationship between the brothers was strained. Success had not eased any of the old tensions, in fact it was creating new irritations for the Reids.

Alan McGee says: 'I don't know if they could ever be happy in a band with each other but in a way they don't make sense apart, musically. Then in the middle of this you had people like Geoff Travis, normal people, un-fucked-up. We didn't even use drugs in these days to get fucked up, we were just all either depressed or drunk. Everyone in that band, and the manager, was a head-case. It was the most dysfunctional team of people ever to get success.'

Douglas Hart remembers the exhaustion both Reids were suffering from. The drinking didn't help, but the added pressure of having to write songs for the next album while on tour was, at times, hard for the brothers to bear. It's the cliché of having your whole life up to that point to write your debut album and generally you're writing in a space you feel comfortable with. But then you're required to write the next one in a matter of months, in hotel rooms and dressing-rooms, on tour buses. Whenever William and Jim had the opportunity, they'd return to East Kilbride to try to write songs in the kitchen.

'That was the creative space for them,' says Douglas. 'But both of them were stressed, they were having . . . not panic attacks, but you could see they were really struggling at that point between *Psychocandy* and *Darklands*. All I had to do was go on tour and have fun, which is probably why they resented me!'

One person McGee remembers handling the often dark times and rising stress levels on tour with detachment and even amusement was Bobby Gillespie. 'Maybe the Reids were having a good time, I don't know,' McGee concludes gloomily. 'I was having a shit time. Douglas was having a shit time. Bobby was probably getting off on the madness. He was probably laughing at it.'

Two things that kept Gillespie slightly removed from the Mary Chain gloom, no doubt, were the fact that he still lived in Glasgow, so there was a physical separation, and the fact that he was developing Primal Scream, who were gathering pace and already had a single out, 'All Fall Down', which boasted a soft naïveté reminiscent of The Pastels and the BMX Bandits. It was co-produced by Joe Foster and released as a 7-inch by Creation Records in May 1985. 'All Fall Down' was well received critically, and Primal Scream now had their eye on the future. It was becoming increasingly difficult for Bobby to commit to two bands in two different cities and make it work.

What followed in the early weeks of 1986 has often been described

as a dramatic ultimatum, but in truth the subject simply needed address-
ing so that everyone knew where they stood. Jim Reid says: 'With Bobby
we'd said, "You can be in the band if you want to, but we don't think it's
going to work being in two bands." We sort of knew he wasn't going to
join the band. Obviously it was lucky for him that he didn't.' Bobby was
'pretty fucking upset', however. He felt he 'belonged' to the Mary Chain
and, at the same time, certainly felt closer to them than Primal Scream.

Douglas, who was closest to Bobby in the band, was also hit hard by
the decision. 'It was a sad day. The whole atmosphere of the band
changed after Bobby left.'

The final Mary Chain release with Bobby on drums would be the
'Some Candy Talking' EP, due for release in July 1986. The group first
recorded the title track on 29 October the previous year, one day after
William's 27th birthday, for John Peel's Radio 1 show. The accompanying tracks on the forthcoming 12-inch would be 'Taste Of Cindy', 'Hit'
and an acoustic version of the track 'Psychocandy', which, contrarily,
didn't appear on the initial release of *Psychocandy*.

For their recording of 'Some Candy Talking', the Reids were keen to
work with Flood, the engineer of choice for the likes of Nick Cave and
Depeche Mode. Flood was based at Trident Studios in St Anne's Court,
a haunted Soho alleyway. Strange noises could be heard in Trident late
at night, noises that couldn't always be blamed on musicians, but that's
another story. Flood, real name Mark Ellis, earned his nickname during
his days as a runner, as he always made countless cups of tea for those
in the studio. (His fellow runner, on the other hand, was not so willing
to get busy with the teabags. He was known as 'Drought'.)

When Alan Moulder, then a young studio engineer working with
Flood, heard that the Mary Chain were coming to record at Trident, he
'went straight to the studio manager and told them I *had* to be the
assistant on the session. I had *Psychocandy* and loved the band.'

The Jesus and Mary Chain were still a little dubious, as Moulder
puts it, about unfamiliar engineers and studios. They hadn't forgotten
that their experience with John Loder was the exception rather than the
rule. But with Flood and Alan Moulder being a similar age to themselves, and simpatico to their mindset, this was a good match.

'There were a lot of engineers who thought there was a "correct" way
of doing things,' says Moulder. 'It was the 1980s and every engineer

wanted to make records that sounded like Trevor Horn, so Jim and William's bright, reverby and violent guitars didn't fit into their ideas of how to do things. I remember Kevin Shields from My Bloody Valentine had the same problems.'

The Mary Chain were as serious as ever when working on 'Some Candy Talking', and if they struggled to get the sound they were looking for, the mood would plummet. 'I just kept supplying cups of tea and chocolate biscuits, which seemed to cheer them up,' Alan remembers. 'They were picky about everything, be it music, sound or food. They were funny once they relaxed a bit.'

One thing that did prove a problem was the bass part. No one could play it, even though, as Jim pointed out, 'it was incredibly simple'.

'Jim couldn't play it, I couldn't play it,' William admitted in an interview with *Select*. 'Douglas was the bass player and he couldn't play it. We got in a session bassist, and *he* couldn't play it. In the end Dick Green from Creation Records came down, and he could play it. So we were like, "Quick! Run the tape!"'

The resulting record would be another classic Reid gem with ambiguous lyrics – it has long been assumed that 'candy' and 'stuff' were allusions to heroin, but William insists it is 'more sexual' than drug-related. 'Some Candy Talking' also has an unusual change in the middle. This is because William basically stuck two different songs together. It worked perfectly.

*

A clutch of tour dates was coming up, and this would mean one last trip to the US with the Mary Chain for Bobby Gillespie. By this time the band had an established following across the Atlantic, particularly in New York. It was no longer a case of playing to Anglophiles and roller-skating regulars who would have turned up anyway; this time The Jesus and Mary Chain would be playing to fans.

'We played at the Ritz in New York City and it was like being in a pop band,' says Jim. 'We arrived at the venue and there were girls standing outside shouting, "Jim! I wanna have your babies!" I was like, "This is weird. This just doesn't happen in the UK."'

The gig in New York was also the night that Jerry Jaffe, former head of A&R at PolyGram and a consultant for Warners, would see the group for the first time. Jerry Jaffe was later to become The Jesus and Mary Chain's manager in the US, but if you had told him at this stage that any involvement with the band was on the cards, he would never have believed you. Jaffe was mildly impressed by *Psychocandy*, not to the extent that his Warners co-workers were, but he agreed to come to the Ritz to see them play. He found himself sharing a table with the then *Village Voice* writer Robert Christgau, and within minutes of the Mary Chain appearing on stage, both Jaffe and Christgau were united in their opinion of the group.

'I thought this was the worst band I had ever seen in my life,' growls Jaffe. 'I thought they couldn't play, they played maybe half an hour – apparently this was a long gig for them at that time – and I looked at Robert and he looked at me and we were basically saying, "What the heck?" I was just flabbergasted. Anyway, that was that. I didn't think about them after that, they were out of my consciousness.' Needless to say, Jerry would not take on the US management of the Mary Chain just yet. (Christgau would also change his tune about the band, giving *Psychocandy* a rave review on its release. 'My favourite parts are the cheapest,' he would later write. 'When the feedback wells up over the chords in perfect pseudomelodic formation I feel as if I've been waiting to hear this music all my life.')

One thing Jerry noticed about the Mary Chain was that, after the gig, they were far friendlier than he'd been warned they would be. They had a forbidding reputation, and there was almost a romance about how rude they were expected to be. The reality was that they were shy, quite serious and didn't suffer fools gladly. But, while Jaffe's Warners colleagues 'wanted their record-company version of S&M', the Mary Chain were quietly accommodating. In fact, compared to artists such as Dead or Alive's Pete Burns, whom Jaffe also managed, 'The Jesus and Mary Chain came off like Graham Norton'.*

'I guess some people who didn't know us thought we were rude or up ourselves,' muses Douglas. 'But it was shyness. Even among ourselves we wouldn't speak much. I remember people sitting in rooms with us, squirming in their seat and then leaving after about a minute because we weren't talking.'

---

* Extremely exuberant Irish comedian, TV host and much-loved motormouth.

This discreet attitude also meant that, in a way, a purity was retained, Douglas observes, 'We kept ourselves to ourselves. Nowadays if you get a band that has the level of publicity that we've had, they'd be going out with kiddies' TV presenters and hanging out at parties, but we were sitting on our own watching the telly.

'Even at the height of the fame we weren't out every night getting wasted on drugs, no way. That helped us focus on the music, but talk about different times! And I think if one of us came in while we were making *Psychocandy* and said that he was going out with a kids' TV presenter, he'd have been thrown out of the band.'

A lot of time on tour in the US was spent listening to music, exploring junk shops and record stores and reading. Jim was an avid reader of biographies, and no second-hand book store was safe when the Mary Chain were in town. 'Jim read about people like Lenny Bruce,' says Laurence, 'people with talent and who were really representative of Americana, but sick. Every time we came back our suitcase would be full of second-hand records, books and things like that.'

The members of the touring party were collectively fascinated by almost everything they saw as they travelled across the US, from the landscapes to the truck stops to the evangelical bumper stickers. Particularly in New York and Los Angeles, the Mary Chain made a point of requesting a few extra days to explore before the tour moved off again.

'When we arrived at any new city in the States, any free time would be spent looking for guitar shops,' adds Laurence. 'It was a total obsession with Gretsch and Gibson semi-acoustics and Les Pauls . . . and go karting. Unfortunately you couldn't bring back many things, but guitars, we did every second-hand guitar shop in every city.'

Back in the UK, the news had broken that Bobby Gillespie was leaving the band, prompting many a sombre, big-haired youth to wonder what it might be like to take his place. John Moore was one of them; he was just more determined than most. He was a huge fan of the Mary Chain, and when he picked up a copy of the *NME* from Knight's, his local newsagents in Reading, and read the story, he knew somehow that this was his chance. It was, as he puts it, his '*Charlie and the Chocolate Factory* moment'. The fact he couldn't play the drums was frankly neither here nor there.

John Moore had already been to East Kilbride to soak up as much in the way of Mary Chain vibes as possible. His father was running a courier firm at the time, and occasionally John would run errands for him. The opportunity to deliver a package to Glasgow arose, and John was all over it. 'I took the overnight train with the package to deliver to Sauchiehall Street by 9 a.m.,' he says, 'and I worked out from the train timetables that I could get a train to East Kilbride and have a look at where my favourite band came from.

'East Kilbride was not what I expected. It was like a new town, it doesn't really have the romance of granite buildings or fog. It was a bit boring, a bit nondescript, a bit like where I came from.'

In order to have the full experience, John went to the high street and bought a black shirt from Topman, where he imagined Jim, William and Douglas had bought their own black shirts. He was going all-out. 'I tell Jim this and he says I sound like a fucking stalker,' he laughs. 'More of a charming enthusiast, I think . . .'

One trip to Topman in East Kilbride does not a future in the Mary Chain guarantee, but fate was on John's side. A friend of his from Reading had started working at Warners in Broadwick Street, Soho, and was intrigued to see pictures in the office of a group of 'young men with a really bad reputation' who looked just like John.

John came into town to take his friend to lunch, and in the foyer of the office he spotted Alan McGee. The wheels were in motion. They'd already seen each other a week earlier at Tottenham Court Road Tube station, McGee noticing John because he looked distinctly Reid-like, and they shared a nod of semi-recognition. This time John decided to intercept McGee and broach the subject of being Bobby Gillespie's replacement.

'I said, "I play the drums." He looked sceptical and he went up for his lunch with Rob Dickins or whoever it was. But then I went to see *Entertaining Mr Sloane* at the Scala in King's Cross, the Joe Orton film. There must have been ten people in the cinema, but among them were William, Jim and Douglas. Then a couple of nights later, at a Sonic Youth gig, there was Jim again. We seemed to be at so many similar events that we got talking.'

Jim says of those early meetings: 'We'd kind of spotted John around the place; he was almost like a weird stalker. At the Sonic Youth gig

John came up and said, "I saw you the other night." I thought, Oh God, is he coming on to me or what? What's going on? He was a bit of a hustler, you could see that. He'd spotted the drumming spot was vacant and he was going to go for it. It was McGee as well, he said, "There's this bloke who looks just like William, and he wears leather trousers. I think you should get him." We're like, "Can he drum?" "Er . . . oh, I don't know about that."'

Part of the appeal of hiring John, from McGee's point of view, was that it would be good for the band to have someone 'normal' who could potentially lighten the mood. Alan arranged a meeting in the pub for John and the group, but when they met Jim laconically stated that they were 'just going to have a friend of theirs from Glasgow, because they weren't very good at meeting people', as John recalls. 'Never a truer word spoken. But they didn't have any friends in Glasgow, didn't have any friends anywhere. They were the most anti-social little clique of people you could ever imagine.'

Jim clearly didn't want to commit before he was sure, but the next time they bumped into each other, at a Primal Scream concert at the Dome in Tufnell Park, they were getting desperate. They had another American tour coming up, and still no drummer. 'McGee said, "Listen, this is serious. Jim's going to be here in a minute, and we really do need a drummer. Can you really play?"' says John. 'And I said, "Well, actually, no. I can't."'

Moments after this bombshell, Jim turned up. After a few seconds spent mulling over the dilemma, he looked at John and said, 'Can you learn?'

16

Besotted Americans and Burst Eardrums

*I expected sex and drugs and rock'n'roll. Pretty much got it. No
point in doing it otherwise.*
John Moore

John Moore was given two weeks to pick up a new instrument from
scratch. He was naturally musical, primarily a guitarist, but it took
time, sweat and quite a lot of plasters to get himself up to *Psychocandy*
standard on the drums. He took advantage of his father's office in Reading after closing time and practiced through the night, a ghetto-blaster
playing *Psychocandy* by his side. His hands blistered up to the point
that they eventually turned into 'one solid wound', as he recalls with a
wince. Still, mission Mary Chain was under way. (His father's business
would later come in handy regarding other matters Mary Chain. 'I
helped Jim and William move house later on, because I had a driving
licence and my dad's courier business had vans,' John explains. 'Talk
about ingratiating yourself . . .')

An audition was arranged at Alaska Studios, where 'Upside Down'
was recorded. Quietly confident in his abilities, John turned up and
duly waited three hours for the Mary Chain to appear. They were still
drunk from the night before and in no mood to play.

Jim has no memory of this audition at all, so John tells the story: 'We
played a few songs, and at the end they said, "Don't know . . . Your drumming wasn't that good," and I said, "Well, nor was your guitar playing!"
"Aye, fair enough . . ." Always a sense of fair play in the Mary Chain.'

The Reids eventually agreed to try him out at the end of the UK tour
at Nottingham Rock City, a toilet-circuit sweatbox and heavy-metal

stronghold known for its Hells Angels bouncers. McGee sent a train ticket to John in readiness for the journey. In the meantime, John practised, attended a couple of Mary Chain rehearsals and had a pre-gig pep-talk from Bobby Gillespie over coffee. 'Bobby was very nice,' John remembers. 'He said, "It's not really that difficult, the main thing you've got to do is duck when the bottles start flying." He was so right.'

The big day would soon arrive, and, after a final nervous primp of his thick black hair and no doubt one last panicky listen to *Psychocandy*, he left his parents' house in Reading for the first leg of his journey to Nottingham. On the train he obsessed about the task ahead, hoping he'd pass the trial. He'd done everything he could to prepare: he'd watched Bobby's last gig at the University of East Anglia, practised until his blisters had blisters, and ultimately he felt as ready as he'd ever be. He arrived in Nottingham five hours early.

Walking up to the backstage entrance of the club, John was met by a pair of enormous hairy men, their arms covered in spider-web tattoos. Fortunately, they greeted him kindly and welcomed him in to wait for the rest of the band. The three Mary Chains finally arrived, like pale, angular apparitions, ambling into the comforting darkness of the club.

John's first gig is justifiably etched on his memory, not least because he would be the only one not drinking; he had to be able to trust himself to get the drum parts right. From the lateness onstage to the roar of the crowd to the shower of glasses that rained upon them when they appeared, every moment is still in bold relief.

'You go from the corridor where there's nothing happening to the stage, people's faces pressed right up. Feedback. It was a really good gig. I might have been musically inept, but it sort of fitted. I'd been playing for about three weeks at that stage. Went on with the Moe Tucker set-up.'

While it was, as Jim puts it, 'a bit like having a fan in the band', having John on board worked well. His cheerful nature quickly made him an asset, just as Alan McGee had predicted. 'John fitted in straight away,' says Laurence Verfaillie, 'I think he had to handle more than he showed but he always came across as a joker, trying to kill a nasty situation with a joke. I liked him a lot.'

'With Jim especially, I became very close,' adds John. 'I didn't hang around with William, he was older and settled down with his girlfriend, and he'd become quite shy. Maybe having all that success had turned him slightly, just shocked him. He kept himself to himself. Jim was more into having a good time, as was Douglas.'

There was something of a cultural difference between Jim, William and Douglas and their new member, but this only served to break the ice – particularly because there had been a recent news story stating that East Kilbride had the lowest life expectancy in the UK, while Wokingham, where John hailed from, had the highest. 'I think they called me a Southern ponce about twenty-five times a day,' says John. 'He was like us though, more or less,' adds Jim. 'He just sounded like a bit of a fop.'

*

The band had entered their next phase when John joined the group, and not just in terms of having a new drummer. The Mary Chain were becoming more 'business-oriented', as Jim puts it. The sets became longer, up to an hour, and the band also decided to commit wholeheartedly to the mission of cracking America.

'It sounds absurd,' Jim admits, 'because we've never been business-like, but we were trying to be. We knew that if we fucked up and fell all over the place, we'd just be a mild curiosity and that would be it. We had no idea what to do, but had decided that a serious approach might be helpful.'

John, meanwhile, had been hoping Rock City wasn't a one-off – no doubt the Mary Chain were as poker-faced as usual after the gig – but any anxiety was allayed when McGee next contacted him. 'He said, "Have you got a passport? We're going to America for a month."'

One of John's useful functions therefore was, he remembers, 'working as a translator. At the time those accents were pretty indecipherable. Once you got past Hadrian's Wall those guys could starve. You know, trying to order something in a café: "What? What's he saying?" "I *think* the boys are saying: two plates of egg and bacon, one cup of tea and a side of fried bread please." "Oh thank you! We haven't eaten for days . . ."'

One thing that surprised John was the fact that the Mary Chain rarely behaved in the way pop stars should, in his opinion. There was little in the way of glamour; the Mary Chain were not, as Douglas said earlier, into attending parties with models on their arms (or, God forbid, children's-TV presenters), and there was a considerable lack of pools, jewels, Mars bars, 'beautiful, doomed people. . . I thought it would be like The Rolling Stones, basically, a rock'n'roll-carnage lifestyle,' says John. 'There were bits that were like that, but it was a bit more prosaic and down to earth. To know that they ate beans on toast, or they had no food in their fridge, or they might have a Pot Noodle . . . pop stars don't do that! You click your fingers and you have filet mignon brought in.'

John's first tour of America with the Mary Chain was memorable, even if it wasn't going to rival the Stones' travelling circus in terms of the antics, or indeed the menu. He'd been to the US before, but not in this context. Jim remembers with amusement watching MTV in the hotel with the rest of the band when the video of 'Just Like Honey' appeared on the screen. 'John took a photo of the TV,' Jim recalls. '"Ooh! Ooh!" Mind you, I was impressed myself. Fucking hell, we're on MTV! I probably took a photo as well.'

'The tour was really good,' says John. 'It was like going from nothing to headlining at the Ritz in New York. This was when we experienced elderly groupies hanging on to the side of the bus, going "We fucked Led Zeppelin, you chickens! Why can't we come with you?" We were terrified. "Get them away! We're innocent! No!"'

The Mary Chain were idolised in the US – they mingled fearsome energy with troubled love songs, sex appeal and a doleful remoteness, and this recipe was proving irresistible. Their popularity soared. But still, if anyone tried to barrel their way backstage after a gig, they would be given short shrift. Or no shrift. Silence.

'People were frightened,' John explains. 'The reputation was more severe than most people's, still is. People would have to be quite brave to approach, so there weren't that many people making arseholes of themselves, coming in and trying to take over, "Let's all have a party!" Actually, you wouldn't want to go to a party that The Jesus and Mary Chain were at. That wouldn't be a party.'

However, this glacial force-field wouldn't always protect the Mary Chain from the lunatics, ranging from boring to terrifying, who trail bands and try to pierce the membrane that separates fans from stars however they can. Jim, being the front-man, was normally the one who had to ward them off.

'Oh, we got the nutters,' Jim confirms, heaving a sigh as the memories flood back. 'More than our fair share. You'd get guys in the front row, so they must have queued up for hours to get that spot, and they'd spend the whole gig going, "You fucking arsehole!" I'd be thinking, Why did you come?'

'There was one guy in New York, I swear to God, it was like Travis Bickle [Robert de Niro's psychotic character in *Taxi Driver*]. He was just staring at me. He looked evil. I thought, Well, what can happen? I just laughed at him. But then, oh God, this guy's climbing on stage. One bouncer comes along and Bickle's kicking the shit out of him, then two, three. I thought, I'm going to get my arse kicked, or worse, in front of a live audience. Thankfully, three or four bouncers managed to hold him down. But we were like a magnet for that kind of weirdo.'

One highlight of this tour, apart from surviving the determined attentions of Travis Bickle, was a gig at the Santa Monica Civic Center, 'where Bo Diddley played on his TV special in 1961', John says proudly, a large picture of himself and Bo just feet away from us on his wall as we speak. 'You know, The Doors played here, everyone's played here and now we're doing it! And we only played for 25 minutes.

'There were people who'd felt robbed, but other people thought that, you know, if we'd tried to do a full set they'd have felt cheated. But 25 minutes was like a lifetime . . . and Bruce Springsteen or The Jesus and Mary Chain? I know who I'd rather see. Bruce Springsteen.'

The Mary Chain's sheer Scottishness, as John observed earlier, was a recurring challenge when it came to making themselves understood, especially in America, where ironically it was more important than anywhere to 'meet and greet' the record label and the press. Jim and William had to show up for daily interviews with magazines or radio stations, and practically every night there would be dinners with Warners representatives that the band could not wriggle out of if they wanted to build on their appeal in the US. This was not the sort of thing that came naturally to the Reids, but they took their responsibilities seriously and duly made themselves available. However, thanks to their Scottish brogue, it was all too easy for them to be misquoted by American journalists. This certainly resulted in some interesting misinformation appearing in the press.

'Once a journalist asked Jim, "Which bands are you into?"' says

Laurence Verfaillie. 'Jim of course mentioned The Stooges. They printed "the Bee Gees". Jim was mortified.'

The Mary Chain returned to the UK and, barely catching their breath, prepared to go straight into another tour, this time taking in mostly the northern cities: Sheffield, Liverpool, Coventry, Glasgow, Aberdeen, Blackburn and, once again, Manchester's Hacienda, the penultimate stop before the tour concluded at London's Hammersmith Palais on 8 May. At the Hacienda and the Hammersmith Palais the group were joined by Alan Moulder, who attempted to handle the Mary Chain's sound. The Reids had surmised that, working in a respected London studio as Alan did, it would be a cinch for him to be their live soundman. It was not. 'I had never done live sound,' Moulder confesses. 'I hadn't a clue.'

Despite this, the Hacienda show went well, and the following night at the Hammersmith Palais was truly great. The venue was packed and the atmosphere electrifying. The Mary Chain's silhouettes loomed out of the flickering darkness, dry ice billowed around them like an eerie, illuminated mist from a horror movie, and the sound of William's guitar feedback was huge. So huge, in fact, that during the Mary Chain's final number, 'Never Understand', all the mid-range speakers blew, largely due to Moulder getting 'a bit carried away' on the desk and turning William up as high as possible, with literally explosive results.

'It sounded like your eardrums had burst; all of a sudden there was no top end at all,' he remembers. 'Fortunately, the song had nearly finished. Most bands would have been furious and fired me on the spot, but they didn't mind. They thought it was funny.'

17

Alcohol, Speed, Farewell McGee

Jim's the rock'n'roll swinger. I'm a pipe-and-slippers man.
William Reid to Adam Sweeting, *Q*

Finally the Mary Chain had a chance to go home and recover briefly from what seemed like an almost endless stint of touring. Relaxing wasn't exactly on the cards back in London, however. It was more a case of retoxing. Or just toxing. To retox, one does have to detox, after all, and there was certainly no danger of them doing that.

John, who had recently moved into a squat in Vauxhall, would hit Soho with Jim to inhale the contents of the bar at the Spice of Life in Cambridge Circus and the famous Coach and Horses, situated just behind it. 'Then,' says John, 'we'd watch Roland Rat on TV:AM at my place after being up all night. There was a lot of breakfast television in those days.' John Moore, incidentally, remains a dedicated Roland Rat fan to this day.

Another haunt that loomed large in the nightlife of Reid and Moore was the Limelight club, just a few yards away from the Spice of Life. Several people who shared John's squat worked at the club, which was convenient, as 'they'd give me piles of free drink tickets. I'd take Jim there and we'd get drunk for nothing.

'I got into a spot of trouble because we got photographed with Bananarama. It was in the *Daily Mirror*, I think. Alan McGee said, "You're leading the boy astray! We don't want to be in the mainstream!" It was great. Getting hammered with Bananarama back in the 1980s . . .'

Another good reason to get smashed in this part of town was that it was a mere stagger away from Speed, a club night run by Douglas every Thursday, situated opposite where the much-missed Astoria used to be. Here Douglas could create exactly the kind of club he had fantasised about when he was a kid. It would also be the conduit to Douglas's future career as a film-maker and music video director.

'The guy who rented us the club said, "What are you going to call it?", and I said, "Speed, you know, because we're into cars and all that." And he goes, "You know it's a name for an illegal drug?" We were going, "Nah, no way!" And he was going, "It is!" He was trying to warn us. We were going, "Thanks for telling us!"

'My Bloody Valentine played there a lot, and that's how I got into making music videos. I had a Super-8 camera, so they said, "Why don't you shoot something for us?" So that was the early stages of that.'

The Mary Chain had severally moved over the river to North London and now William was in Stoke Newington, Douglas in Stamford Hill, and Jim had found a place on Kentish Town's Leighton Road, where he would stay for the next twenty years. He often pined for Fulham, but life had changed. The Jesus and Mary Chain were now famous. They were pop stars. They were the alternative pin-ups of choice for thoughtful teenagers left unmoved by the images of tanned young men with Princess Diana haircuts that usually greeted them in *Smash Hits*.

This new status, and the knowledge that their shadowy visages were being Blu-tac'd to walls and wardrobe doors the world over, must have been at once flattering and confusing. It wasn't exactly what the Mary Chain aspired to and underneath the public bravura, Jim in particular found it vaguely worrying. (Or so he says, anyway. On the subject of girlfriends, Jim declared at the time that they 'welcomed as many as possible'.)

'We left Fulham when we started to get well known,' he explains. 'I'd started getting Japanese girls who'd spot me on the bus, and they'd wait for me to get off, and you'd have to run around the block, shake them off. I didn't enjoy that side of it. We were never really *that* famous, but we did get to the point where you'd walk down the street and people would look round. I was never interested in all of that, it was about the music.'

*

The new single would soon reach number 13 in the UK: a proud moment for McGee – it was the first time a Creation band had had a hit in the charts. But it wouldn't be long until he was given his marching orders.

'They wanted rock'n'roll management,' says McGee. 'I was haphaz-ard, mental management. They wanted someone who could answer the phone, not some bum who would let it go straight to the answering machine and pick it up at two o'clock in the afternoon when I got out of bed.'

But the band also felt they still had a stigma after the unrest that had plagued their gigs and the consequent troublemaker status they had earned. This was the image presented to the press during their formative years in the public eye, and while it worked from one point of view, it was not easy to brush off. It soon became obvious that, if they wanted to be taken seriously for their music, this would have to change.

Douglas Hart describes the feeling within the Mary Chain camp at that time: 'With all the talk of the violence and the spectacle of it, Jim and William felt there weren't enough people talking about the songs. Maybe they thought it was time for a Stalinist purge, a changing of the guard. As much as we liked playing the music-business game, the balance wasn't always right, and maybe that's why it had to end. The publicity Alan generated for us obviously did a lot of good but when you're the subject of it, you wonder . . .'

Alan McGee says: 'It was strange. I was so in their camp. If they'd said, "We want McGee to be our manager forever," I would have been. It kicked me in the balls when I got the sack, but it was the best thing that ever happened to Creation Records. It made me go out and find The House of Love and The Valentines, Ride, break the Primals, find Oasis . . .

'They sent Jim round, and I *knew* I was going to get the sack. But he came round and he couldn't bring himself to sack me. He left after about ten minutes. Jim never left after ten minutes. I thought, That's too fucking weird.'

After Jim sheepishly went home and told the others he hadn't had the heart to do the deed, William grabbed the reins, contacting McGee to say they wanted to meet him in Oxford Street. It helped that it was somewhere neutral, although McGee was not impressed that the Mary Chain chose to sack him in a Wendy Burger outlet.

What happened next, oddly enough, was, as McGee remembers it, 'one of the most civilised moments that we'd shared . . . There was no screaming or shouting. I played my part and that was the end of the part.'

McGee had cut his management teeth with the Mary Chain, and in a way they had all grown up together. But what took him by surprise was learning, in the years to come, how much of a good time other bands were having in comparison.

'You think, "OK, rock'n'roll, you might not make much money but it's good fun." Well, with the Mary Chain, we got plenty of money, we just had a shit time. I'd say, "The *NME* has done three pages on you, it's amazing!", and they'd look at you as if you'd told them that someone had died.

'The House of Love and the Primals were just, "Give me the drugs, give me the drink, give me the girls and let's go on tour!" "Fuck, *this* is what rock'n'roll's about! This is what they said in the books!" I'm not digging at the Mary Chain, they're brilliant guys. They were just so miserable. I love Jim, I really like Douglas, I haven't seen William in years but I have no bad feeling towards him, any of them, but it was not fun managing them.'

The Mary Chain might have been dysfunctional, something they'd admit themselves, but they wouldn't be the worst offenders from that point of view in McGee's experience. He had all of that to come with Pete Doherty.

'The Libertines were actually, truly unmanageable – and my filter for mental cases is quite high – but managing Doherty was on another level. We had to wrap him up in carpets and bring him to the gig. If we couldn't wake him up we'd just roll him up in a rug.'

In the long run, the split between McGee and the Mary Chain wouldn't lead to a lifelong rift. Just a few years down the line, McGee would be happily off his face on Ecstasy with Jim at the latter's Kentish Town flat, their differences very much in the past. But what would have happened if The Jesus and Mary Chain had not decided to part ways with McGee?

'I'd probably now be in a mental institution,' says McGee flatly. 'But I'm in Wales, in the country in my big fucking house, you know? I don't think in life you can regret anything. Shit happens and the art form is to deal with it and go forward.'

It's natural to draw comparisons between the Reids and Noel and Liam Gallagher, who would be working with McGee just a few years later when Britpop burst lairily into life. For McGee, having worked with the Reids, nothing the Gallaghers could do could faze him. Admittedly, the Gallaghers are more extrovert than the Reids and more prone to jab at each other in the press, something the Reids tend to avoid save the odd sparring match when they're together. The Reid brothers might have been more inclined to brooding silences and dark moods, but what is also clear is the fierce loyalty they have to each other. As Douglas Hart remembers it, the Reids could count on each other, no matter how stormy their relationship became – often to the exclusion of others around them.

'It was like a solid rock underneath it all,' Douglas says. 'Going into that second period with all of the stress, they held on to each other. At the time it was a bit hard, but now I can totally understand it. They weren't much older than me, not that worldly, not the most naturally well-adjusted characters, so it must have been difficult for them.'

Of course, there was a period of adjustment, and a period of hurt, after the Mary Chain and McGee parted ways. McGee admits it was 'difficult, because there were a lot of people around me all slagging them off.' He gave an interview to a French journalist soon after that fateful afternoon at Wendy Burger, and the Mary Chain were naturally curious as to what he was saying. Thanks to Laurence, the interview was translated and one sound-bite really stood out. Even though McGee appeared to be having a dig, the Mary Chain couldn't help but admire the cut of his jib.

'He said this amazing thing,' Douglas recalls. 'I suppose it was an insult, but we loved it: "If it wasn't for me, the Mary Chain would still be at home, videotaping adverts off the TV." It scanned amazingly. If I was a kid and read that, I'd have thought it sounded great. I mean, we used to do that. We'd always have a videotape in, and we'd just record and make these mad compilations.

'We lent McGee a tape, but because we couldn't afford videotapes there'd be a documentary and then mad adverts and little clips, so he'd watch the documentary and these things would come on and he'd be, "What the fuck?" He couldn't get his head around it. He was thinking, These guys are freaks!'

Cutting ties with McGee had been hard, and the Mary Chain weren't ready to think about who might take his place. It seemed prudent to take the opportunity to get away from London and the inevitable press intrusion. Jim headed to Paris with Laurence for a much-needed break, and this was when the next in a long line of Mary Chain thunderclouds decided to burst.

18

White Noise, Black Moods

'I want to make as much money as Phil Collins. I don't think mass appeal always has to be bad. People think: "Football stadiums? Crap! It can't be any good." I'd like to be the band that proves that isn't true.'
William Reid to Nina Malkin for *Raygun* magazine

When the BBC Radio 1 DJ Mike Smith heard 'Some Candy Talking', which was, at this point, safely residing in the UK Top Twenty, he was incensed. He believed the song was clearly a love song to heroin and refused to play it on his show, fearing that the nation's Radio 1-devoted youth would be corrupted if they heard it. The press required a response from the Mary Chain, and McGee was no longer there for them to deliver a statement. Jim became the voice of the group, whether he liked it or not.

'"Some Candy Talking" is not about heroin,' Jim confirms. 'When that whole thing kicked off, I was in Paris. I got a call and they wanted me to go live on Radio 1. I'm having a holiday, let somebody else do it. William didn't want to, so it ended up being Rob Dickins. At the end of it I said, "Did you tell them that the original recording was commissioned by the BBC? That it was originally recorded as a John Peel session?" "Ah, no, I never thought of that."'

When a record is banned it generally becomes a sure-fire hit, but the Beeb had made this mistake before, and they weren't going to make it with the Mary Chain. The record, therefore, was never officially axed; Radio 1 just starved it of airplay, letting it sink. 'They'd got wise because of all the stuff with Frankie Goes To Hollywood and "Relax",' Jim explains.

With regard to any narcotic references in the Mary Chain's songs, Jim has always been dismissive, at least partly because it is no one else's business unless he or William chooses to be explicit about those themes. But also, people are famously quick to pin the blame on stars when their fans, in a supposed attempt to emulate their heroes, choose to experiment with drugs.

'Sometimes people see drug references that aren't there,' Jim offered in an interview with *The Aquarian Weekly*. 'I'm not saying there's none at all, but some fans go over our lyrics with a fine-tooth comb. People should take responsibility for their own life. If someone in a band says, "Yeah, I took smack," then if some fans take it because of that, they're just idiots.'

★

The Mary Chain still had no replacement in mind for the position of manager, so they tried their best to make their way without one, organising their affairs on their own. Jim's then partner Laurence was an invaluable support; she was a strong but approachable character, she knew about music, and obviously she was close to the band. However, once the music press discovered that Laurence was helping out, they immediately wrote about it as if the Mary Chain had turned into a *Spinal Tap*-style operation, which was some way off the mark.

Jim says: 'There was a classic thing in the music papers saying, "In true *Spinal Tap* tradition, the Mary Chain have sacked their manager and got the singer's girlfriend in." I thought it was quite funny. I think Laurence laughed.' She didn't.

'I was really offended by that,' says Laurence. 'It wasn't the attention, it was just that my role was to kind of be a glorified personal assistant more than anything else. I wasn't going to be making any decisions but I went with Jim to meet people to make sure I knew what was going on. So that was not very nice.'

Laurence was also trying to maintain some domestic balance for Jim because the tension within the group was reaching seemingly impossible new heights. The Reids wanted to start working on their next album, but *Psychocandy* had been such a success that the pressure was on to make an album that would be just as good, if not better.

'Shortly after I moved to London, they had to start *Darklands*. Oh my God . . .' says Laurence. 'The process was painful, to say the least.'

'I remember being a lot more uptight,' William admitted in a 2009 interview with *Pitchfork*. 'Once we made *Psychocandy* we were burdened, and it put a lot of stress on the relationship between me and Jim.'

The Reids had already started writing songs and forming the concept of *Darklands* – Jim, who felt like 'a rabbit caught in the headlights', relaxed a little when he heard the quality of William's song 'Darklands' – but they also needed space in which to come to terms with their rapidly changing lives. It wasn't just about the loss of McGee, and the inevitable if temporary animosity between them, but the simple fact that they were now very much in the public eye and, therefore, targets. Not just for libidinous teenage girls, either.

'Jim would get people wanting to hit him,' John Moore remembers. '"You're that guy with the shit band . . ." He got beaten up at a Birthday Party gig, someone just decked him. I think Jim and William needed a bit of time away to come to terms with what had happened with McGee too.'

On being asked about their next tour by *Smash Hits*, Jim warned ominously that, whatever happened, they couldn't go away together for longer than a month. 'If it was any longer than that, I don't even like to think about what might happen.'

The Reids admittedly spent most of their time on the road screaming at each other; it's no wonder they had to press 'pause'. 'William is the really intense one,' says John Moore. 'Jim would be fun, but then when he was working with William it was like a battle. You know the *Scanners* film, where one of their heads is about to explode? They were scanning each other. They say you shouldn't get involved in a boy-girl fight; well, don't get involved in a Reid-Reid fight.'

There was no use in trying to work out what the triggers were either. According to William, it took next to nothing to tip them over into savage combat and they would argue about anything and everything – 'Whether it was a grey day or a slightly sunny day. Whether the new McDonald's vegetarian burger tasted like Mexican food or Indian food . . . that actually was one of the big fights.'

★

The Mary Chain had six months until their next major shows: two nights at the National Ballroom in Kilburn, North-West London. By this point another change had taken place: John Moore had moved from drums to guitar, his main instrument. The Reids were keen to move on from the two-drum Moe Tucker set-up, and this change would soon herald the Mary Chain's drum-machine era, although this was really nothing new for the Reids; their early Portastudio demos had programmed drums, after all.

In the meantime, Laurence Verfaillie put the Reids in touch with a drummer called James Pinker, playing with the Australian fusion band Dead Can Dance at the time. He was booked to play drums for the Mary Chain at the Ballroom on 15 and 16 December. It felt like he was in the band for 'a minute – but a long, fun, scary minute,' from which, he jokes, he 'never fully recovered'.

'I was pretty scared as I had to learn all of their songs in a week,' Pinker remembers. 'It was daunting. Jim and William were like twins. Douglas was like a brother too. Lovely bloke. They carried a box of SM58s [microphones] with them as Jim smashed up a few at each gig.'

Mary Chain gigs may have been chaotic, but it was an organised chaos. Much was deliberate and carefully decided, particularly the elements that were seemingly accidental or out of control. 'They had it worked out perfectly,' says John Moore. 'On one occasion they'd forgotten their fuzz pedals and they didn't have anything to make feedback with except a cassette recorder onto which they had already recorded feedback. They just held that up to the microphone. That's preparation, isn't it?'

James Pinker's tenure didn't last beyond those two pre-Christmas gigs, but the Reids hadn't yet decided for certain that they definitely wanted a more electronic sound. They actually wanted a drummer, but they couldn't find anyone who was right.

'We auditioned dozens of drummers,' says Jim. 'Purely on ability, we could have got one easily, but we wanted somebody we could spend ten weeks on a tour bus with. We kept getting these guys that started going on about what type of sticks they would use. We didn't give a fuck what type of sticks they were going to use! It's a bit of wood, you moron!'

One contender was the now sadly departed Nick Sanderson, some-time drummer in The Gun Club, a group the Reids and Douglas had always loved. Nick would join the Mary Chain in later years, and all who knew him recall his boundless charm and energy, but his first audition for the band did not go well. To be fair, considering the perversity of the Mary Chain, this makes it hard to imagine why they didn't instantly fall in love with him. He was more appropriate in terms of attitude, feel and humour than many drummers who would later work with the Reids.

'We're all a bunch of wasters, but Nick was the king of the wasters,' Jim says. 'He turned up to the audition hungover as hell. I said, "Right. Do you know "Never Understand?"' "No, how does it go?" "Er . . . do you know any of our songs?" "No." So I said, "Well, just start playing a slow beat." "I haven't got any sticks." He didn't pass the audition.'

Eventually the Reids decided to quit the search and opt for drum tapes instead. Drum machines don't go on about their favoured brand of drumstick. They don't drink the rider or throw in unnecessary drum fills. You can switch off a drum machine. But this change also reintroduced a cooler, mechanical sound to the Mary Chain's music. Jim just wishes they'd made a better choice of drum machine.

'I love tinny, biscuit-tin drum machines,' Jim says. 'But we made a mistake. We should have used one that sounded more like a drum machine. We used a 1980s drum machine that just sounded like a crap drummer.'

In the studio it soon became clear that *Darklands* would be a Jim-and-William-only operation. The songs they chose for the album reflected a different kind of light and shade to that of *Psychocandy*, and there was a distinct lack of white noise – perhaps a sign that the Reids were becoming more assured in their voices and their playing. They no longer had to hide behind an opaque wall of protective distortion, like a roaring sea separating themselves and the listener. They also didn't want to do what people expected of them, and they had no intention of making *Psychocandy: The Sequel*, which is, of course, what the label was hoping for.

This very different sound and mood on their latest studio recordings would be a revelation to Douglas and John as well as to the fans, not least because the Reids' bandmates were not involved in the proceedings. Douglas says: 'When they were about halfway through, I realised, "I haven't seen them for a while, what are they doing?"' I'd started making films, I was always doing something. I'd visit them in the studio a couple of times, and it was very much the same sort of thing as with *Psychocandy*: tea and toast, not cocaine or anything. That came much later with the Mary Chain.'

The Reids would concur; they were as fond of getting obliterated as the next man – in fact they were arguably quite a bit fonder – but when it came to writing songs, stimulants were wisely eschewed because, as William puts it, 'when you get drunk or stoned or do speed, the stupidest ideas make you feel like a genius. I've written songs in that state that I've thought were fucking brilliant. Then I've woken up the following day and realised what shite they are.'

The new album would feature 'April Skies', the song that would become their biggest hit in, naturally, April 1987; the slow, obsessive 'Nine Million Rainy Days'; the lighter 'Cherry Came Too'; 'Happy When It Rains', and one of their earliest songs, 'On The Wall'.

'On The Wall' was originally to have appeared on *Psychocandy*; the Reids took their Portastudio demo of the track to Rob Dickins, who instantly loved it. And so, in true Mary Chain style, they forgot all about it. 'Another classic Mary Chain shooting-themselves-in-the-foot situation,' says Jim. 'Rob raved about it, he was saying, "That's a number one hit single!" We just went away and recorded the album without the track that the chairman of the company was raving about. I think at the time we thought we couldn't do it justice.'

The demo would be included on the 7-inch release of the single 'Darklands' in October 1987, and also in 1988 on the Mary Chain's much-loved *Barbed Wire Kisses – B-Sides And More* collection. Even the demo version is a nugget of 1980s alt-pop perfection, a clear example of how the Reids were crafting pop gems years before they'd even left their shared bedroom. Echoing, sparse chords turn towards and away from each other like moving figurines on a Black Forest clock. William's guitar drones shimmer and the track concludes with dripping rainwater and moaning guitar wails that rise and fade. For all the beauty of the *Darklands* version, there is a purity to the demo which sets it apart.

For *Darklands*, the Reids were under pressure from the label to work with a producer. They had found a way of recording that worked for them, but it was clear they had to at least try to play the game to keep Warners happy. One suggestion from the Warners camp was that they team up with Chris Hughes, who had produced Tears For Fears. Hughes worked with Tears for Fears' keyboard-player Ian Stanley as a production duo, and so the Reids duly travelled to Bath to stay at Stanley's house to record some demos. It didn't go well.

'One of the demos we recorded with them was the song "Darklands", says Jim. 'We weren't getting into this at all. They'd be getting super-enthusiastic about things we didn't give a fuck about, and by the end of the week we'd just had it. They had some idea they wanted to try, so we said, "Oh, just help yourselves," and went to bed. We got up in the morning, these idiots had been up all night, and they were going, "You've got to hear this! This is going to blow you away!"

'They played us "Darklands" and they'd been up all night recording a double bass on it. William and I looked at each other, and we just burst out laughing. You know when you can't control yourself? I was nearly wetting myself.'

Word immediately got back to Warners about the Mary Chain's dismissal of Hughes and Stanley's best efforts, and the usually composed Rob Dickins lost his rag with the Reids, which set them off again. 'Rob called us and went, "You fucking losers! You had a world-class producer, and what did you do? You laughed at him!" And then we started laughing *again* . . .'

Fortunately, the suggestion of working with Bill Price on 'April Skies' was more successful. 'They liked the association with the Sex Pistols,' says Laurence. 'I remember going with Jim to meet Bill at the studio in Highbury, Wessex Studios. He looked like a middle-aged geezer, but musically things worked out.'

'I was there when they recorded "April Skies", says John Moore. 'Even contributed a line to it. *Sun grows cold, sky turns black* . . . In this day and age, you know, "change a word, get a third". Ah well. I think I'd had enough from the Mary Chain without that.'

Naturally, the whole process from the writing to the artwork was painstaking and considered. Laurence remembers being at home with Jim as he crouched in front of the TV with a video of cult 1971 movie *The Jesus Trip* in the VCR. 'He was trying to find the perfect freeze-frame of the guy on his cross for the cover,' she remembers. 'How many times did I see that gesture of the hand coming out and the gun being pointed?'

'April Skies' reached number 8 in the UK, their highest singles chart position, and, despite the only musicians on the actual track having been the Reids, the video still featured the four Mary Chain members playing along with the song in an abandoned building, the sight of John thumping the snare and floor tom proving somewhat incongruous with the electronic drum track.

Psychologically, a line had been drawn in the sand. The Mary Chain was, now, truly the Reid brothers. *Darklands* was solely their production, and, to be fair, much of the work on *Psychocandy* had been executed by Jim and William too. From this point forth the group, as it was, became more of a touring line-up. As William once admitted, it was only in the early days with Bobby that they were really 'a band'.

'It must have been hard for Douglas,' says John. 'It was hard for me, and I wasn't an original member. Any involvement I had would have been a bonus. What can you say? We're talking about a time in musical technology where, all of a sudden, using a drum machine becomes the favourite tool. Everything became very exact, very clinical.'

That said, for many – even within the band itself – *Darklands* is the preferred LP. It is unusual for the 'difficult second album' to eclipse the first, but there was a maturity that shone through on this record. Something new and bewitching had burst out of the chrysalis. 'My favourite album is *Darklands*,' says Douglas. 'The songs were better. But I wasn't really involved in it. I don't blame them, they were young and things were happening. It was just different.'

The Reids played *Darklands* to their loved ones, who were impressed by the new sound, not to mention the songwriting, the clarity, the contrasts, the humour. 'Nine Million Rainy Days', an obsessive love song augmented by a wry reference to the Stones' 'Sympathy For The Devil' with its 'ooh-ooh' backing vocals, was a particular favourite.

'The Rolling Stones thing was to lighten it,' William explained to Steve Sutherland at the time. 'We thought "Nine Million Rainy Days" was brilliant but too heavy, [so] that last bit we thought was quite a good little joke. Nobody seemed to get it, though. I think everybody thought we'd done it with deep frowns. Oh well . . .'

'I loved "Nine Million Rainy Days",' says Laurence. 'But people were shocked. "Where's the feedback?" Jim and William were like, "We are not performing monkeys. That's what we wanted to do, that's how it is." *Darklands* really was the album they wanted to make.'

The lack of feedback would prove a shock to the press and many of the band's fans. More than one journalist would refer to the Reids 'doing the unthinkable' and creating an album that was, basically, not *Psychocandy*. Their debut album had, like the Mary Chain themselves, seemingly burst out of nowhere, a startling, fully formed force of nature and noise. However, as William suggested in an interview with Sky TV at the time, why should the Reids repeat themselves when they had simply been using feedback 'the way other people use keyboards'? White noise was just another instrument at their disposal.

'Simply Red used keyboards on their last single and they didn't use them in this one, and it would be a weird situation for people to say, "Where's the keyboards?"' said William. 'That's how it sometimes feels to us.'

The Reids were also more than aware that their greatest strength was their songwriting, and as their confidence continued to grow, they were less inclined to drown out their songs with distortion. But part of the thrill of releasing an album as unexpected as *Darklands* would be that, just as people were getting used to the Mary Chain's penchant for cranking out the kind of metallic, industrial screams one might otherwise hear at an international welding convention (maybe William's time working with sheet metal was not entirely wasted), they could then yank the rug unceremoniously from under their feet and present something that no one had predicted. The songs had always been there, and yet even in later years William would have to defend the Mary Chain's more melodic output. They were hardly 'going soft', there were just two sides to the Reids' songwriting and they wanted to express them both, even if the pop world would have preferred to tidy them into a narrow box labelled 'noisy' and be done with it.

'Probably fifty per cent of our music is slow and very melodic and not at all noisy,' William explained. 'It wasn't a conscious effort but we have the same kind of songwriting sensibilities as the Beatles, who could write "Helter Skelter" and "Penny Lane" and be the same band – it's two different aspects. That's something a lot of people don't appreciate. Whenever we play something slow and melodic, people turn on us and say we're soft. We've always done that, but there seems to be a side of us that we're not allowed to be comfortable with.'

19

Do Not Smile

'Pop star' is just a byword for 'pile of crap'.
William Reid

Thanks to the success of 'April Skies', the Mary Chain would finally have two dreams fulfilled in 1987: they would at last grace the cover of *Smash Hits* and they would also appear on *Top of the Pops*, admittedly for the first and last time. The music press might have loved the Mary Chain but, as former press officer Mick Houghton remembers, radio producers didn't like them, and TV producers liked them even less.

'I was never sure if even John Peel really got them,' ponders Mick, 'but they certainly were never playlisted on Radio 1. I also think they had a plugger in-house at the label who probably didn't give a toss about them, so he didn't fight their corner.'

Even so, to BBC Television Centre they would go, to mime to 'April Skies' on *Top of the Pops*, and they were genuinely excited, although you might not have known it to look at them. 'Do not smile' was Jim's solemn command to the rest of the group before they went on, as if they needed telling.

'I couldn't believe we were there,' says Jim. 'As it turns out, we completely put noses out of joint and we were never asked back. We got drunk. The usual. Stumbled around.'

Tension was no doubt high from the minute the band arrived, such was their reputation. But the heat really began to rise when the Mary Chain were about to start their camera rehearsal. 'The guy said, "Do exactly what you're going to do,"' Jim explains. 'And I said, "I don't know exactly what I'm going to do. I'm just going to sing the song, is that all right?" And he said, "No, we've got to get the camera angles." I thought, You're taking the piss.'

After the rehearsal, the Mary Chain set off to the BBC canteen to kill time and do a bit of off-duty Dalek-spotting. However, they were to meet with further hostility before they'd even passed through the door.

'Paul Weller was there with the Style Council,' says Laurence. 'We crossed paths because they were on the show, but of course, no exchange whatsoever. When I turned around, he was like that [sticks up middle finger] to us. No idea why.'

By the time they returned to the studio, the now inebriated Mary Chain were getting increasingly uncomfortable, not least because the presenter, Peter Powell, 'couldn't pronounce the name of the band,' Douglas remembers. 'He had to do about twenty takes. He was wearing a home-knitted jumper made for him by someone in a mental hospital that had been sent in, you know, with a BBC *Top of the Pops* logo on it.'

The time had come, and the camera swung around to the Mary Chain, a gaggle of cheering children at their feet. William was inscrutable in sunglasses, John straight-backed and on his feet at the drums, Douglas inclining his head to his three-stringed bass. Jim, like a big-haired beacon in leather strides and white shirt, confused the cameramen as he swayed, swooped and inadvertently drove the crew crazy. What he was doing was putting more energy into the performance of the song than he had at rehearsal, but the producers were on a hair-trigger to hate the Mary Chain and this was all they needed.

Mick Houghton says: 'The producer just bawled them out afterwards. People thought they were trying to be difficult, trying to make a point on *TOTP*, but they weren't. They were essentially banned from that point.'

This wouldn't be the last time The Jesus and Mary Chain would accidentally put television producers' backs up. A year later, the group were about to perform 'Darklands' on the short-lived Tyne-Tees pop show *The Roxy* but, as Jim explains, 'The stage manager meant to say "roll the track", but he actually said "roll the crap". We fell about laughing, and the producer was so pissed off that we were thrown off the show.'" The producer should have been relieved they were so good-humoured about it.

On another occasion the crew from Channel 4's *The Tube* turned up to see the Mary Chain play a gig in Liverpool. As associate producer

Ken Scorfield later told music journalist Max Bell, 'I quite honestly didn't like them.' Despite this, they would appear on the show in October 1985, a 'highlight of an otherwise lacklustre show', according to *The Hit*'s Richard Lowe, but the Mary Chain weren't happy. 'We weren't very good,' Jim sighed afterwards. 'We phoned home afterwards because we couldn't tell what it was like. Our little sister said we were a wee bit tame.'

TV shows did, admittedly, offer up the opportunity for mischief in the presence of rock gods and uptight producers, when the Mary Chain were permitted to appear, anyway (the producers of the US version of *Top of the Pops* refused to allow them on the show on account of their name alone). The Mary Chain appeared in the same episode of *The Tube* as Pete Townshend, who at the time had Pink Floyd's Dave Gilmour in his band. Just as these guitar greats were about to soundcheck, Gilmour caught William Reid doing something so awful, in his opinion, that the moment that followed was, in Jim's words, 'one of the highlights of our career'.

'William had a vintage Gretsch Tennessean guitar that was a horrible coffee-table colour,' Jim explained to *Select* magazine. 'A classic guitar, you know? Dave Gilmour walks past and sees William with a pot of black paint, painting this wonderful vintage Gretsch guitar black. Ruining it. When he sees this, he [looks horrified] and hurries away. Probably to tell Pete [Townshend]. I wish I'd had a video camera.'

At least when the Mary Chain's path crossed with that of the irreverent *Smash Hits*, they were among like-minded souls – the writers were fans, evidently excited to have the Reids on board. The Reid brothers in turn were funny and erudite in their double-page interview and looked wilfully dour on the cover, a place usually reserved for grinning popstrels with perfect skin. Accompanying their cover photo were the scrawled words 'loud, spotty and weird'. Jim and William were pleased, not least because they'd heard that, when Spandau Ballet realised the Mary Chain were the cover story and not them, they withdrew their interview – something Jim considers to be up there with the Mary Chain's finest achievements. 'I was thinking, Wow!' Jim laughs. 'If my life ends today, I'll be happy. That's fantastic, great!'

*

Meanwhile some vital new blood was about to be injected into Blanco Y Negro; Jeannette Lee, now co-owner of Rough Trade, was about to start working with Geoff Travis, both on Rough Trade and the Warners imprint. Jeannette had punk-rock form, unparalleled dynamism and savvy, not to mention considerable style. She had initially worked with Don Letts at his shop Acme Attractions on Chelsea's King's Road during the punk era. The shop was close to Vivienne Westwood and Malcolm McLaren's boutique Sex, and was another hub for young punks; Sid Vicious used to come in and consult Jeannette on what he should do with his hair.

Out of this scene grew, amongst other groups, the Sex Pistols and eventually Public Image Limited – John Lydon, Keith Levene and Jah Wobble – with Jeannette going on to work with them during the early 1980s. By the time Geoff approached her, however, Jeannette was raising a child with her husband, Pop Group/Rip Rip And Panic founder Gareth Sager. One of the first bands that Geoff played to Jeannette was The Jesus and Mary Chain.

'It instantly felt like home to me,' Jeannette reflects. 'It was completely in sync with everything I'd ever loved. I wanted to work with Geoff, but musically speaking it was the Mary Chain that made me feel this was somewhere I could be.' Geoff and Jeannette agree to this day that the Mary Chain were 'one of the most important bands we have ever worked with'.

Jeannette was thrown into the cut and thrust of working on the release of *Darklands*, which was due in October 1987. Her earliest memory of working with the Mary Chain is of spending time with the Reids going through options for potential artwork for the album. At that time the relationship was uncomplicated. 'I loved working with them,' says Jeannette. 'But because of their shyness and because they were so intense, I always felt like they weren't that good at expressing themselves verbally to people they interacted with. It all seemed to go into the music.

'I think that's part of the reason it ended up with things being kicked over and them going mad at each other onstage, because they had a lot of stuff they couldn't get out, so it all poured into the music. It's the only time they seem able to get it all out. They've got a lot to say, they just have trouble saying it.'

★

The Jesus and Mary Chain still didn't have a manager – Jim had no choice but to man the phone and be the point of liaison, and the stress was overwhelming. Both Geoff Travis and Jeannette Lee helped all they could, as did Laurence, but the time had come to find someone to fill that role.

'It was hellish,' Jim admits. 'We were a bunch of fuck-ups and I was the least fucked-up of the fuck-ups, so it would be my phone that would ring every five minutes. Honest to God, I felt like I was going to have a nervous breakdown. It couldn't go on.'

As unlikely as it might seem, considering his initial reaction to the band, the person who would step in and take them into the future was Jerry Jaffe, former PolyGram A&R executive, and Warners consultant. Jerry was working with UK music manager Chris Morrison, taking care of the US side of business for him. He is also the man who, let's not forget, had proclaimed the Mary Chain the worst live act he'd ever seen just months earlier.

Jerry was working one afternoon in the New York office of Warners when he heard a song being played in the adjoining room. It immediately arrested his attention, to the point that he leaped up from his desk and burst into the neighbouring office where the music was coming from. He was interrupting a meeting, but he didn't care. Inside the room he found, among other people, Geoff Travis. 'I said, "Man, that is a great song, who the heck is it?" Geoff said, "The Jesus and Mary Chain." I said, "You've got to be kidding!"'

The song was 'April Skies', and as Jerry listened to the track play out, Geoff added that they were looking for a manager. 'Now this is how my mind works,' says Jerry. 'This band was the worst live band I'd ever seen, and they made "April Skies", so they're doing something that I don't know, and they're so big in England . . . this is definitely a Jerry Jaffe thing. I don't get it but the music is great, that's all I care about.'

Jerry arranged a meeting between himself, Chris Morrison and the band as soon as possible. The Mary Chain were in the midst of a European tour, and would be playing Dublin that September (1987). This provided the perfect opportunity for Jerry to take Chris to their show and schmooze the group afterwards.

Jerry Jaffe: 'I said, "This band are huge in the UK, they have a great song, Chris, it's going to be number one all over the world." That's how much I believed in that freakin' "April Skies". I still think it's one of the best songs of all time. That line, *Making love on the edge of a knife* . . . The imagery, the changes . . . Anyway. I arranged with Chris to fly to Dublin.'

That evening at St Francis Xavier Hall, Chris Morrison climbed the stairs of the venue with Jerry to watch the gig from the production office, which overlooked the stage. Chris didn't know what to expect, but Jerry was enthusing constantly. He hadn't yet realised that the group now used a drum machine on stage, something that wouldn't be to his taste, to put it mildly.

Laurence had been given the job of feeding drum tapes into the Portastudio by the sound desk on the *Darklands* tour. This was not without its stressful moments. 'Jim was very drunk on that tour. Some of the songs start in quite a similar way, and there were a few incidents where I'd put on a track and Jim started singing another song. A few times I'd stop the tape, but Jim would turn round and say, "Don't fucking stop it!" It was so funny.'

'Everything was on cassettes,' says Jerry Jaffe, aghast. 'Cassettes! I was a real purist, I hated that. So there's three guys looking completely bored and a drum machine.'

Chris Morrison had glanced at his watch one too many times. 'I just said, "Chris, there's 2,500 kids going crazy there!"' says Jerry. 'Anyway, after the show we met at the hotel in the lounge, and the next thing I know Chris had put the deal together. We were managing The Jesus and Mary Chain.'

Jim Reid says: 'We thought it was good to have someone like that representing us. There was a breakdown in communication between us and Warners, but Chris understood how people like Warners work. And Jerry Jaffe's a wonderful guy. He's been in the music business for years. He signed Bon Jovi. Don't hold that against him.'

Chris Morrison liked the group, and kept them entertained with his dry sense of humour and tales of managing Thin Lizzy, but he was initially dubious as to how suitable he was for the Mary Chain. 'I said to Jim, "I'm not sure I fit your thing. I mean, you've come from Alan McGee,"' says Chris. 'And he said, "We need someone who is organised so we can be chaotic." Very smart.'

They now had someone onside who could take care of business so that they could focus on the music. One thing their new management couldn't control, however, was the way Jim and William would react to the reviews that were coming in for *Darklands*. Most of them were excellent – 'nines and tens out of ten,' Mick Houghton remembers. 'But I don't think William thought the press got it. It's a very deep record.

'*Darklands* was my favourite record of theirs to work on. I think it's the best album they made, it's a brave album. They made something that's a much more lasting statement than *Psychocandy*, in a way. William felt it was a better album, and I'm sure I remember them actually being disappointed in the reviews.'

Laurence picked this up too, and it taught her a valuable lesson that would take her forward into her own successful career as a music PR. 'The guys took things very personally. It helped me learn to look after the artist rather than the record label. It was hard for them to read reviews – you know, you bare your soul, and these guys were so reserved, so baring their soul was huge. Being open to criticism was something they were never good at.'

All the same, good reviews continued to flood in as the Mary Chain travelled around Europe before heading to America, but the Reids were blue, thanks no doubt to a combination of feeling misunderstood musically and, in William's case particularly, a hatred of being on the road. It didn't help that they were also coming up against widespread dissent regarding their decision to tour with a drum machine, something the Cocteau Twins' Robin Guthrie had warned Jim about after bumping into the Reids at the Hammersmith Palais.

'Robin said, "You're going to go to America with a drum machine? They won't like it. Don't!" He was absolutely right,' Jim says. 'We got there and it was, "Hey! Where's the drummer? I don't get this." So straight, 1980s America. They want to see a bassist, a singer, a couple of guitarists maybe, and a drummer. They want to know where those drums are coming from.'

Unfortunately this was also the tour that parted Jim from his beloved Vox Phantom, the guitar he bought from McGee two years earlier. Another of Jim's guitars was also stolen, but the Vox Phantom was his favourite. To add insult to injury, not only did his guitars get taken, but the thief also left something behind. 'We'd played in Detroit,' Jim explains. 'We were driving to New York, and there was this horrible stench in the van. I was thinking, No, I've had a bath . . .

'We were all talking about it, "What is that smell?" We get to New York and start unloading the gear, and there's half a pig's head in the bass drum. The guys took the guitars and left us with that. What's more, I think I know who stole the guitars. There was a guy there a few days earlier and he'd been desperately trying to buy the Vox Phantom off me, but I said, "No, it's not for sale." It could be a coincidence, but it's a hell of a coincidence.'

It's not surprising, perhaps, that the vibe on this tour might have been low, but at least on stage the Mary Chain could vent their frustrations and transcend everyday life. That short time on stage also connected them directly to their earlier years, when they just wanted to play live and 'grab people by the throat', as Jim put it, with none of the music industry complications, cynicism or bullshit in the way. Laurence, technically the 'drummer' on this tour, remembers: 'You could see William really letting it all go while he was playing guitar. You'd see him crouched and looking at all the pedals, and you could feel that energy – anger, in a way.

'Everything was going as well as it could with the guys going, "I don't like touring, I don't like playing, I don't like doing this . . . I don't like nothing", basically. There were funny moments, but there were moments when it was quite hard. They became depressed very easily.'

Some people believe dark thoughts beget dark incidents by sheer energetic magnetism. If that were genuinely the case, the Mary Chain would have to be more careful. The power of negative thinking is potent indeed, but whatever you believe, an incident that was to shake their foundations was just around the corner.

20

Meatheads, a Mic-Stand and the Drunk Tank

*'Sidewalking' reminds me of things that get you wasted. I think
1988 was the year I really discovered I was an alcoholic . . . and I
liked it.*
Jim Reid to Marc Spitz in *Spin*, 1998

The Mary Chain still attracted what Douglas Hart describes as 'the
meathead contingent' at their live shows, and their now outdated
reputation for troublesome gigs still preceded them in some parts of
the world. Even though the Mary Chain had and continue to have a
huge fan base in Toronto, Canada, there were a number of said meat-
heads in the audience on the night of 15 November 1987 at the RPM
Club. One individual in particular had, of course, elbowed his way to
the front and was hurling abuse relentlessly at Jim. Jim was used to
this and generally managed to shrug it off, but this time it went too
far. Already feeling thin-skinned after a long period of touring and
championship-level drinking in the often gloomy world of the Mary
Chain, Jim cracked.

'You'd be playing and a dark shadow comes flying towards your
head,' Douglas says. 'You get through it most times, but then you just
fucking break. That's what happened to Jim that night. To be wound
up like that all through the gig, I'm amazed he only hit him towards
the end of the set. So yeah,' concludes Douglas evenly, 'he quite rightly
hit the cunt.'

Jim shares his memory of that night: 'This idiot was just calling me
a cocksucker all night. Sober, I can handle it, but when I get a bit drunk,
I think, "Well, fuck it."

'I remember stepping to the side of the stage and saying to security, "If you don't get rid of him, something's going to happen." Nobody did, so it just got to breaking point. I hit him over the head with the mic-stand.'

Jim's intention was 'just to frighten the guy'. He knew he hadn't hurt him and, after the gig, he put the incident from his mind and made his way back to the coach with the others. But the bus didn't move – their way had been blocked. The 'fan' who had been hit had complained to the promoter. The Mary Chain were going nowhere.

'We couldn't get out,' says Jim. 'Someone said, "Call the cops." And that was it. I got arrested.'

As Jim was taken away, Laurence rushed to the hotel to collect a toothbrush and gave it to the tour manager to pass on to Jim, before returning to their hotel room alone. During the night, Laurence put on the TV to distract herself from her rising anxiety, but every few minutes the phone would ring. Groupies.

'For some reason they'd managed to call through to the room, and it was extremely annoying,' says Laurence. 'I remember getting these phonecalls from girls trying to talk to Jim while I was watching *Apocalypse Now*.'

Jim, meanwhile, had been taken to the police cells, and his mood momentarily brightened when he realised he had the cell to himself. 'I thought, Well, this is all right, I might not get raped in jail after all. Because I'm standing there with a pair of leather trousers on . . .'

*

Somehow Jim managed to fall into a doze, but, at 4 a.m., the police burst in and moved him down to the courthouse. This was when the situation became particularly surreal and nightmarish for Jim.

'I'm handcuffed to a down-and-out and a guy who has blood gushing out of his face,' he remembers. 'Then I got put in this drunk tank, and, during the course of the night, loads of people came in; there were about thirty of us in there by the end of the night. Nobody said a word to me except when I got bailed out in the morning. "Hey, leather pants! Where are you going?" It was quite entertaining on some level, but bloody scary.'

By the time word had reached the UK, the incident, in news terms, had largely blown over. Had this happened twenty years later, it would have been all over the internet and on the front pages of every red-top. But this wasn't the end of the story for Jim, who would have to return to Toronto for his trial three months later. Jerry Jaffe immediately organised a defence lawyer, but the tour manager, who had stayed behind to bail Jim as the rest of the touring party moved on, was starting to unravel psychologically. By the end of the tour he had a nervous breakdown, running away and flinging all of the Mary Chain's documents into a skip as he went.

★

Jim returned to Toronto in February 1988, Jerry Jaffe by his side. Both Jim and Jerry wore suits, but the complainant, whose repeated verbal assaults had driven the singer to violence, dressed down in a Metallica T-shirt. 'Weird guy,' Jerry Jaffe recalls. 'Jim hadn't hit him in a way that was going to cause any physical pain. He was big, hardcore. Anyway, he was going to press charges and we had to show up to this court case. I remember how amusing it was, before we even got there, the fix was in, but we had to go through the process to make it look like justice was being meted out.'

During the two-hour trial Jim had to sign a handful of Jesus and Mary Chain records for the judge's daughter. 'That was part of the penalty,' Jerry laughs. 'Part of it was that he had to show remorse and say he was sorry, and then we had to pay a token fine and pay the defence attorney, even though this was completely frivolous. If you did that in the US the judge would be thrown off the bench. It was the equivalent of a Cold War-era show trial. It was scary.'

Once the trial was over and Jim was free to go, he and Jerry had some time to kill, but all Jim wanted to do was get back to the airport. 'He didn't want anything to do with Toronto.'

★

Amid the drama, the Reids were still writing fluently, William in particular, and among the songs he had 'kicking about', as Jim puts it, was 'Sidewalking'. The Reids were always soaking up new influences as they travelled the world, and they were especially inspired by hip-hop. 'We wanted to experiment with those kinds of drum beats,' Jim explains. 'The drum beat on "Sidewalking" was sampled from a song by Roxanne Shante called "Roxanne's Revenge".'

It took a single afternoon in the studio to develop 'Sidewalking', extemporising over beats and a riff, and the Reids were proud of the result. The only problem was that they felt it was too different to the sound their fans were used to. They considered releasing it under a different name, or inviting a female hip-hop star to sing on it instead.

'But then we spoke to Geoff Travis,' Jim says, 'and he said, "You're nuts. It's just a great record. Just put it out as the Mary Chain." So we did.'

The Reids released 'Sidewalking' as a stand-alone single in March 1988 and it reached number 30 in the charts. 'Live, "Sidewalking" became such a phenomenon,' Laurence says. 'They'd expand on it and do it as an encore with white noise on it and beats. It was stunning.'

Another release that had been in the works was the now classic collection *Barbed Wire Kisses (B-Sides And More)*, released just one month after 'Sidewalking'. *Barbed Wire Kisses* is a box of shady delights, it contains the ones that (almost) got away: the obscure songs, the flip-sides, stand-alones and sketches. The entire compilation boasts an experimental spontaneity due to the tracks, in many cases, having been belted out quickly rather than agonised over. Of course, as fans will testify, a B-side courtesy of the Reids is often stronger and more arrest-ing than your average A-side, and Jim and William, especially in years to come, would compete with each other when it came to their B-sides, ratcheting up the quality even higher.

Jim says: 'We thought the B-sides shouldn't disappear because we thought they were good – although, to be honest, the early B-sides we didn't give a toss about. One was called "Cracked", and it was literally a track from *Psychocandy*, "The Living End", I think, slowed to half-speed with another vocal on it at the right speed. It got us out of jail. But later, and not much later, we started to take B-sides seriously.'

The Jesus and Mary Chain wear their influences proudly on their sleeve; most obviously the Velvets, The Stooges, Phil Spector's 'Wall of Sound', surf pop and dance music. But here the band also display their reverence for Bo Diddley with the track 'Bo Diddley Is Jesus', and the oft-covered 'Who Do You Love?' Lyrically, this song couldn't be more Mary Chain, with its cobra-snake neckties and miles of barbed wire.

'Bo Diddley wrote "Who Do You Love?" in 1955, and I don't know if you can make out the words on our version, but they're like pure evil,' William enthused. 'These days they would be considered offensive, too evil for mass consumption. And this was released in the day of Doris Day and Perry Como.'

Also featured on *Barbed Wire Kisses* is a dark cover of 'Surfin' USA', The Beach Boys' rip-off of/homage to Chuck Berry's 'Sweet Little Sixteen'. 'Kill Surf City' (the B-side of 'April Skies') also subverts the surf, the devilish vocal seemingly unfurling upwards from the depths of hell. While the Mary Chain's take on 'Surfin' USA' gives a nod to The Beach Boys, 'Kill Surf City', as the title may hint, kicks sunshine well and truly up the arse and brings on a total eclipse. 'Just Out Of Reach', the B-side of 'You Trip Me Up', meanwhile, is a thick fog of troubling sound, pierced by what sounds like a guitar being attacked by a gleeful maniac. When the record was released, there was a question mark over whether 'Kill Surf City' was 'anti-American', but William Reid insisted it wasn't. 'It was basically our weird twist on a surf song,' he explained. 'We sang about a guy fucking his girl to death while being fucked to death by another guy, and we were singing about nuclear bombs and wanting to shoot someone in the face . . . we just thought it was kind of funny in the midst of a surf song. Not what you usually get. We loved surf music but couldn't handle most of the lyrics or the sensibilities.'

Barbed Wire Kisses (B-Sides And More) rocketed to number 8 in the UK charts, giving the Reids another gold disc for their collection alongside those for *Psychocandy* and *Darklands*. Meanwhile the marathon *Darklands* tour was coming to an end, and the Mary Chain played Glasgow's Barrowland venue, linking up with their families in East Kilbride, who proudly attended the show.

John Moore, the self-confessed 'lone Sassenach' in the group, remembers spending time with the Reid and Hart families very fondly: 'All the relatives were in the dressing-room having a wonderful time,' he remembers. 'Imagine your sons being the toast of the nation.'

The Reid family invited everyone to a party at their house after the show – an unusual occurrence after a Mary Chain gig – and John scoured the living room for photographs of the Reid brothers. He didn't find a single one. Jim had taken them all down. 'I said to their mum, "No photographs of Jim and William?", and she was complaining that they were so conscious of protecting their image,' says John.

'But she said, "I've got some here, come and have a look at these." She got me this photograph of Jim with the Celtic football manager, Jim as a kid with curly hair. Jim came in and said, "Mother! What are you doing? Don't give him a photograph, he'll sell it to the newspapers!" I would have, as well.'

This unusually warm experience on tour with the Mary Chain was all the more poignant because, as it happened, John was preparing to bow out. He'd been working on his own demos – which, he jokingly admits, 'probably sounded rather like The Jesus and Mary Chain' – and had started to get major-label interest. 'With my matinee-idol good looks and complete lack of morals, I was probably quite attractive to record companies, because I'd do anything.' The Mary Chain had an extensive tour of Australia and the Far East coming up, and John had to make a decision.

'I had these deals on the table that I couldn't walk away from, so I had to leave at the end of the Darklands tour,' says John. 'I didn't go to the after-show party because I was really sad, and Jim was upset. I don't think it was because he thought he'd lost a friend, but because he had to audition a new bloody person.'

John wanted an opportunity to write and record, which, other than the occasional contribution, wasn't going to happen with the Mary Chain, very much a Reid/Reid operation by now. But he'd observed how it was done, and in his own time had worked out that he could do it rather well. There was nothing to stop him going solo and heading up his own group, The Expressway. He signed with Polydor.

With hindsight, however, John feels that perhaps he left the Mary Chain too soon; he was young, and going it alone was quite different to being in a band that was already a going concern. 'I don't think I was ready,' admits John. 'I hadn't lived enough to write songs . . . so I should either never have joined the Mary Chain and just waited, or stayed longer and learned more, because they were as good as it gets.'

Jim and William Reid in a cold, dark room with some barbed wire, 1987. Just a regular evening chez Mary Chain.

Colin Smith

Above. 'Stonehenge with windows' (Douglas Hart). Also known as East Kilbride. This is the Scottish new town in 1975.

Right. Hair, cameras, action. Jim Reid photographed in Douglas Hart's bedroom in 1983, the year it all started.

Douglas Hart

Douglas Hart

Laurence Verfaillie

Jim Reid photographed by
Douglas Hart, Glasgow, 1983.

Douglas Hart ponders the nascent
Mary Chain's options for world domination.

Douglas Hart

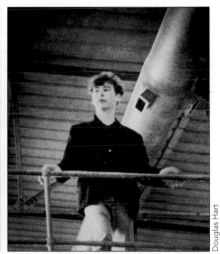

Douglas Hart

Jim Reid recording 'Upside Down' at
Evenlode, East Kilbride, this being the band's
(then the Daisy Chain) first ever studio
recording. Douglas Hart's school friend
Norman Wilson was hauled in to play drums.
He was the only person they knew with a kit.

Jim Reid at the abandoned paint factory
in East Kilbride, 1983. The paint factory
was a sanctuary to the Mary Chain,
providing the ideal place to drop acid,
listen to incredibly loud music and,
most importantly, smash things up.

Kevan Price

Photo-montage poster created by the band themselves for the Jesus and Mary Chain's first Glasgow gig, 10 June 1984. The 'live' pictures were actually staged in Jim's bedroom.

Robin Kennedy

The Mary Chain portrayed in all their glum glory on the cover of *Slow Dazzle* fanzine, 1984.

-DEAR ALAN
          THIS IS THE
MASTER TAPE FOR THE SONG
ON THE LP. SORRY IT
TOOK US SO LONG TO SEND
IT, BUT WE'VE HAD A
LOT OF PROBLEMS GETTING IT
DONE. WE DIDN'T HAVE
VERY MUCH MONEY SO WE
WENT INTO AN 8 TRACK
STUDIO AND RECORDED IT LIVE
(MORE OR LESS) BUT IT SOUNDED
FUCKING AWFUL, THE GUITAR
SOUND WAS TERRIBLE AND
THE WHOLE THING WAS VERY
TAME, MAINLY BECAUSE OF
THE STUPID BASTARD ENGINEER
WHO DIDN'T UNDERSTAND WHAT
WE WERE LOOKING FOR.
   SINCE IT WAS SO BAD
WE ALL DECIDED THAT THE
~~XXXXXX~~ FIRST 4 TRACK VERSION

OF THE SONG WAS MUCH BETTER
SO THAT IS WHAT WE HAVE
SENT. WE ADDED A FEW
LITTLE BITS ONTO IT
   HOPE YOU LIKE IT.
IT IS CALLED "UPSIDEDOWN" AND
~~WAS~~ WAS WRITTEN BY JIM REID
                    AND WILLIAM REID
          THANKS.
                 JIM REID

P.S.
   THE JESUS AND MARY CHAIN ARE

   JIM REID - VOCALS
   WILLIAM REID - GUITAR
   DOUGLAS HART - BASS
   MURRAY DALGLISH - DRUMS

The original letter written by Jim Reid to Alan McGee after the recording of 'Upside Down' didn't quite go to plan. Note that Murray Dalglish has now been recruited on drums, and the band name 'Daisy Chain' has been changed to 'The Jesus and Mary Chain'.

DEAR ALAN

THIS IS THE MASTER TAPE FOR THE SONG ON THE LP. SORRY IT TOOK US SO LONG TO SEND IT, BUT WE'VE HAD A LOT OF PROBLEMS GETTING IT DONE. WE DIDN'T HAVE VERY MUCH MONEY SO WE WENT INTO AN 8 TRACK STUDIO AND RECORDED IT LIVE (MORE OR LESS). BUT IT SOUNDED FUCKING AWFUL, THE GUITAR SOUND WAS TERRIBLE AND THE WHOLE THING WAS VERY TAME, MAINLY BECAUSE OF THE STUPID BASTARD ENGINEER WHO DIDN'T UNDERSTAND WHAT WE WERE LOOKING FOR.

SINCE IT WAS SO BAD WE ALL DECIDED THAT THE FIRST 4 TRACK VERSION OF THE SONG WAS MUCH BETTER SO THAT IS WHAT WE HAVE SENT. WE ADDED A FEW LITTLE BITS ONTO IT.

HOPE YOU LIKE IT. IT IS CALLED "UPSIDE DOWN" AND WAS WRITTEN BY JIM REID AND WILLIAM REID.

THANKS

JIM REID

P.S.
THE JESUS AND MARY CHAIN ARE
JIM REID – VOCALS
WILLIAM REID – GUITAR
DOUGLAS HART – BASS
MURRAY DALGLISH – DRUMS

Jim Reid and Douglas Hart survey the chaos unfolding at their feet at the Ambulance Station, Old Kent Road, London, in November 1984. 'The police were called . . .' remembers writer Neil Taylor.

Getty Images

Jim Reid in Southern Studios, London, recording *Psychocandy* in 1985. The Mary Chain worked hard in the studio, and the atmosphere was frequently tense. 'I threw William against a door and knocked it off its hinges,' Jim recalls. 'Can't remember why. But back then it was all about the music. Ten minutes later we'd be fine with each other.'

Douglas Hart

William Reid on stage, 1985. 'You'd see him crouched and looking at all the pedals, and you could feel that energy – anger, in a way,' recalls Laurence Verfaillie.

Jim, Douglas and William on stage during their European tour, 1985.

Douglas Hart, and Bobby Gillespie on drums. Three strings on the bass, a kit consisting of no more than two drums – less was always more.

· B I O G R A P H Y ·

(The Jesus and Mary Chain do not want to participate in the
writing of a biography. Instead, we present a writer's
impression...)

THE JESUS AND MARY CHAIN

Passion. Invention. Fire. Brilliance.

Just four little words sum up a startling new musical discovery
... The Jesus And Mary Chain. Now ready to launch themselves
on an unsuspecting public, here are four lads with talent in
abundance PLUS the hunky good looks to challenge Wham!, Duran
Duran and the rest for the hearts of the nation's teenagers.

There is no doubt that this group means business despite - or
perhaps even <u>because</u> of - extremely humble beginnings. All
products of the slum district in East Kilbride, JIM REID (vocals),
WILLIAM REID (guitar), DOUGLAS HART (bass) and BOBBY GILLESPIE
(drums), know only too well what it's like to go without.

"We may have been in the gutter," says Jim, "but we were looking
up at the stars."

Inspired by Iggy Pop and the punk explosion, the foursome got
together with a view to musically document the social deprivation
and bureaucratic hypocrisy which was all around them. Beginning
with equipment borrowed from mates, the band quickly evolved
a totally unique sound - low on pretension and meaningless pop,
high on melody, bite and sheer rock and roll aggression.

Their rise was rapid. In no time they had a ferociously
loyal fan following around their home town. "After just a couple
of gigs I knew that this was something special," says charismatic
guitarist William. "I can't even say why...I just knew."

Instead of rushing to London to try and quickly cash in on their
talents, the band instead travelled to Europe, winning hearts
and minds on a major tour across Germany, Switzerland and France.
An independently-released single, 'Upside Down' c/w 'Vegetable
Man', increased the momentum and, by the time the group arrived
in London in January, '85, they found themselves the talk of the
town.

Blanco Y Negro Records won the race to sign them up, and they
are currently readying a new single, due for a February release.

Though they are clearly poised for great success, here is a band
with both feet planted firmly on the ground, as blond, tee-total
Douglas explains: "We never had any intention of being 'Superstars'
when we started out. We just do it for the music...and the kids.
The money and fame means nothing to us..."

Prepare to be converted to....The Jesus And Mary Chain!

January, '85

Robin Kennedy

WEA's (unreleased) band biog of The Jesus and Mary Chain, 1985, shortly after being signed
to Blanco Y Negro. 'Hunky good looks', eh? Are you *sure* you didn't write this, chaps?

The Jesus and Mary Chain looking insouciant in Tottenham swimming pool, 1984.
The Mary Chain, still living in Scotland at the time, had been staying at Alan McGee's
flat nearby. Non-swimmer Douglas Hart admits he 'appreciates a drained, abandoned
swimming pool far more than a full and functioning one'. Works slightly better for
Mary Chain photo-shoots as well.

Derek Ridgers

Mike Laye

Bobby Gillespie in Portugal, where the band had flown with director Tim Broad to shoot the video for 'You Trip Me Up'. The idea was to film the band in a sunny location. It rained.

The Mary Chain looking positively bereft beneath a palm tree in Portugal in 1986. (Actually they had a very nice time.) 'It was special,' remembers Jim Reid. Although 'nobody knew what we were about. Everybody thought we were some kind of freak show that had rolled into town. Which, of course, we were.'

Jim and William Reid in a field of flowers.

Douglas Hart, Jim Reid in the background, 1986.

The Jesus and Mary Chain on stage at the Tic Toc Club, Coventry, 6 September 1990. Douglas Hart would leave the band the following year.

Tom Sheehan

The advent of the magnificently coiffed (and, crucially, quite cheerful) John Moore, replacing Bobby Gillespie on drums. This image was taken in press officer Mick Houghton's office in 1987, around the time of the band's second album *Darklands*, Mick's favourite JAMC album: 'I think it's the best album they made. They made a much more lasting statement than *Psychocandy*, in a way.'

William and Jim Reid backstage in Glasgow during the Rollercoaster tour, 25 March 1992.
It was never, as Douglas Hart and John Moore both attest, a 'party' atmosphere after a
show. 'Actually, you wouldn't want to go to a party that The Jesus and Mary Chain
were at,' says Moore. 'That wouldn't be a party.' The band would, Douglas confirms,
'sit in silence and then go home and watch the telly'

Getty Images

The Jesus and Mary Chain on stage with Scarlett Johannsson, Coachella, 27 April 2007, singing 'Just Like Honey'. Former Mary Chain member John Moore thought it hilarious that 'in true Mary Chain style, they didn't even bother to introduce her'.

21

Acid House, Sugarcubes and
a Trip behind the Iron Curtain

*If the public don't like 'Sidewalking', I'll be utterly pissed off and
my view of the public taste will go even lower.*
William Reid to Steve Sutherland, 1988

The Reids had to find a replacement guitarist, but they were reluctant to
advertise, didn't want to have to go through the audition process, and
didn't have anyone in mind. 'Perfect example of their sociopathic
tendencies,' says John Moore. 'They got Dave Evans, their former
roadie.'

Dave Evans, an erstwhile member of Biff Bang Pow! and the Mary
Chain's sometime sound man, had taken a year out with the Shop
Assistants as a backline/guitar technician but had returned to the Mary
Chain fold for the upcoming tour. The Reids now had just two weeks
before the tour started, but, as Evans recalls, 'they spent the first week
in the studio and there didn't seem to be any enthusiasm on anyone's
part to find someone. I offered my services and they said "Yes". We
didn't have any rehearsals whatsoever.'

It was a solution, but the decision to include Evans in the line-up was
not universally popular. He was well liked and could play guitar, but, as
Douglas observed, it was strange that the Reids spent so much time
perfecting their song-craft but would put little or no effort into finding
just the right people to play it live. Whether it was a lack of confidence
that prevented the Reids from being more outward-looking when it
came to line-up changes, or just sheer indolence, their fellow founding
member found it hard to reconcile.

'It's weird,' says Douglas. 'They cared so much about everything else. Dave Evans, lovely guy, but it's just because he was there. That's something that would occasionally confound me. Mary Chain laziness . . . "He'll do!"'

The cloistered process of making *Darklands*, the advent of a more businesslike manager, and some ostensibly lackadaisical decision-making had all caused Douglas and the Reids to grow apart. But while the brothers worked together on new music, Douglas had been developing new ways of expressing himself, particularly through film-making and making music videos for artists such as My Bloody Valentine and the Cramps/Gun Club sideman Kid Congo.

Douglas was also inspired by acid house in its formative years, which led to some musical experimentation of his own. He made his first record away from the Mary Chain, under the name of Acid Angels, with Peter 'Pinko' Fowler, an associate of the late John Loder and an instrumental part of the alternative music television series *Snub TV*. The result of their collaboration was a sprawling dance record called 'Speed Speed Ecstasy', which featured a sample of Donna Summer's iconic disco hit 'I Feel Love'.

'In 1988, way before *Screamadelica*, I went to some gig at the Astoria,' Douglas recalls. 'My girlfriend at the time said, "Let's stay here, there's a club coming after, they play dance music." And I'm going, "What, a fucking disco?" But it was an acid house night.

'It was an important moment. Andy Weatherall was DJ'ing, and he was like, "What are you doing here?" He was surprised to see one of the Mary Chain, I was still in that indie world. So I made a dance record really early on, just a one-off, came out on Mute. Of course, two years later everyone was doing it.'

William too had been making solo dance tracks in his bedroom, but as Jim observed, he didn't have the confidence to release them. But the Reids were both influenced by acid house, and the next Mary Chain album, *Automatic*, would be their most dance-orientated record yet.

*

The summer of 1988 also saw the rise of music festivals across Europe, and this ensured that the Mary Chain would cross paths with other groups of a similar mind-set, such as the Cocteau Twins and Iceland's Björk-fronted indie band The Sugarcubes.

Laurence remembers: 'At Roskilde, not far from Copenhagen; we were booked in the same hotel and they all went out. I think the Icelanders are pretty good at holding their drink, they beat the Scots flat out.'

This experience clearly bonded the two bands; eccentric Sugarcube maverick Einar Örn (now dividing his time between his group Ghostigital and his day job on the Reykjavik city council) was especially friendly to the Mary Chain, and this connection would lead to The Sugarcubes inviting the Reids to remix their hit 'Birthday'. The result is compelling and mysterious, interweaving Björk's yelps and wails with some trademark Jim Reid 'Hey, Hey, Heys'. It was, as Laurence recalls, 'really the first time the Mary Chain had done anything like this'.

Another memorable music festival the Mary Chain played that June was Tallinn Summer Rock in Estonia, still firmly behind the Iron Curtain at this point. The Mary Chain were put up in the now infamous Hotel Viru, a high-rise hotel where it was compulsory for all foreign visitors to stay, and where they were monitored closely by the KGB. Agents recorded guests and listened to every conversation in every room from their secret hub on the wind-blown top floor, which is now open to the public as a KGB museum. The door that leads to the old secret recording rooms in Hotel Viru bears the ominous and highly unconvincing sentence: 'There is nothing behind this door' in Russian.

'Every floor had a concierge who reported back to the KGB on what you were doing,' says then Mary Chain manager Chris Morrison. 'You were noted every time you went in and out of your room. So I went in and out of my room about six times. Give them something to do.'

'I imagine we were followed everywhere on our trip,' Douglas adds. 'Wouldn't it be a blast to have a look at the KGB's Mary Chain files?'

It sure would. Although, as Jim observes, 'they probably got rid of them for being too fucking obscene'. The conversations crackling up the line from the Mary Chain's rooms to the top floor of the Hotel Viru would certainly have made for interesting listening. 'I remember a bizarre fetishistic conversation I had with Douglas and Richie (drummer Richard Thomas) in the hotel room,' recalls Lincoln Fong, who was working with the Mary Chain as a technician. 'It's probably best not repeated.' There's a good chance that the KGB wouldn't have been able to decipher their accents, of course.

'Tallinn was a pretty weird trip,' says Jim. 'There were all these dodgy high-rise constructions that looked like they would have fallen down if you sneezed near them, and it was totally run on bribery and corruption. You'd go to a restaurant and they'd say, "It's fully booked," and you'd look and there'd be loads of empty tables. The promoter would bung this guy a load of roubles and a table would appear.'

On one occasion, on his way downstairs from his room, Chris Morrison was approached in the lift by two young women who suggested he take them to dinner. He politely declined. When the lift reached the ground floor and the doors slid open, he was met by Jim and William and their Estonian guide, who was extremely perturbed. She warned Chris that some American tourists had also recently been propositioned by the same women. Their 'dinner date' culminated in the women spiking their drinks with drugs and, the following morning, the hapless Americans woke up naked in an alleyway not remembering anything of the night before.

Chris remembers, 'I said, "My God, all of my life I've wanted to wake up naked in an alleyway not remembering where I was the night before. Where are they?" Jim said, "Forget the women, how do we get the drugs?"'

*

Tallinn Summer Rock took place in a vast football stadium, and the Mary Chain walked on stage to see about 200,000 Estonians staring back at them – one of the biggest crowds the band have ever played to. The bill was somewhat incongruous in terms of style: blues singer Robert Cray was also appearing, as were 'a bunch of Finnish heavy metal bands,' says Douglas. 'The strangest Mary Chain show ever. Such gigs were rare, so everyone from Tallinn under the age of 40 came along. We played to thousands of bemused Estonians, many with mullets and bum-fluff moustaches.'

'They were just standing there like frying sausages,' says Jim. 'All these bands they'd never heard of doing what they do. It was quite bizarre.'

The Jesus and Mary Chain performed, as they always did, with maximum noise, concentrated energy, and, in Jim's case, the usual attack on the equipment. But when he looked up, mid-frenzy, Jim noticed that the crowd appeared to be in a collective state of shock. Their reaction, as Douglas recalls, 'was similar to that of the audience in *The Producers*, at the premiere of *Springtime for Hitler*'. You get the idea.

'I was as off my tits as it was possible to get in Tallinn,' Jim explains, 'and I did my standard smashing-the-monitor thing that I used to do. These people had no reference points as to what it was I was doing. They were just standing there thinking, What the fuck is that guy doing? Looking back on it, I was smashing up their gear that would have taken them about eight lifetimes to buy. Maybe it wasn't such a great idea.'

In the not too distant future, Jim Reid would increasingly leave the gear unscathed during a live show. His initial feeling was that the destruction was theatre; 'you have to put on a show,' he said in later years. 'It's something to do besides playing the songs.' Sometimes the violence was borne of nerves, desperation or genuine frustration, other times it was 'unnecessary, or sometimes you go on speeding out of your head and there's a guitar and a floor to smash it on.' The point at which it had to stop was when audiences started to expect it. There was no point in being predictably unpredictable, and the Mary Chain didn't need a gimmick. 'It dawned on us that what's good about the Mary Chain is it's not about glitzy showbiz stuff,' said Jim. 'Now we push the music to the front.'

As summer waned, it was time for the Mary Chain to set off to Australia to continue the 'Sidewalking' tour; two more gruelling months on the road. But there was a light at the end of this particular touring tunnel, an Iggy Pop-shaped light, to be specific. Once they had completed their dates in Australia, they would travel to the US for a run of shows with one of their lifelong heroes. Meanwhile, to accompany the Australian tour, Blanco Y Negro released a 7-inch of the Mary Chain's jagged cover of 'Surfin' USA'.

*

There were difficulties on the tour from the off: an argument erupted between Lincoln Fong and a drunken Jeffrey Lee Pierce from The Gun

Club; a riot broke out on an early Australian date when Perth's finest The Triffids set the stage alight (literally); and the Mary Chain's gigs were the subject of a public protest in New Zealand when two goths died in an unrelated suicide pact the week before. Protesters tried to have the Mary Chain shows cancelled, but they didn't succeed and the band escaped New Zealand unscathed. More trouble, however, lay ahead in the US.

The Jesus and Mary Chain were trepidatiously excited about whom they were soon to share a bill with. They had revered Iggy Pop since they were teenagers, listened to his records, waged joyous trails of destruction in the abandoned paint factory to the sound of 'I Wanna Be Your Dog', and now they were about to meet the sinewy dark lord of proto-punk himself. Unfortunately, but perhaps unsurprisingly, disaster ensued.

'Oh God,' Jim sighs, cringing at the memory of it. 'One of the main reasons the Mary Chain exists is because of Iggy and The Stooges. We were asked if we wanted to "co-headline with Iggy", which basically meant we were the support band. Anyway, we're big Iggy fans, so we do it.'

The Mary Chain arrived at the California Theater in San Diego and prepared for a soundcheck, but Iggy was still on stage. 'We thought, Good, let's watch Iggy soundcheck,' says Jim. 'Not allowed to watch Iggy soundcheck. Even then, that's cool, I hate people watching me soundcheck. I've never stopped anybody doing it, but I know how that feels.

'But Iggy is soundchecking not for half an hour, not for an hour, but for about three or four hours. And suddenly we're told, "There's no time for you to have a soundcheck." We're like, "What happened to this 'co-headline' shit?"'

Despite the way the tour had been sold to the Reids, the Mary Chain were hardly treated as equals by Iggy's crew. 'Iggy had this Scottish tour manager, a real hard nut,' Jim continues. 'He thought that if he sent Iggy into our dressing-room to hang out for about ten minutes that it would make everything OK.

'I don't want to put the guy down here, because I still love him and I love his music, but he came in and said, "Have you got everything you need?" I said, "No, not really." He said, "What do you want?" And I said, "A soundcheck." And he went, "Gee, I was really looking forward to meeting you guys . . ." He stumbled out and that was that. Then we were told, "You can have a sound-check for ten minutes."

Once the Mary Chain were on stage, an argument broke out between William and Iggy Pop's roadies about how much of the stage they could use. The disagreement concluded with William spitting angrily on Iggy's 'Marley', a large vinyl mat used on stage that the Mary Chain were not allowed to go near, let alone gob on.

Jim says: 'One of Iggy's crew came up with a towel and said, "Clean it up." We told him where to go and all hell broke loose. During the show I was so furious that I literally wrecked all of the onstage equipment. I smashed up the monitors and kicked them all into the pit at the front of the stage.'

Mid-set, Mary Chain tour manager Scott Rodger (now Paul McCartney's manager) sidled up to Jim and quietly conveyed that as soon as they'd finished the show, they were to run, not walk, straight out of the fire door and into the waiting van. 'If you don't,' he said, 'you're going to get the shit kicked out of you.' Jim looked up to see Iggy's crew standing in the wings with baseball bats.

When the debacle reached the ears of the press, however, promoter David Swift took Iggy's side. The Mary Chain were, according to Swift, 'very demanding about using Iggy's lights and wanting more stage room,' he told the *LA Times*. 'Logistically, Iggy couldn't do that for them.'

★

Work would soon begin on the Mary Chain's third studio album, *Automatic*, the brighter, harder, synth-heavy record that William refers to as their 'driving across America' (and away from Iggy's baseball-bat-wielding crew) album. The Reids holed up in Sam Therapy, a studio on Kensal Road in West London, and the ever-supportive Geoff Travis and Jeannette Lee would visit occasionally to check in on them. As Jeannette remembers, the atmosphere was often strained.

'You wouldn't know what the vibe would be; maybe they'd have been working on something that hadn't gone well and they'd had a row, so you could walk into a very black mood. One could storm out as you were walking in.'

Although the Reids had long had a combative relationship, this ominous studio atmosphere provided a preview of things to come. The mood of the record, from the song-writing to the glittering programmed drum sound, seems to reflect where the band was at personally too – while *Darklands* was softer, more sensual and more introspective, *Automatic* has clean, sharp lines and, at times, a glaring cocaine confidence compared to *Psychocandy*'s acid-inspired haze. As David Quantick concluded in his review for *NME*, it was 'cruel, but fun'.

The album was released in September 1989, reaching number 11 in the UK album chart. Arguably it is more loved now than it was at the time, featuring as it does such enduring songs as 'Blues From A Gun', 'Halfway To Crazy' and 'Head On', famously covered by The Pixies. However, some critics and fans, no doubt hoping for *Darklands* or *Psychocandy* part two, did not take to the release.

'*Automatic* was probably their least well-received album,' admits then Mary Chain press officer Mick Houghton. 'Not that it's for me to talk about how a record should be produced, but I thought the mistake was not having the proper drum sound. The songs were great, but the production lacked something, they kind of worked it too much. But later they came back with "Reverence" as a single. When that came out in 1989, it blew people away.'

Just before the *Automatic* promotional tour started in October 1989, with three months of British and European dates stretching out ahead of them, the Reids decided, apparently at the last minute, that Dave Evans was not the guitarist they wanted to take. As much as they hated auditioning musicians, this time it couldn't be avoided. Nobody suitable was springing to mind.

Jim says: 'We auditioned what seemed like hundreds of guitarists. When I look back on it, it was probably about four. We narrowed it down to two, and that was Ben Lurie and Phil King.'

Philip King, later of shoegaze band Lush fame, first met the Mary Chain when he was playing with See See Rider, an indie group also originally from East Kilbride (although King himself is a Londoner). Some members of See See Rider, Philip included, also shared a flat with Douglas, who had a hand in producing some of their material. 'Total keep-it-in-the-family Mary Chain thing,' says Douglas.

London-born Australian Ben Lurie, on the other hand, was working as a receptionist at Rough Trade when Jeannette Lee, who knew he wanted to join a band, suggested he try out for the Mary Chain.

At first it seemed that Philip was the ideal choice – he looked right, played well and was already part of their extended circle. Ben Lurie admits that he 'did everything wrong' at the audition. Apart from anything else, 'he had a *ponytail* . . .' Jim shudders. However, the Reids appreciated his contrariness and his blithe disregard of the groups he was supposed to revere.

'We asked him what music he liked,' says Jim. 'He started going on about The Police. We were like, "What? Are you fucking kidding?" Then we said, "You're Australian, what do you think about The Birthday Party?" And he said, "They're pretty funny." We thought he was amusing. When it came to musicianship, he and Phil were neck and neck.'

'Jim says they flipped a coin and Ben won,' Philip adds. 'William says I didn't get in because my shoes were too pointy. So, somewhere in between the two . . .'

As October loomed and rehearsals were arranged, Ben Lurie and his ponytail were absorbed into the Mary Chain line-up, which would stay as it was for three years after a long period of all too frequent changes. Also joining the tour of Britain and Europe would be Richard Thomas on drums, who had played with the Mary Chain on the 'Sidewalking' tour. The drum sound on the Reids' latest output sounded more mechanical than ever, and yet the drum machine on the road had, perversely, been scrapped in favour of a real drummer.

The *Automatic* tour is remembered by all as a difficult, exhausting period for the band. However, despite the usual touring melancholia, Jerry Jaffe recalls a heartwarming moment that would doubtless change anyone's opinion of the band. (Unless your opinion of them was that they were well-mannered young men with a soft spot for old ladies.)

Jerry Jaffe recalls: 'My mother was in her eighties. She'd never been to Europe, and I took her to Amsterdam during the tour. The Jesus and Mary Chain were very big on meeting my mother. I mean, *I* had trepidation about meeting this band, so the thought of them meeting my mother . . . But they said, "No, we want to meet Mrs Jaffe." It was kind of sweet, but I was apprehensive.

'They told me to meet them at a certain Italian restaurant at a certain time. I was thinking, I can't believe I'm doing this, my mother's not going to talk to me for the rest of my life . . . But they were all there, and they couldn't have been nicer – they made her feel like a million dollars, honestly it was the nicest time of her life. She was saying, "You know, you'd be so handsome if you cut your hair . . ."

'William said I was his third favourite American Jew behind Bob Dylan and Lenny Bruce. That used to make me feel good. And they made my mother feel good, so there you go.'

22

Crash and Burn

A lot of bands say, 'When it stops being fun, we'll give it up.' But
we betrayed ourselves, because we never did. We should have given
up playing live in 1990.
William Reid to *Uncut* magazine

The Mary Chain had been to some dark places together, but 1990 was
the year the fun-to-stress ratio seriously changed for the worse. The
tour for *Automatic* was heavy going, and the Reids, William in particular, had already been in a tailspin for some time. All you have to do
is listen to some of the lyrics from songs such as 'Halfway To Crazy'
– *That's me being torn at the seams . . . catch me, 'cause I'm falling*
apart – to get an inkling of the general feeling. Chris Morrison helped
as best he could, but the drunker the band became, the less he was able
to do anything.

'Have you ever tried to talk sense to anybody who is drunk? Or high?
Let it all go down and I'll bail them out in the morning, hopefully they'll
still be alive, but I can do nothing when they're drunk,' Chris says.
'Being on the road is unhealthy, physically and mentally, it's stressful,
exhausting, and then you have the drug dealers, the parasites, the sycophants. It's a difficult environment for anyone to survive in.'

Laurence Verfaillie remembers that, for William at least, anything
approaching happiness could only really be found at home, 'with his
girlfriend and his cats, his TV, his video, the latest games . . . Tetris was
probably cutting-edge back then.' On tour, William would find it
increasingly hard to communicate with people, and he quickly became
remote. 'Or,' Laurence adds, 'he'd get pissed and misbehave. But

William could also be the funniest guy. He had this really surreal humour.'

'William has an insanely interesting worldview,' says Geoff Travis. 'It may just be insane. He'd say things like, "Brian Wilson had nothing to do with The Beach Boys! It was Carl!" He probably meant Carl Wilson sang lead on the songs that you think are all to do with Brian, but it's just a great thing to say.'

Chris Morrison remembers going backstage after a show to look for the band, only to discover William in the green room, on his knees and seemingly in tears. 'He was going, "It's terrible, Jim! He never got the recognition he deserved! He was so badly treated." I'm wondering what's going on. I said, "Who's he talking about?" Someone said, "Bob Dylan." I said, "What's William on?" They said, "Three Es . . ."'

★

A certain unravelling started to happen to the Mary Chain towards the end of the 1980s and into the 1990s because, while they had pioneered a sound and an image, the Reids were being overtaken commercially by their contemporaries. My Bloody Valentine ('Gerry and the Pacemakers with noise', as Jim Reid referred to them in their earlier years) and Sonic Youth in particular had the arty slant covered, and tapped into the zeitgeist perhaps more successfully and with greater determination than the Mary Chain. The Reids were also happy to nail their colours to the pop mast, which still confused people. Indie and rock were supposedly worthier and more serious than pop.

'The Jesus and Mary Chain had this brief flirtation with being the hippest band in the world,' says writer and musician John Robb, 'but as the years went by they got pushed to the side. They weren't seen to be as cutting-edge, not like Sonic Youth. The Mary Chain didn't get slagged off, they just weren't in the middle of the thing any more.'

Mick Houghton observes that, while Sonic Youth, who were certainly allies of the Reids, were branded as the 'US Mary Chain', the two groups just couldn't be compared. 'Sonic Youth were middle-class Americans, very art-school,' Mick says. 'The Mary Chain never had pretension or artifice. And they were working-class.' The other problem for the Mary Chain, Mick observes, was that The Smiths were increasingly stealing the Mary Chain's thunder as the decade wore on. 'People began to see The Smiths as the band of the 1980s,' he explains. 'But I still think *Psychocandy* was one of the albums, if not *the* album, of the 1980s.'

*

The epic upcoming tour of America would be vital for the band's future, securing and increasing their fan base in the States, but it was, as Douglas remembers, draining in almost every conceivable way. The tours had been getting longer and longer and there was greater pressure on the Reids to do even more press. To make matters worse, it was also nigh on impossible to get a good cup of tea Stateside.

'The longest tour we ever did in America was with Nine Inch Nails,' Douglas remembers. 'It was funny; as the tour went on, they started to dress more like us. It was quite freaky.'

This support slot would give Nine Inch Nails, an emerging band from Ohio, their first big break. Jerry Jaffe made sure they were on the tour after checking them out because, having endured the Mary Chain's previous choices of support act, who were not to his taste to say the least, he felt it was time to take the reins.

Jerry says: 'The support bands were like irrelevant jokes, they had no talent. Bands like Art Phag. One of the guys played washboard, another played a ukulele, it was just awful.

'I was friends with the label that had just signed Nine Inch Nails, TVT. The guy played me this stuff and I said, "Yes, that sounds like a band that should open for us." I sent the records to Jim and William. They couldn't care less: "Hey, you like them? Fine." Couldn't give a shit.'

Nine Inch Nails were evidently in some awe of the Mary Chain, and frontman Trent Reznor was shy around them. This didn't bother the headline act, who weren't exactly angling for a group hug. What the Mary Chain did find strange was that the members of Nine Inch Nails were complete health freaks. Douglas recalls: 'They were all doing exercises and drinking those whey-protein things that body-builders have. Some contrast. We were ingesting quite different liquids, and crystallised solids, before going on stage . . .' It was, therefore, relatively rare for either group to venture into the other's dressing room to hang out, not that they'd have known what to say to each other if they had – Reznor remembers with amusement that 'one of the Reids might have grunted at me once, but that was about it'.

One of the dates on the tour took the bands to Cleveland, Nine Inch Nails' home-town. Reznor and his band-mates took the Mary Chain out to a local club, marking one of the few times they socialised. Douglas, as previously noted, has something of a gift for being able to stroll up to someone intimidating and ask for whatever he wants. Three sheets to the wind on a winter's night in Cleveland, he spotted something he wanted and cheerfully asked for it, much to his friends' concern.

'There was a mad biker there and he had this amazing Coca-Cola T-shirt,' Douglas remembers. 'I just went up to him and said, "Hey! Can I have your T-shirt?", and they were all going, "He's going to fucking kill you!" But the guy was like, "Sure!" and took his T-shirt off.

'We didn't interact much, though. We weren't comfortable in social groups. That's why I always say that the Creation thing was never a scene. To have a scene you have to have lots of people who are quite well adjusted. That wasn't us.'

Chris Morrison can confirm this. While in the US, he had organised a meeting with the acclaimed video director Sophie Muller, who would later go on to create the artwork for the Mary Chain's 1994 album *Stoned & Dethroned*, and the videos for 'Come On' and 'Sometimes Always'.

'I was uncharacteristically ten minutes late,' Chris recalls, 'but the Mary Chain are already there, and they and Sophie are in this room. I walked in, nobody's talking, so I went, "Hi! You got it all sorted, then? Terrific." And Jim said, "Actually, we haven't talked yet." They hadn't even spoken!'

They might not have been the greatest verbal communicators, but simply because the Mary Chain were playing so often they were arguably at the peak of their powers as a live band at this point. They'd even started rehearsing more, not least because they had new members to bring up to speed. But while they were feeling more assured about their live sound, there was a fresh sense of friction. After an awkward start, Ben Lurie had become friendly with Jim, but Douglas wasn't at ease with the new situation.

'We were such a bunch of weirdos,' Ben recalls. 'I thought we were getting along famously, but I'm not sure that Douglas did. But he was a lot of help to me. I'd follow his lead for learning the tunes.'

'The dynamics change and there's a new relationship,' Douglas muses. 'I don't think it was that I was jealous of his and Jim's relationship, just a bit disappointed. Later there would be tensions between Ben and William too, definitely. But that's just travelling together. It's difficult to spend that much time with the same people.' Separate tour buses, à la Mötley Crüe, were not an option.

As far as the fans were concerned, particularly in previously uncharted territory such as Brazil, the chaos and creativity of the shows were life-changing. But after three arduous months in the US, the Mary Chain were at the end of their tether. The group went straight from America to Japan and, as Laurence remembers, 'the pressure was building and building. Jim could communicate more easily than William, and William was getting frustrated that he couldn't do that. They had a huge falling-out in Tokyo before a show.'

'I don't even remember what it was about,' Jim admits. 'But it got to a point where things were said that couldn't be taken back. We agreed that that was it. "Fuck you then!" – "Well, fuck you as well!"'

Laurence then remembers watching what was, as far as she knew, the last ever Jesus and Mary Chain show later that night. There was no interaction between anyone on stage, they were just going through the motions. Japanese Mary Chain devotee Mihoko Kimura was in the audience and remembers seeing the group in a state of deep inebriation, and radiating sheer unhappiness. The fans weren't aware until after the gig that, according to a local Tokyo publication, the band had 'quarrelled' – they just seemed 'too plastered' even to perform, says Mihoko. 'I wasn't pleased to say the least, but remained their fan even after that.'

After the show, the band returned silently to the dressing room, unable to even look at each other. 'That was our first major break-up,' Jim says, 'but it never got as far as us actually telling anybody. Still, for a few weeks, the Mary Chain didn't exist.'

Both Jim and William were ragged after years of psychic warfare, not to mention self-medication to dull the considerable pain. They just wanted to move on with their lives, preferably with as little contact with each other as possible. Obviously it could never be that simple.

By Christmas the brothers still weren't talking, and it really did look as though there would be no way back for the Mary Chain. They'd had a good run, with a clutch of hit albums and singles to their name, gold records on the wall, well-thumbed passports and overworked livers. But while it might have been healthier for the brothers to stay apart, musically they were at their best together, and those close to them knew they had to sort out their differences.

On Christmas Day, Jim and Laurence travelled to East Kilbride to spend the day with his parents. William would not be joining them, but he called home to speak to his family. The phone was thrust at Jim, and the brothers grumpily called a truce. I think we can probably call that a Christmas miracle.

23

Remake, Remodel

They write up these histories of the 1980s and we're not even in there. We were the fucking 1980s ... but we feel a lot more comfortable with the 1990s.
Jim Reid to John Robb in *Sounds*

By 1991 the Reids were communicating a little more fluently with each other, and had started developing material for their next album, *Honey's Dead*. While *Automatic* had proved to be their hardest, 'most rock'n'roll album' as William put it (later describing it as 'a compromise to get on American radio'), *Honey's Dead* was reflective of their whole career up to this point, 'everything rolled into one'. The future finally glimmered with a spark of hope and expectation. Some of the changes within and around the band, however, would be hard to take for some.

The Mary Chain had burned themselves to a cinder before rising from the ashes to rebuild themselves, and, after the painful break-up in Tokyo, it was time to begin a new chapter. Said chapter, however, would not include founding member Douglas Hart. The Jesus and Mary Chain was very much a Reid-Reid operation in the studio now, and the brothers were also becoming even more insular after the decision to sack McGee. Their buffer had gone and, as the pressure mounted, Douglas was increasingly excluded from the proceedings until it inevitably reached the point of no return. Jim and William drove to Disgracelands, the squat Douglas shared with Philip King, to break the news.

'It was terrible,' Jim remembers. 'I hated doing it, but he was really good about it. Douglas wasn't really a gifted musician, nor were any of us. Well, William plays guitar like nobody else. But Douglas didn't record on *Darklands* and he played on about half of *Psychocandy*. I used to play bass. We'd go to the studio and Douglas hadn't heard the song. You'd be going, "Do this . . ." and then I thought, I'll just get here early tomorrow and do it.

'But he was a big part of the band in the same way that Bobby was,' Jim concludes. 'We were so tuned into each other, Douglas understood it the way we did. That was worth everything.'

Douglas, who was already busy making videos at this stage, was philosophical about the decision, but after having practically grown up with the Reids and having gone through so much together, he felt as though he'd 'lost a lover'. He agrees that it was time to move on, but leaving the Mary Chain was 'emotional, very sad.

'From 1983 to 1991, we saw each other almost every day,' Douglas says. 'But, you know, I was their first fan, so to be a kid and to be playing in your favourite group for eight years . . . not fucking bad! You'd have to be a real petty bastard to get bogged down in the crummy details. When you look back at the whole picture, it's amazing. And the insanity in every direction . . . I've seen a lot of bands as a film-maker and I've never seen anything like the Mary Chain, never.'

Douglas Hart would stay in touch with his former band-mates, and also with Geoff and Jeannette, making videos for artists (including, in later years, Pete Doherty) under the Rough Trade umbrella. But, as Mick Houghton says, even though Douglas had not been involved in the recordings since *Psychocandy*, there was something vital about The Jesus and Mary Chain that, inevitably, altered when he left.

'They lost something,' says Mick. 'The dynamic within groups is really important. Douglas's role was much greater than anybody realises.' The Reids would bring in the rhythm section from The Starlings (Barry Blacker and Matthew Parkin) to replace Hart and drummer Richard Thomas, who had moved on to join the electro group Renegade Soundwave.

On a positive note, the Reids finally did what they'd been muttering about since *Automatic* and bought their own studio in Elephant and Castle, just south of the River Thames – 9a Amelia Street, to be exact. They named the studio 'The Drugstore', and there they could create their own environment, stay all night if they wanted to, and, crucially, there would be no more haemorrhaging of cash while the clock ticked ominously in the background.

'When we were making *Automatic*,' Jim explains, 'even though we got the studio [Sam Therapy] reasonably priced, we just kept thinking, Why are we paying all this money? We'd be thinking, rightly, that the budget on your average album is the same amount to buy an average studio, so we thought, Well, let's not do this again.'

The Drugstore was a bright, sunny studio in a modern red-brick building. A mixing desk was already in place, so the Reids just brought in effects equipment and made themselves at home in their own time, with no one breathing down their necks. David Cavanagh of *Select* magazine visited the studio in 1992 and, as the Reids were mid-rehearsal, he took the opportunity to nose around.

'The loo downstairs, contrary to nervous premonitions,' he wrote, 'is a model of sophistication and hygiene. The kitchen is pristine white and user-friendly. There's a packet of herbal tea with some digestives nearby and – for those occasional moments of ill-health – some sachets of Lemsip.'

Most days would begin relatively late, with the brothers meeting at either one of their respective homes in North London before William drove them down to the studio, having recently learned to drive. (He was rather put out by the number of people who appeared surprised by the idea of him behind the wheel of a car. 'I couldn't help feeling insulted,' he told *Vox*. 'I mean, there are people I know who I can't imagine driving a car, but that's because they're pretty much semi-retarded.')

Alan Moulder, now the Mary Chain's go-to engineer, would make his own way there to help the Reids set the studio up. He recalls that the Reids' first priority was to get a television set installed in the control room. 'They had the TV on constantly. We made the studio really homely. We spent some days just assembling Ikea furniture.'

William was in his element; finally the Mary Chain didn't have to be 'creative on demand'. As William observed, it seemed ludicrous to have a studio booked for a specific date, only to hope that they would be feeling creative and productive that day. The Reids would develop their songs together in the studio rather than turning up with finished songs, ready to record. 'You can find yourself with a week's studio time booked, but no ideas to work on,' William explained to *Vox*'s Alan Jackson.

'Now we can work when we want and for however long it takes. I know we're not the first people to think of it, but I'm surprised this way of working doesn't occur to more bands.'

*

Laurence Verfaillie, meanwhile, who had been at Jim's side since 1985 and had helped the band however she could, started to pull away. She'd been offered a job by Alan McGee to take care of PR for Creation Records, replacing Jeff Barrett, who founded the Heavenly Recordings label.

Laurence says: 'My interview with Alan went like this: "Alan, I don't speak good enough English, and I hate the press . . ." "Great! You're hired!"'

It had been some years since Jim Reid and Alan had crossed paths, and, while Jim was not entirely comfortable with Laurence's new post as a PR for other bands, ultimately her new role would be a factor in bringing the former friends back together.

'I never felt comfortable about them falling out,' Laurence says. 'Jim was missing Alan a lot. But they all became friends again at a secret gig by The Sugarcubes at the Borderline. Jim was a bit drunk, Alan was also a bit drunk. They ended up talking and things got back to normal.'

However, one of the problems ushered in by Laurence working with Creation was that The Jesus and Mary Chain were increasingly seen as the old guard, while a new wave of so-called shoegazing groups was emerging. The Reids felt left out, and the fact that Laurence, their ally, was furthering the careers of up-and-coming bands led to increased paranoia.

'They started feeling threatened, stupidly, by the new bands,' Laurence explains. 'And what was I doing? It might be a bit over the top, but it felt like while I was getting all these front covers for the Creation bands, I was digging the Mary Chain's grave a bit deeper.'

Laurence would agree that the press had largely dropped the Mary Chain in favour of newer, younger groups such as Lush (with Philip King on bass), Curve, St Etienne and Ride – all groups who, ironically, were influenced by the Mary Chain. Primal Scream meanwhile, the jewel in Creation's crown at this point, had released *Screamadelica* – an instant hit now rightly hailed as a classic, their shift from indie to acid house proving to be a fortuitous move. Creatively and in terms of profile, this was proving to be a golden era for Creation (although financially it couldn't quite be described thus; My Bloody Valentine album *Loveless*, released not long after *Screamadelica* in 1991, left the label teetering towards bankruptcy, a merger with Sony hauling Creation back from the brink). The early 1990s would also be defined by the birth of Britpop – with Blur, The Charlatans, Supergrass, Inspiral Carpets and, most notably, Oasis (soon to be picked up and given their big break by McGee) as its swaggering kings, booting aside everything in their path.

Neil Taylor says: 'Many of the more studious, inward-looking pioneers of what went on to be called indie, their ideas were taken almost lock, stock and barrel by Britpop, polished up and expanded. The Britpop bands got the lot, the riches, the spoils.'

The band's US manager Jerry Jaffe felt it didn't help that the Mary Chain were so adamantly anti-showbiz. This is, of course, a rare quality – basically, they had integrity. But in terms of staying afloat, as Jerry observes, they didn't always help their own cause. 'Almost everybody else walked the tightrope between being anti-establishment and commercial,' says Jerry. 'I don't think the Mary Chain knew how to walk that line, and so they never really got the following that they should have.

'If they were in the internet era, perhaps they could have got a viral following and they would have been big enough to counteract what they did to not ingratiate themselves with the powers that be.'

*

The most recent release for the Mary Chain had been the 'Rollercoaster' EP; it was unveiled in September 1990 and included a cover of Leonard Cohen's 'Tower Of Song'. By the end of summer 1991, work began in earnest on *Honey's Dead*, 'the last sober album,' says Jim. 'Sober and without drugs. We still had that industrious, do-the-job thing. That record was made relatively quickly, in about two months.'

Still, the Reids were enjoying having their own studio to work from; they had time and space to just play and experiment, something they couldn't do to the same extent in a studio before. 'We were teaching each other things and learning together,' Alan Moulder says. 'We were messing around with loops and synths, sampling and triggering guitars and vocals. It was great fun and we felt we were doing something new.'

A new addition to the Mary Chain periphery, later joining the group as a touring musician, was Curve drummer Steve Monti. As always, the degrees of separation were few – not only had the Mary Chain's paths crossed with Curve in the past, but the lead singer, Toni Halliday, was in a relationship with Alan Moulder. Monti was, according to Jim, 'a great drummer, but I'm not sure whether he was right for the Mary Chain'.

Jim adds: 'Monti reminded me a bit of what Murray Dalglish might have been like as a grown-up. He was a nice bloke, a bit too much into the musicianship. I believe that the vibe and attitude is everything. You can learn to play guitar and sound like Eric Clapton, but why would you want to when you can pick up the guitar and not know anything about it and just do something really mental? That's my brother. He's done things that nobody would think of had they had a guitar lesson.'

While, as always, the Reids relied upon those in the inner circle to put them in touch with potential band members, they already knew Monti's playing and could trust him to record his drum parts without them having to hover over him. Quite the opposite, in fact. 'This is why I was able to do nine tracks in such a short time period,' explains Monti. 'Jim and William were laid back and let me follow my own drumming ideas without interfering. That was something I always liked about them.'

Despite recording generally being a stressful process for the Mary Chain, there were light moments and, most importantly, some classic Mary Chain songs were recorded during the making of *Honey's Dead*. The album, which remains a favourite of the Reids, would include songs such as 'Far Gone And Out'; 'Almost Gold'; 'Teenage Lust', a sleazy portrait of virginity lost; and the brilliantly profane 'Reverence'. Several sacred cows slain with one swipe.

'"Reverence" is a wannabe song,' William explained to *NME*'s Simon William. 'There's a glamour in dying, like Jesus Christ and John F Kennedy are two of the most glamorous deaths in the history of the world. I certainly don't want to die like a 75-year-old man in a bedsit in Hackney.'

'Reverence', the first single from the album, was released in February 1992, reaching number 10 in the UK chart. (And, as Alan McGee points out with pride in *Creation Stories*, the Mary Chain were flanked by Ride at number 9 with 'Leave Them All Behind' and Primal Scream at number 11 with their *Dixie-Narco* EP. A 'royal flush' of bands signed by McGee.) This admirably perverse choice of single was a deliberate two fingers to everyone who had shrugged them off, stonewalled them, banned them. Now they were at least giving the music industry a real reason to get hot under the collar. This track had it all: controversial death-wish lyrics (*I wanna die just like Jesus Christ . . . I wanna die just like JFK*) delivered in orgasmic moans. A menacing groove that whacked sneering Britpop around the head before calmly pushing it straight out of a high-rise window. A heavy, hypnotic middle eight that paid tribute to Iggy's 'I Wanna Be Your Dog'. Uncompromising religious themes being more mercilessly subverted than ever. But it wasn't blasphemous, according to William.

'To me, "blasphemous" means to show disrespect, even hatred, toward God,' William told *Interview*'s Bradley Bardin. 'I've never felt that way . . . Another thing these middle-class Bible-thumpers forget is that Jesus was a man. Jesus maybe had an affair with Mary Magdalene. I mean, Jesus had a hard-on, Jesus was flesh and blood and bones.' In reality, there was little for said 'Bible-thumpers' to complain about at all if they really listened to the lyrics. The Reids made references to religion, and that was seen as subversive in itself, but the words themselves weren't disrespectful. 'Even a lyric like "I want to die like Jesus Christ" from "Reverence",' argued Jim. 'I mean, that's probably a fantasy of 100,000 Catholic priests. They probably go to bed at night and dream of being nailed to crosses.'

Ultimately, when it came down to the matter of personal faith, the brothers were divided.

Death still seems to be as much of a taboo subject as religion when it comes to songwriting, and it irritated the Reids that, thanks to the 'Walt Disney attitude' in pop music, it was acceptable to write a book about death, but not a song. 'I don't see any reason why pop music can't be more than three-minute throwaway rubbish,' Jim said at the time. Whether you believed death was final or a portal to another plane, the certainty and also the mystery of our own expiry is a perennially fascinating theme – and thanks to the output of The Jesus and Mary Chain, pop had its very own musical memento mori. While other groups gave nary a nod to existentialism, the Reids and their admirers (such as the Pixies, Nine Inch Nails and Nirvana) could be relied upon to remind us of the old inevitable.

'Maybe that's why death creeps into our songs a lot,' said William. 'Everyone runs around as if it's never going to happen, everything else seems to be important in people's lives – sex, money, love – but death's one of the things people don't respond well to. It's going to happen to you, me . . . It doesn't depress me.'

Jim declared religious belief to be a 'sort of mental illness', while William insisted he believed in God, 'but it's like, "What if there's no God? What if God doesn't like me?"'

★

The Reids were stunned by the success of 'Reverence', although it was still banned from *Top of the Pops*. The Mary Chain were never invited back after they upset the show's producers five years earlier, drunkenly miming to 'April Skies', but even the video for 'Reverence' was snubbed. Infamous pop-culture series *The Word*, however, could be relied upon to embrace the single, and they even had the band on to play it live. (It's worth finding this on YouTube for obvious reasons, but also because, thanks to the studio audience, it's a masterclass in early 1990s dancing. There are flapping elbows and flopping fringes and a great deal of loping on the spot. Thankfully, the Mary Chain themselves abstain from this sort of caper.)

'Reverence' also provided proof that The Jesus and Mary Chain were still pop's most radical provocateurs. While mainstream audiences slavered over rock bands such as Guns 'n' Roses, a band Jim Reid shrugged off as clichéd, moronic nonsense, the Mary Chain were courting genuine danger with a song like 'Reverence'. The Reids believed they were particularly risking their lives in the US, not least because of the fate-tempting line 'I wanna die just like JFK'. The accompanying video also features the American flag being riddled with bullets. 'Never mind drinking Jack Daniels for breakfast and sleeping with a snake,' Jim sniffed, referring to Guns 'n' Roses guitarist Slash, a renowned reptile-fancier. 'We're inciting someone to shoot us on stage, and knowing our fucking luck it'll happen. Lee Harvey Oswald's cousin will show up in Dallas and we'll be killed. Meanwhile everyone will continue to call Slash "dangerous".'

More mainstream acceptance was due for *Honey's Dead* after its release in March 1992 – *NME*'s Stuart Maconie concluded in his glowing review of the album that 'all is well with the unholy family' – and the release was shortlisted for the inaugural Mercury Music Prize alongside Primal Scream's *Screamadelica*, Jah Wobble's *Rising Above Bedlam*, U2's *Achtung Baby* and St Etienne's *Foxbase Alpha* among others. Primal Scream would win the award. Gongs aren't particularly Mary Chain anyway, but deep down they must have felt at least an amused sense of vindication at being short-listed, considering how left out in the cold they had been feeling around the time of making this album.

After the release of *Honey's Dead*, the Mary Chain would be back in the States for an appearance on *The David Letterman Show* to perform 'Far Gone And Out'. Letterman has always been a fan of the Mary Chain, despite what happened on this particular occasion.

Ben Lurie recalls: 'The first thing was that Jerry Jaffe threw us a great big celebratory party, but due to some mix-up in scheduling he threw the after-show party the night before we went on the show.'

'There were all sorts of temptations,' Jim adds. 'Drugs, all the things that rock'n'roll bands have at their disposal. We got seriously fucked up. I didn't sleep at all that night, I was just twitching around at five in the morning thinking, I don't know where I am . . . I don't remember what city I'm in . . . I don't know if I know what my name is . . .'

William was 'totally freaking out', as his brother puts it, calling Jim's hotel room repeatedly throughout the night to report that he'd been possessed by the devil during the night, then saved by Jesus, only to be possessed by the devil again. The Letterman show was certainly going to be interesting.

A car came to pick up the band from the hotel and take them to the studio, Jim feeling 'as fragile as I've ever felt in my life'. One of the first things they had to do was liaise with the very sober and very chipper house band, who would be playing the Mary Chain's music. The Reids delegated Ben Lurie to communicate with them as best he could.

'I said, "Just play what's on the record." Well, they weren't having any of that,' Ben says. 'They were jazzing it up, and I remember having to tell the bass player to just calm down.'

The bass player was clearly an excitable fellow, and not only were his bright red blazer and gleaming white trousers proving painful for the excruciatingly hungover Reid brothers, his exuberant manner nearly tipped them over the edge.

'This ultra-cheerful bass player came up to me and went, "Wooh!" I literally jumped in the air,' Jim groans. '"Arrgh!! Can you just . . . not do that?" I could hardly talk. I looked over at William and he looked like a little pussycat who'd been run over by a tractor. I looked at Jerry and said, "Get me alcohol or this is not going to happen."' Jerry Jaffe hurried off, returning with two pints of beer. It was all he could find. Jim necked them both.

'It was enough to make me remember who I was and what I was there to do,' says Jim. 'We did it. And you know what? I look back on that and it looks totally together. How? We seriously got away with it.'

Jerry Jaffe remembers that William, still hiding under his trademark explosion of black hair, kept his back to the audience. Meanwhile Jim, furrowing his brow under his auburn Caesar-cut, 'looked like he wanted to be anyplace else. When they finished and they had to shake Letterman's hand, I guess Jim didn't think he was going to do that. David Letterman ended up shaking thin air. I remember him saying, "Oh, what's with these kids?"'

'Oh well,' says Ben. 'It was nice to be in New York anyway.'

24

Rollercoaster, Lollapalooza, Cocaine Blues

The two key words for The Jesus and Mary Chain this year are
'Reverence' and 'Rollercoaster'.
Select magazine, 1992

After the release of *Honey's Dead*, the Mary Chain embarked on one
of their most famous and extensive outings, the Rollercoaster Tour.
Chris Morrison had come up with the concept after being inspired by
Lollapalooza, the pioneering American touring festival, which
features several bands on the same bill as they travel the country – a
'travelling Woodstock', as Jerry Jaffe puts it. Also, as it turned out,
the Mary Chain would end up joining the Lollapalooza line-up itself
that same year.

'For Rollercoaster, we got Dinosaur Jr, My Bloody Valentine and
Blur, equal billing,' Chris Morrison says. 'Total respect to the Mary
Chain's modesty, they didn't think they could do it.' The idea was to
represent three distinct genres in the bands they chose – American rock
with Dinosaur Jr, indie noise with My Bloody Valentine, and Blur were
there as champions of the Baggy phenomenon which bridged the gap
between dance and Britpop.

Laurence Verfaillie, still working with Creation Records, was a veritable queen of indie at this point and, having fallen in love with Blur,
had introduced Jim to their music. During Blur's early days she knew
the band were looking for a manager, and passed this information on to
Chris. 'The rest is history,' says Laurence.

Chris's concept for Rollercoaster was that the Mary Chain would
close the show every night, and the other three groups would circulate.
They would have the same lights, same sound and the same treatment.
He was always amazed that support bands weren't always treated well,

and were generally expected to put up with technical limitations. Apart from anything else, those groups are there to entertain the audience to the best of their abilities, to get the crowd warmed up.

Tickets were priced at a paltry £12.50, and all in all the Rollercoaster tour 'worked', as Chris puts it. 'We played small arenas and we'd have 5,000 people in, so I was quite pleased with the outcome.'

Jim liked the concept for Rollercoaster largely because it was reminiscent of the punk crusades of the late 1970s. 'It reminds me of when The Clash and the Buzzcocks used to do tours together,' he told Miranda Sawyer for *Q*. 'Hopefully, that's the way it'll be and that's the way people will see it. It'll be a good night out. This alt-indie line-up appealed strongly to the fans, although the decision to include Blur was seen as something of a curveball. 'They were the band we took the most flak for,' Jim remembers. 'Everybody was going, "Great line-up, but why Blur?" They were on the way down at that time and it did them the world of good, they came out with a good record after that, *Modern Life Is Rubbish*. The combination of a good record and that tour resurrected them.'

★

For most people, a year like this – with Lollapalooza sandwiched between two long tours – would be hard-going. For the Reids, it nearly sent them out of their minds. Lollapalooza itself was a spinning planet of stress around which everything else circled and occasionally collided. Little about Lollapalooza was appropriate for the Mary Chain, not least the fact that they were given an afternoon slot. Playing in broad daylight would ruin the Mary Chain experience, render the lights and visuals redundant and destroy any chance of creating an atmosphere. The Mary Chain, of all groups, should be allowed to take you over after night has fallen, not in glaring daylight as sun-hatted festival-goers wander about, squinting and aimless.

Jerry Jaffe remembers: 'Lush opened up, whom the Mary Chain were friends with, then second on the bill was Pearl Jam, Jesus and Mary Chain, Soundgarden, Ice Cube, Ministry, Red Hot Chili Peppers. The Mary Chain just thought everybody on this tour was pure mainstream bullshit rock'n'roll.'

'The tour was just unbearable,' says Jim. 'We'd signed up to do it because Lollapalooza was the thing to do. We were worried that we had to go on at two in the afternoon; we relied heavily on our light show and we used to use movies and stuff like that. But you know, fuck it, let's live a little.'

They should have followed their instincts, if only for the sake of their physical and mental health, but they went for it and ended up anaesthetising themselves to the point of near-oblivion to blunt the effects of bombing repeatedly in front of 10,000 people every day for more than two months. 'Lollapalooza knocked the shit out of us,' said William in an interview with *Uncut*. 'It messed with the fragile parts of our minds. We always felt our music was huge, and there it just felt tiny.'

Lollapalooza kicked off on 18 July at the Shoreline Amphitheater in San Francisco for two nights before heading off around the country, taking in Cincinnati, Detroit, Boston, Long Island, Phoenix and everywhere in between before returning to California at the end of August. The Mary Chain would be just about holding it together health-wise, but many of the other groups on the bill, including the Chili Peppers and Soundgarden, were not dissimilar to Nine Inch Nails when it came to how seriously they took their health and, most importantly, their general buffness. The Mary Chain, being more of the pale and determinedly unhealthy persuasion, could not relate.

'The other bands would work out and go to the gym,' Jerry Jaffe says. 'I guess The Jesus and Mary Chain thought alternative bands were supposed to die young, not do push-ups and have personal trainers and be on vegetarian diets. They felt they were the odd men out on that tour.'

Grunge band Pearl Jam, Seattle's energetic rivals to Nirvana, went on before The Jesus and Mary Chain, just after lunchtime. Not the best slot in the world either, one might argue, but this was the tour that launched Pearl Jam – not least because, as Jim admits, 'We made them look great.'

Jim continues: 'The singer, Eddie Vedder, was really dynamic. I kid you not, he climbed up on the lighting rig and was standing on the canopy. People were going nuts. Then the Mary Chain stumble on and scowl at everybody and go "Rrrrgggh" for half an hour and then leave. You could see people leaving and you'd think, "Oh God, we've got ten weeks of this." We tried to switch with Pearl Jam and they didn't want to, obviously.' 'Every single gig was like a little death,' William admitted in an interview with *Raygun*'s Nina Malkin. 'We couldn't create the atmosphere we wanted. Everybody has tricks when they play live; we need darkness, for a start. Playing in the sunshine, the light shining in your eyes and lighting up your red, sweaty face – it was horrible. I felt exposed. I felt that everybody could see the cracks.'

In addition to the indignity of being upstaged by Pearl Jam, and playing to an indifferent crowd, the Reids were disappointed that the so-called democracy of Lollapalooza was not quite as it seemed. All artists were equal, but some were more equal than others. Jim remembers: 'We were told that Red Hot Chili Peppers were bringing an extra PA, so we said, "Can we use it?" "No, they're paying loads of money for it." So we said, "Can we pay loads of money and bring in our extra PA?" "No." What happened to the democracy?

'We started to realise it was a mistake. We tried to get out of it, but then we realised we'd lose our insurance. So that's when I got into cocaine in a big way. I didn't even know what an eightball [a nominal eighth of an ounce of cocaine] was until 1992. I just got off my tits for the whole ten weeks. That was the most unhealthy tour I've ever done.'

Def American (now American Recordings) boss Rick Rubin was present at one of the band's Lollapalooza shows as the drama unfolded yet again, like *Groundhog Day*, for the Mary Chain. Rubin was intrigued by the Reids and saw how difficult it was for them. He suggested to Jaffe while watching from the wings that, instead of trying to play their set to an disinterested crowd, they should just play a 40-minute version of 'Reverence', complete with feedback, and then leave the stage, the guitars still screaming long after their owners had gone.

'Of course we didn't do that,' says Jerry. 'But in hindsight, we should have. That's why I think Rick Rubin's kind of brilliant, he understands the essence of everything. The essence of the Mary Chain is to play that song and let it go on and on with feedback and say, "Fuck you".'

Another element of Lollapalooza that was hard to enjoy was that, although they were travelling across the country, the hotels were almost all attached to out-of-town shopping malls. 'Very grim,' Ben Lurie remembers. 'And Jim and William were fighting a lot. There were times when I'd just disappear to the back of the bus and you'd hear things crashing. Sometimes the vibe in the dressing-room was so bad that I'd just take myself out of it. I think most people did. It was incident after incident.'

One of the main incidents to which Ben refers was the disastrous clash between William and rapper Ice Cube, or rather Ice Cube's posse. 'This was the first time that I saw the whole thing of an entourage,' says Jerry, who was on damage-control duty whether he liked it or not.

William became increasingly irritated by the often abrasive presence of Ice Cube's ever-present gang of sycophants, who would, as Jerry recalls, occasionally stride into the catering tent and knock people's food to the floor, like school bullies. What shocked Jerry the most was not that William lost his patience with them, but that nobody else dared say anything. 'There was no malevolence on William's part, certainly no racist overtones,' says Jerry. 'It was just: "Leave me alone."'

This grating behaviour unfortunately combined with the usual maelstrom of Mary Chain ill-feeling, unlocking something in William and letting a very angry genie out of the bottle. 'This was when William's crazy behaviour started to become an issue,' says Jim. 'Ice Cube's crew were going about with water-guns and soaking everybody. It was irritating, but you've got all these liberal types from the record companies who don't want to upset the rap band.

'They soaked either William or Rona, and William tried to pick a fight. Anyway, it turned out they were quite tough. The guy bottled William, and William came up to me covered in blood saying, "The guy from Ice Cube did this!" I said, "Right, let's go and get those so-and-so's." I can't fight my way out of a paper bag, but when you're drunk, you're Superman. We started looking for the guy that had done this, and then we were told that they were all tooled up on their bus with guns, waiting. I was thinking, Er . . . maybe . . .'

This was not the only Ice Cube-related occurrence on the tour. Ben Lurie doesn't remember it himself, but he was told on good authority that the following story is true. 'Ice Cube's posse used to have fake guns on stage, like assault rifles made of rubber. Apparently I wandered off with one of these guns and into the production office, where the tour managers happened to be doing a cash settlement for the day.'

Stunned at the sight of a wild-eyed, long-haired lunatic wielding what appeared to be an assault rifle, everyone panicked, and Ben almost got shot by someone who had whipped out a real gun. 'One of the US tour managers was packing,' he mutters ruefully.

The tour ended on 28 August 1992 and the Mary Chain, exhausted and somewhat mentally scarred, headed back home. They had two months until they had to return to the US for the second leg of their Rollercoaster tour, this time with Spiritualised and Curve. But this was far from an opportunity for rest and recuperation. 'I still wouldn't get drunk when I was at home, but when we got back I made a few contacts to get coke,' says Jim. 'I'd say by the mid-1990s cocaine was ruling all of my decisions.'

Ben Lurie too was hoovering up copious amounts of cocaine at that time, which cemented the bond between himself and Jim even more firmly. William, on the other hand, preferred weed. Inevitably, this would split the band down the middle. 'There were little camps, those who liked to snort and those who liked to smoke,' says Jim. William apparently started to resent Ben's presence, referring to him as 'Smithers' to Jim's 'Mr Burns', according to Douglas.

'William and Ben loved each other,' says Jim. 'But in my opinion William was a bit unreasonable at that point, and I think anybody who was sane would have agreed with me. Ben called it as he saw it, and William saw that as Ben siding with me. It wasn't like that.'

The Rollercoaster tour swung round again, by which time depression reigned supreme and William's dope-smoking was hitting a peak. The flight between New York and Philadelphia would be action-packed, to say the least. That day, William had bought a sizeable bag of marijuana, and he understandably didn't want to throw it away before boarding. So before they left their hotel, he smoked it. All of it.

William was rather quiet for the rest of the day, although this would soon change. Ben would be sitting next to William on the plane, and, as the long journey wore on, everyone was soon either asleep or gazing silently at the video screens in front of them. All was calm. Until:

'William starts screaming "*Fire!*"' says Ben. 'It's not a good thing to yell on a plane. He'd woken up in this semi-stoned psychotic state and they were showing a news story on the screen – Windsor Castle had had a fire. Everybody was waking up on the plane and Jim's sitting a few rows away thinking, Thank God I'm not sitting next to him. William just wouldn't shut up.'

After a polite but firm request from a steward to 'calm your friend down', Ben finally managed to convince William that the fire blazing in front of his eyes was not incinerating the plane but just one of the many homes of the royal family, and peace was restored.

The Rollercoaster tour was also notable because it would mark the first time Douglas Hart would see the Mary Chain as a member of the audience, with Bobby Gillespie and the KLF's Bill Drummond in tow. It was a strange experience on many levels for Douglas: not only did it sting to see someone else playing bass with the Reids, but he also experienced the funereal backstage Mary Chain atmosphere as a relative outsider.

'It was like going to a wake,' he says. 'If you'd walked in the room and had been blindfolded, and someone asked, "What's just happened here?", you could be given 150 guesses and you wouldn't guess that these guys had just played a rock'n'roll gig.'

'On many tours that's just what it would be like. Sometimes I'd go, "That was a great gig!" and it'd be like, "He humiliated me there!" It wasn't always like that, it was great fun as well. But it just shows you the difference between them and a lot of groups, and thank fuck for that.'

25

Stoned and Dethroned

A couple of times on tour I felt my real role was to stop the Reids
from killing each other.
Steve Monti

Soon after the Rollercoaster tour concluded, plans were afoot for the
recording of a new album: *Stoned & Dethroned* – a title that poetically
but succinctly described the way the Reids were feeling at that time.
This luminous collection of slow, stoner grooves would appropriately
take quite a long time to complete, during which time, according to
Mick Houghton, they were somewhat left behind. 'To some extent, they
had been dethroned by Oasis and Britpop, then grunge put the lid on it.'
The Reids might have taken more kindly to the situation had grunge not
turned out to be something of a disappointment in itself. William Reid:
'When *Nevermind* first happened, people said, "Things are going to be
different now; there are going to be other bands like this." What did you
get instead? Stone Temple Fucking Pilots! Sorry, but I've got enough
money to hire a fucking hit man . . . (Music) is probably healthier now
than it was ten years ago, but not healthy enough.' Creativity aside,
however, the Reids weren't especially healthy at this point themselves
thanks to their now day-long proximity to the pub. The plan was originally to go into the studio for two weeks and record an acoustic album.
But 'it took about two years,' Jim says, 'and we spent most of that time
in the Queen's Head across the road.'

William claimed that, at the time, both he and Jim were also suffering
'breakdowns', and the making of this album was simply 'one long bad
dream'. Jim seems inclined to agree. 'My personal life was starting to

slide, broken relationships and stuff like that, likewise with William. He got it on with Hope [Sandoval, Mazzy Star's lead singer] during that record, but he was still going out with Rona. That got messy, as it would.' William himself would later explain in an interview with musician and friend Dimitri Coats that while he had fallen in love with Hope, 'it was the unhappiest time in my life. It was horrible, horrible, horrible.'

Going into the studio had always been a time of abstinence for the Reids in the past, and that clarity had served them well. But, for the first time, this sober industriousness went well and truly out of the window with *Stoned & Dethroned*, as the title itself indicates.

'We must have got tanked up one day and then did a good day's work,' Jim surmises. 'Then you think, "Fuck, that's the answer!", and you spend three weeks at the pub and then think, "Why are we in Elephant and Castle again? Oh yeah, that record!" It was a hard way to go about getting it, but it was a bloody good record.'

William's difficult split from Rona, his girlfriend of nine years, also gave the elder Reid an excuse to 'dive headlong into fucking degeneracy', as he admitted in his 2000 interview with *Uncut*'s Nick Hasted. But incredibly, neither bouts of depression nor alcohol abuse affected his ability to write songs. 'Music comes from your higher self,' he explains. 'I never lost the drive to make music. I'd be lying in a pool of vomit, wake up feeling like the biggest piece of shit in the world, play a tape of what I'd done the night before, and be amazed it worked.'

With Alan Moulder, producer/engineer Dick Meaney, Ben Lurie and drummer Steve Monti in tow, the Reids created something that would become an enduring classic. The record was certainly worth the wait as far as fans were concerned, even if it wasn't immediately lauded by the press. One especially compelling element of the new record was that they had finally decided to go back to a live sound after making three albums with mostly programmed drums.

'We didn't use click tracks or machines,' says Monti. 'Sometimes it was just me playing with William on guitar. It was an enjoyable process, sparse and organic compared with the recording of *Honey's Dead*. Dick [Meany] was quite experimental, and we set up my drums in different places to get a different sound. At one point I was playing in the stairwell.'

Honey's Dead might have been the Mary Chain's 'last sober album', but there was still an element of discipline in the making of *Stoned & Dethroned*, or at least something of a routine. Those keen to preserve the rock'n'roll myth in their minds, look away now.

'We'd turn up at the Drugstore,' Ben remembers, 'and then, around 12.30, go up the road to Marks & Spencer and buy lunch, go back and work all afternoon. Microwave our dinner, have half an hour off – Dick liked to watch *Brookside* – and then work for a few hours and go home. Then on Friday night, there wasn't really anywhere to go, so we'd go to Pizza Hut for a treat. If fans knew, it would have totally blown the mystique.' Mystique duly blown. Oh well.

The relationship between the Reids was deteriorating, however; even their relationships with themselves seemed to be on a downward turn. The melodic strength of *Stoned & Dethroned* is balanced by bittersweet themes and quiet cry-for-help songs such as 'Save Me', 'God Help Me' and 'Hole'. But something that helped the brothers rein in their mutual irritation was the presence of those from outside of the usual circle during these sessions. *Stoned & Dethroned* would be the Mary Chain's first album to feature collaborations with other artists, most famously on the bright, velvety boy-girl ballad 'Sometimes Always', sung by Jim with Hope Sandoval (although Jim would get quite irritated by her too). Hope was already a 'good friend' of William's at that point, to quote the party line, but the rumour that they were dating soon proved to be correct.

The other collaboration on *Stoned & Dethroned* would be 'God Help Me', a tender ballad reminiscent in both melody and sentiment of Television's 'Guiding Light'. Shane McGowan of The Pogues would take care of vocals on 'God Help Me,' or at least he would once Jim Reid finally pinned him down. When it came to drunkenness, the Reids had met their match in MacGowan, and it took time to secure him for a session.

'We sent him a demo months before,' Jim says. 'I would call him up. I'd go, "Shane? It's Jim," and he'd say, "What? Jim who?" "Jim from the Mary Chain. Did you get the demo?" "What demo?" I'd go, "We sent you a demo, you said you would sing with us . . ." "Oh! No, I haven't listened to it yet." So I'd say, "I'll call you tomorrow." And for about a month it would be exactly the same every time I called. "Shane? It's Jim." "What? Jim who?" Over and over again.'

A meeting was finally arranged at the Good Mixer pub in Camden, then a haunt of the boozed-up stars of Britpop, and Jim, William and Mick Houghton turned up to meet possibly the palest man in rock'n'roll. Nervous, Jim downed a few whiskies and 'was swaying by the time Shane arrived', as he remembers, safe in the knowledge that Shane would probably arrive in the same state. 'But Shane arrived stone cold sober,' Jim laughs. But after buying Shane his drink of choice – a quadruple whiskey – the plan to record 'God Help Me' was soon arranged. However, Shane still hadn't learned the song by the time it came to lay down his vocal.

'It was, "Shane, shall we go for a take?" "What does it go like?"' Jim says. 'Anyway, after many takes and playing the tape to Shane, he got it and it was fucking magic.'

Another stand-out track on *Stoned & Dethroned* is the song 'Bullet Lovers', inspired by a news clip William had seen while on tour in Los Angeles two years previously. 'It was bizarre,' he told *Melody Maker* in 1994. 'There were two guys being interviewed, without any disguises, and they were drive-by killers. I was lying in bed having breakfast, and I was thinking, This is live, the police could be on their way to get you, you dumb motherfuckers. One of them, when he shot people, his girlfriend got so horny that they'd go off somewhere and fuck.' Sex and death: inspiring William Reid's songwriting since 1982.

While *Stoned & Dethroned* was in the making, the Mary Chain released the compilation *The Sound Of Speed*, their first collection since *Barbed Wire Kisses*. *The Sound Of Speed* featured singles and rarities including covers of 'Little Red Rooster', 'My Girl' and 'Guitarman', an acoustic version of the *Honey's Dead* track 'Teenage Lust', and 'Write Record Release Blues', which deftly describes the Reids' weariness at the perpetual dilemma of being in-demand, pressured pop stars who don't relish the schmoozing side of the business.

Also on the compilation, which would come out in August 1993, were 'Snakedriver' and 'Something I Can't Have', two tracks recorded with The Gun Club's Nick Sanderson, the drummer they had rejected at audition some years before. The EP *Sound Of Speed*, featuring the tracks with Nick, would be unveiled just prior to the collection and the Mary Chain, therefore, had to greet their public, something they were in no mood to do. Antagonism behind the scenes was mounting, not least because of William's new relationship and a growing wariness regarding the machinations of a music industry that was moving on without them. They emerged into the limelight growling, wired and paranoid.

To coincide with the release of *Sound Of Speed*, The Jesus and Mary Chain were invited to appear on the long-running, hugely popular music show *Later . . . With Jools Holland* to perform 'Snakedriver'. The show would provide excellent exposure, and the Mary Chain were even looking forward to it. It was good to be back at BBC Television Centre. They might have been banned from *Top of the Pops* back in 1987, but they were older now and more experienced, although that didn't mean they were drinking less. Unfortunately, technical difficulties, gallons of booze and the resulting turmoil culminated in yet another entry in the Mary Chain's 'catalogue of fucking disasters', as Jim puts it.

'We got there all bright-eyed and bushy-tailed,' says Jim. 'We did everything we were told to do, but there were technical problems when it came to the Mary Chain. We did a rehearsal in the afternoon and it was spot on, and then you do the show. They go round everybody, and then when it came to us it was, "Ah right, fuck it, we can't fix this."'

'At first everyone just thought it was the Mary Chain being difficult but it was the monitors that the show had hired in,' adds Ben. 'So they did the show as if it was live, introduced the Mary Chain – except we weren't there, because they couldn't film our bit. Once it was all over, at around 10 or 11 p.m., they were going to fix the problem and film our bit as though we were part of the show.'

The Mary Chain had been at Television Centre for twelve hours by this point, and through sheer boredom, much of that time had been spent drinking. By the time they were required again, Jim was, unsurprisingly, 'slaughtered. By midnight I can hardly stand, and then I start getting paranoid: "How come everybody else got treated OK?"'

One of the other artists featured on the show was Paul Weller, who had, as you may remember, bumped into the band six years earlier at the BBC when they were both on *Top of the Pops*, making an obscene gesture behind their backs as they passed. During the hours of downtime, the Reids wandered outside into the iconic 'doughnut' courtyard and an argument ensued. As always, no one remembers why it happened; perhaps it was just something to do. Just in time, Weller, who had noted their technical difficulties during the rehearsal, decided to wade in to offer some helpful advice.

Jim says: 'Me and William were screaming at each other, then Weller came by and went, "Mate, you shouldn't put your hands on the microphone, that's what makes it feed back." And then he walked away. Me and William just fell about laughing. It defused the situation.'

Finally it was time to try for a take. 'By that time I'm wobbling,' Jim says. 'And I was feeling hard done by, and I'm swinging at these £50,000 cameras . . . But we did it. William's guitar was great, my singing was awful, everybody was fucked off with us. Everybody. Management, record company, the BBC . . . I remember waking up with the most horrendous hangover the next day, and that feeling when you can't remember exactly what you did, but you know that you made an absolute fucking disgrace of yourself.'

*

By the following year the Mary Chain would still be completing the B-sides for *Stoned & Dethroned*, but they had at least put out 'Sometimes Always', sung by Jim and Hope, in July 1994 as the lead single. It reached number 22 in the charts.

'I'd written this song that sounded to me like Lee Hazlewood and Nancy Sinatra,' William told *Melody Maker*. 'We'd always liked Hope's voice. We asked her years ago to be on one of the records, but there was never a song that suited. Then this one came along and it felt right. At first I felt it was a bit too cute, too light a story. But when we recorded it, Hope and Jim sang and they just transcended it.' The demo was still 'bleak', though, in William's opinion, and even when they had recorded the track the Reids were surprised it worked as a single.

It was decided that a new bass player was called for in time for the album launch on 15 August 1994 (almost exactly ten years since the band's first gig at the Living Room), with Ben Lurie moving back to guitar. As usual, the auditions weren't the easiest of processes, and Lincoln Fong, formerly their live sound engineer, was eventually brought back into the fold. At that point Lincoln had been working with a group called Moose, who were 'having a quiet period'.

The launch took place at the famous Soho club Madame Jojo's, formerly a louche, colourful haunt for drag queens but now frequently used for gigs and club nights. Shane MacGowan joined the Mary Chain to sing 'God Help Me', turning up to rehearse at the soundcheck with, Steve Monti recalls, 'a clinking Sainsbury's carrier bag full of booze. He was swaying, and I was convinced he wouldn't make it on to the stage, let alone sing the song. He managed it.

'After we played I said, "I'll buy you a drink,"' continues Monti. 'But he was reluctant to go out there because he didn't want to be mobbed.' Monti headed backstage to the dressing-rooms, used more frequently by kitsch cabaret performers than moribund rock stars. It was full of all manner of disguises, albeit conspicuous ones. 'I put a wig on Shane that I found among the transvestite gear and he went out with me, wearing this huge camp wig,' says Monti. 'Of course everyone recognized him, but he wore the wig all night.' Comedy toupees at a Mary Chain gig. This had to be a first. And no doubt a last.

The *NME*'s David Quantick hailed *Stoned & Dethroned* as 'Iggy Pop's country album or Bob Dylan's Lou Reed tribute,' but Mick Houghton, whose final press campaign for the Mary Chain was for this album, felt that while the record was great, 'it never got appraised properly at the time. They made a beautifully crafted record, but it was a record the press didn't want them to make. Had they not taken so long and stuck to the plan, it might have been different.'

The Mary Chain worked in their own sweet time, but the media had meanwhile been swept off their feet by a new wave of Britpop, shoegaze and grunge bands. Things had changed. William, however, now felt relatively serene about the shifts that had taken place while they were making their album. 'I think we always felt more connected to what was going on than we do now,' he told *Melody Maker*'s Kevin Westerberg. 'Now I realise we've always been disconnected from everything. So if we go away for two years, and there's five new fashions in that time, I feel like it doesn't matter to us.'

Stoned & Dethroned, in a way, seems to draw a line in the sand – there's a feeling of the Reids rising above the past; the Mary Chain were coming of age. Talking to *Interview* after the album's release, Jim admitted the record reflected 'the end result of the old lifestyle', and William expanded on the theme: 'On a song like "Girlfriend" which is about drugs and junkies, the guy's leaving the girl because she's fucked-up, and he's decided he's not any more. Maybe you see that as us saying, "Enough is enough". You can only be fucked-up for so long before you realise you're gonna have to not be so fucked-up or you're gonna die. It has something to do with getting older.'

On *Stoned & Dethroned* it was possible to detect at times a growing sense of self-acceptance, packaged in self-deprecating humour – such as in the slow, swaying 'Feeling Lucky' ('I've got someone who knows me/ And still wants to hold me'). The youthful arrogance that the Mary Chain did so well had morphed into something a little mellower, albeit still powerful.

While the Reid brothers were feeling philosophical about some aspects of their lives, something they weren't too comfortable with was the fact that Chris Morrison, then their manager, was also managing the now hugely successful Blur. The Reids liked Blur – they had invited them on the Rollercoaster tour when others wrinkled their noses at them, after all – but the Reids finally decided to let their manager go, because, as Chris remembers it, they felt they would be overshadowed.

'Which was a mistake,' says Chris. 'I was gutted to see them go. I was very fond of the Mary Chain. They're a couple of complete lunatics. They made great music. Some of their stuff was remarkable. There were idiosyncrasies that were a nightmare at first, but it was a great time.'

There was no replacement in mind; in fact, William didn't want a manager at all. They attempted to work with Charlie Charlton, Suede's manager, and Bennie Brongers, who used to be the Mary Chain's tour manager, but as Ben Lurie remembers, 'William was really against it, and in the end he put his foot down and said, "I don't want anyone to manage us." And really, we were just an unmanageable mess at that stage.'

An American tour was booked for October and November. The support act? Hope Sandoval's group Mazzy Star. As a result, William and Hope wouldn't have to be separated, which didn't sit well with Jim. One concern was that this latest development made William hard to track down as the couple kept going off on their own. This was also the first time Steve Monti had toured with the Reids – he'd been part of the Rollercoaster tour with Curve, but beyond sneaking into the Mary Chain's dressing-room to polish off some of their rider, he hadn't really had the Mary Chain touring experience.

'The tour didn't get off to a great start,' Monti admits. 'It was a different vibe to what I was used to. They didn't seem to get a buzz from performing, even when it was a great gig.'

On 18 October, Monti was celebrating (as best he could) his birthday, and he had every intention of enjoying the gig that night. Dream on, birthday boy. 'William got pissed off with something, kicked one of my cymbals and said something abusive,' Monti says. 'After the gig, they were all sitting around being morose and I did something I never do: I got really angry, I even punched a hole in the ceiling. I accused William of never enjoying gigs. It was the start of the tour and it already felt like a year. I was worried that the rest of the seven weeks was going to be hell.'

Monti concluded his tirade by announcing that he would be leaving the band the following day, which apparently shocked William into trying to placate him and Monti completed the tour. There would be no dreaded drummer auditions mid-tour for the Reids.

However, a Reid-Reid fight was on its way that would have the other members of the band concerned that it was over for good. On 27 November the Mary Chain and Mazzy Star were booked to play the Roxy in Los Angeles, Hope's home city. Jim says: 'The period after *Stoned & Dethroned,* that was when William and I started to not understand each other's direction. He was going out with Hope and I didn't hit it off with her. Maybe I was a bit hard on her. She could be a bit prima donna-ish, but a lot of it was naïve and innocent, although I didn't see it at the time.

'I remember in LA, after the sound-check William was going back to Hope's and I said, "You're not going to have time to go there and come back for the gig." He said, "No, I'll be all right." He rolled up about five minutes after show-time and I was so pissed off, I screamed at them. Hope just kind of stamped her foot and marched out.'

'William just said, "Fuck you. I'm not going on stage until I'm drunk," Monti adds. 'So we all had to sit there in the dressing-room watching him drink Jack Daniel's while the clock ticked. Every now and then I dared to ask, "Are you drunk yet?" Finally he was ready so we could do the gig.'

Seething, Jim marched on stage and growled into the microphone, 'William's had too much to drink.' Not to be outdone, William retorted, 'And Jim's a fucking prick.'

'They were the kings of stage banter,' says Lincoln Fong, who was watching it all unfold just feet away from him on stage. 'Sometimes it was hard not to laugh when it kicked off. The show went well though.'

Looking back, Jim is philosophical, not to mention contrite. 'I think I was the idiot there. I think back to what the Mary Chain was about – so what that he rolled up five minutes late? There was no harm done, I just wanted to make a point.

'There were a lot of things like that with Hope, and I don't think she meant any harm, but it ruffled my feathers, and I would make stands over things that, as I look back on them, I don't think were important. I probably should have cut her some slack.'

26

Love, Hate, a Departure and a Homecoming

By the time it got to [final album] Munki, *we'd argue about anything. It was 'Do you want a cup of tea?' 'No, coffee.' 'Why do you want coffee?' It just wasn't going to work.*
Jim Reid to Thomas H Green of *The Arts Desk*, 2010

The Mary Chain were soon 'pregnant', as Laurence Verfaillie put it, with their sixth studio album, and it would be the longest and most difficult birth yet, with neither Reid prepared to hold the other's hand throughout the anguish. Still, there was an abundance of powerful songs to choose from for what would be the last Mary Chain studio album to date.

The brothers were more divided than ever, and William's seething dissatisfaction with the music industry was never more evident; he even wrote a song to prove it: 'I Hate Rock'n'Roll'. Released in May 1995, it detailed starkly how William had increasingly been feeling over the past decade. The Reids were always honest in their lyrics, but while William's words in particular were usually open to interpretation, this time the message was cold and literal.

William doesn't flinch from naming names either – MTV, BBC . . . ('I love the BBC/I love it when they're pissing on me/And I love MTV/I love it when they're shitting on me.') Euphemisms and thinly veiled references would have no place in this song. Some would feel he was biting the hand that had kept him in beer and weed for quite some time, but William wanted to reveal the other side of the music industry for all to see.

'When you work for a living,' he explained, 'you get fucked with from nine to five. When you're in a band, you get fucked with 24 hours a day on every continent in the world. Even when you're sleeping you're being fucked with somewhere. I wish I didn't have to write this type of song.'

It was of course the business of rock'n'roll, rather than rock'n'roll itself, that William was lambasting in this song, which poured out of him in five minutes flat. 'I came into this industry as an idealist,' he told *Rolling Stone* in 1995. 'I thought I was going to make art, but I got that kicked out of my system after about ten minutes, when we did our first single for Warners and they asked us to turn down the feedback and turn up the voice and drums for a radio mix. That felt to me like somebody saying, "Hey, Picasso, could you redo this painting, because there's a nipple in it, and we want to show it to schoolchildren."'

William felt resentment towards the music industry not just because he didn't want to compromise his art, but because their success – and the Mary Chain really did want success – largely depended on how much money could (or would) be spent on promotion.

'I have an acquaintance in an American record company who is in charge of Sheryl Crow,' William said in an interview with *Rockin' On*, 'and I hear that, if you're lucky, you can spend $1.5 million on promotion for one record. But we can only spend $180,000. If we had had that amount of money at first, we would have sold hundreds of times more records. I envy big bands like REM; sometimes I'm driven by envy and think, damn it, I want to sell twenty million copies too, but this is the way this business is.'

'I Hate Rock'n'Roll' would be the first single released from the Mary Chain's third compilation album, *Hate Rock'n'Roll*, which included the tracks 'Snakedriver' and 'I'm In With The Out Crowd'. This compilation, released in September 1995, would also, although they didn't know it at the time, be the band's final release on Blanco Y Negro.

'I Hate Rock'n'Roll' launched a new chapter for the Mary Chain in that it marked the inclusion of the band's newest member – Nick Sanderson. Nick locked in with The Jesus and Mary Chain more than most despite a shaky start to their relationship, although that undoubtedly had more to do with the circumstances around the Reids at the time. 'We were on a tour after Lollapalooza, and Nick was back in the picture,' Jim explains. 'Everybody was tense. For some reason we still didn't hit it off with Nick, but Nick, I didn't realise, was nervous and trying to impress us. We hardly said two words to him. He bore a grudge about that for years. Sorry, Nick . . .

'But Nick was one of the greatest drummers I've ever met. He wasn't a great technical drummer, but it came from somewhere in his gut. It always sounded just right for the Mary Chain.'

'Monti was great, but Nick was the most exciting drummer I've ever worked with,' adds Ben Lurie. 'I mean, he'd speed up incredibly during a song. There was one song on *Munki*, "Degenerate", and he did this fantastic take, but it just got so fast. The engineer sent off the tapes to have it duplicated with somebody slowing it down as it went. It just brought it back on track.' Whatever works.

By this time Nick's own group Earl Brutus was well underway. Combining influences such as The Fall, Kraftwerk and glam-rock, their live shows were something to behold, always highly visual, high-octane and loud. They remain one of Jim's all-time favourite bands, and their gigs had plenty in common with the Mary Chain in terms of the atmosphere – there was always an underlying sensation that, as Jim says, 'something bad might happen'.

'Nick said, "We're playing at the Café de Paris on Saturday." I said, "What's your band like?" And he said, "We wear pastel-blue safari suits and have our names written in neon in front of us." They spent a fortune on these neon signs, then they all got drunk and broke them; it was great! But when he said "safari suits", I thought, That sounds awful. That sounds bloody *awful*.

'They'd get these weird gigs. They played at the Austrian embassy one time and there were people coming up to the stage trying to punch them – it was surreal. They were brilliant, they should have been bigger.'

By the time 'I Hate Rock'n'Roll' hit the charts, reaching number 61, the Mary Chain were on their latest tour, which did at least guarantee them some time in the sun. The band initially flew to New Zealand to play the first date of the tour in Auckland, only to discover the gig had been called off. This gave the Mary Chain a chance to relax in warm, idyllic surroundings; an unusual way to start a tour.

'Auckland is a beautiful city on the water,' Ben explains. 'We thought it would be nice to rent a little boat, so we set off down the road and pulled in at this little marina.

'When I think about it, three guys wearing black, wandering out of some hired car, and Jim and William asking in strong Scottish accents if they could hire someone's boat . . . it's no wonder no one let us have one.' Ordinarily, the Mary Chain weren't adept at making the most of the sometimes heavenly locations they found themselves in. Perhaps angst and exhaustion made it harder to enjoy the beauty around them, perhaps it was because they assumed they would probably return, or, perhaps, as Ben Lurie suggests, they were 'just idiots', we can't know for sure. A perfect example of this would be their trip to Hawaii: on a day off, the crew rented a car and explored the island, however, Jim and Ben went to the cinema and sat in the dark, watching a movie about the island instead.

*

The summer of 1995 would also see the Mary Chain crossing paths with Paul Weller yet again, this time at the Dessel Graspop Festival in Belgium. The Jesus and Mary Chain were headlining, but, as Ben recalls, 'We got word that Paul Weller was having a hissy fit because he wanted to headline. I remember sitting at a table in catering next to his dad, a big ex-boxer, saying if he got his hands on the Mary Chain he was going to . . . whatever. I was sitting there thinking, I'm right here, dude! That's how well known our faces are.'

After some considerable bristling of egos, Bennie Brongers, the Mary Chain's tour manager at the time (now managing Suede), discovered that whoever did headline would be going on very late, by which time the public transport taking people away from the festival site would have finished for the night. 'He was of the opinion that most people were going to leave after the second to last act anyway,' says Ben Lurie.

When Bennie explained the situation to the Mary Chain, it was agreed that this was a solution that would ensure everyone had their way, supposedly. By the time Weller realised going on last at Dessel wasn't maybe such a great idea, the Mary Chain would already have left. And so Weller was informed that the Mary Chain were graciously giving up their headline slot for him.

'So, we did our show and were about to leave, then it started raining,' Ben Lurie says. 'Some rain dripped into the desk, which blew, and they had to delay Weller for a couple more hours.' Sure enough, thanks to the rain and lack of public transport, everyone had left by the time Weller hit the stage. Be careful what you wish for.

★

Work slowly continued on the new album once the Mary Chain returned home and reconvened with engineers Alan Moulder and Dick Meaney at the Drugstore. The Mary Chain's sixth album would, like *Stoned & Dethroned*, feature guest appearances from other artists, including Hope Sandoval (on the track 'Perfume', with William), Gallon Drunk's Terry Edwards on trumpet, and the Reids' younger sister and official peacemaker Linda, who would sing the song 'Moe Tucker' on a later session. Linda, also known as Sister Vanilla (so named by William because of her ice-cream-pale skin) had been present at the recording of most of her brothers' previous albums, but this time she would also provide the title of the LP, *Munki*. The Reids wanted something 'un-Mary Chain-like', which meant no honey, no candy and no guns. The idea was also to have something 'less dark, miserable, rain-drenched, all the things we're usually seen as,' Jim explained. Linda was going through a phase of being 'obsessed with monkeys', as she puts it, and the phonetic spelling gave it an odd, ambiguous quality.

Terry Edwards, a well-known multi-instrumentalist from East London who began his professional career playing with The Higsons, had long been a fan of the Mary Chain. He'd even made an EP of cover versions of Jesus and Mary Chain songs in 1991, titled *Terry Edwards Plays The Music Of Jim And William Reid*. The EP quickly reached the ears of the Reids themselves thanks to Laurence Verfaillie passing the cassette on after Edwards sent a copy to Creation. The band approved, ordering a boxful to give to people they knew. Terry was an obvious choice when it came to looking for a horn player.

The tracks Terry would play on were 'I Love Rock'n'Roll' and the eerie ballad 'Man On The Moon', a silvery paean to alienation, both written by Jim. 'I Love Rock'n'Roll' was a direct answer to William's 'I Hate Rock'n'Roll', and while William was convinced this response was a deliberate dig, Jim simply felt that, after years living as rock stars (which, at times, probably wasn't *too* bad), it was 'worth showing the other side of the coin'. William's furious swipe at the music industry got Jim thinking.

'I thought, I love rock'n'roll, and I do love rock'n'roll – so does William. But to this day William still thinks I only wrote that song to piss him off. At the time, though, I might have given him that impression. "Yeah, you're right. I did . . ." But I didn't. Rock'n'roll changed our life.'

When Terry Edwards first arrived at the Drugstore, he was, he admits, 'uncharacteristically five minutes late'. This prompted everyone immediately to head to the pub. 'Five-minute grace period,' laughs Terry. 'I got there and the pints had just started. That was my memory of first getting in there to play.'

Once it was finally time to return, lubricated, to the studio, Jim explained to Terry what he wanted for 'I Love Rock'n'Roll'. It was just three notes. 'It was funny,' Ben Lurie remembers, 'because Terry was ready to score out a horn section, but we said, "No, just these three notes." That worked out well, so we brought him back for another day, another three notes. Probably the same notes but in a different order.'

'It's a very simple line,' Terry adds. 'They just wanted it to be played on a trumpet rather than a guitar. Sound-wise we thought, instead of having an artificial reverb, we'd play it in this concrete stairwell and quadruple-track it, so there are four trumpets playing single notes. "Man On The Moon" was, again, a very simple line, and it just has that great feel to it.'

Another memory Terry has of the Drugstore was that, even while they were mid-session, Jim and William were taking Polaroids for use on the album artwork. As always they were considering the whole, and the visual side was vitally important to the Mary Chain.

'They took a picture of me with my trumpet and screwed with the colours,' Terry remembers. 'At the time it wasn't usual to have your photo taken while sitting on the settee, not even posed, just "bang", that was that. These days I make sure I wear suits . . .'

The initial sessions for *Munki* went as well as could be expected, and the Mary Chain managed to record a lot of material relatively quickly, although the tracks they had weren't quite ready to be revealed to Blanco Y Negro. But the fact that the band had been playing well live, and were musically as match-fit as they'd ever been, meant the process of laying down the tracks they had chosen was quite straight-forward, and the record had an immediate 'live' feel.

However, in direct contrast to the early fluency of the *Munki* sessions, Jim and William's relationship was grinding to a halt. They could barely be in the same room as each other, and soon Jim and Ben were coming in to record in the day, while William took over the studio at night to work on his parts with Dick Meaney. It was with Meaney that William made the track 'Nineteen666', a song that seems to collapse into an accidentally perfect slumped position of sensual, wasted nonchalance. On *Munki*, perhaps more than ever, we hear the distinct personalities of the brothers in bold relief, their individual expression more defined as a result of their increased segregation from each other in the studio. One morning, Jim and Ben came into the studio to find the ceiling had been burnt – William had spilt whisky on some of the channels on the desk, and the resulting fire shot up to the ceiling. 'Fortunately we had lots of channels,' says Ben dryly.

'I know William had stuff going on with Hope, but William just stopped showing up when we would,' Ben Lurie continues. 'It was like we were making two records at the same time. I know William sometimes felt that Jim and I were ganging up on him, but he wasn't around. He was bringing this on himself. There were lots of little incidents. Silly stuff. You look back and think, God, what a bunch of children.'

★

The Reids' sister Linda's role in the history of the Mary Chain is far greater than many realise, particularly at this point in the band's fractious story. The brothers had reached a near-stalemate, but Linda was, in Jim's words, 'the Kofi Annan of the Mary Chain', which was no easy feat. She could receive a phone-call from either brother at any time of the day or night, and frequently did. As their sister, Linda couldn't take sides, but 'she tried to steer us in the right direction,' Jim says.

'The band would have split up a long time before if it wasn't for Linda's UN peacemaking deals,' continues Jim. 'Poor Linda, she was always getting calls from me or William saying, "Do you know what the fucker's done now?" I stopped doing that after a while because I realised it must be fucking hard for her. But when you're wasted and you're in this situation, it seems like life or death.'

The music press would merrily grab on to the idea that 'Jim nearly killed William' during the making of *Munki*. It went perfectly with the 'Brothers Grim' tag the Reids had earned, and perhaps it wasn't far from the truth. But 'brothers are *supposed* to love and hate each other at the same time,' as Jim said in an interview with *Option* in 1998. 'We're cooped up together in this space called The Jesus and Mary Chain. There's about enough room for a midget, but there happens to be two non-midgets fighting for the same little piece of territory.'

The two non-midgets were avoiding each other completely while still managing to record *Munki* at this point, and, although the tracks weren't quite finished, Jeannette Lee was eager to hear how things were going. The Reids reluctantly agreed to let Jeannette hear the tracks at the studio. What happened next would sadly mark the end of the Mary Chain's association with Blanco Y Negro.

'This was awkward for me for many years,' says Jeannette. 'They played me some songs which I thought sounded great. Not radically different, but good. I came back and told Geoff, and then they sent us the tracks. But then Geoff told them that we didn't like the songs, because collectively we decided we weren't going to do it.'

'William seemed to be in not that good a state,' recalls Geoff. 'Speaking personally, I don't think *Munki* was a very good record, and so we said, "No, thank you."'

The news was a bombshell. Jeannette had enthused, genuinely, about the songs she'd heard in the studio, but when Geoff took a dislike to the album and the collective decision was made not to pick up the option, the Mary Chain felt they'd received something of a mixed message. 'They felt betrayed,' Jeannette recalls.

Jim says: 'Nobody [at the record company] seemed to be into *Munki*, and for the first time neither was Geoff Travis. Geoff was like, "I don't get it, I don't hear any singles." I said, "What do you mean in particular?" He said, "The lyrics don't make sense, for a start." I was like, "What are you on about?" It shook us.'

Rob Dickins, to his credit, stepped in and suggested the Mary Chain should go back to the studio and record some singles. William duly recorded the menacing 'Cracking Up', which, appropriately, detailed 'relationships that were once there and then not', Jim explained at the time, referring no doubt to the label's sudden rug-pull and also William's volatile romance with Hope Sandoval. 'Mentally it's been like Vietnam for William over the last couple of years,' Jim added.

The song, imbued with sinister confidence, casts a glowering eye back on what 'they' said of him (*They said I was weak . . . One said I was a priest . . .*) overriding all claims, good or bad, with the spectral but defiant affirmation *I am a freak*.

For Jim's part he decided to record the track that would become the energetic 'Moe Tucker', introducing his sister Linda as a singer for the first time, a typically spontaneous development that injects an insouciant freshness into the Mary Chain sound. Linda was still living at home in East Kilbride while studying English in Glasgow, but she came down to the studio when they were about to record the track. Originally titled 'Suck My Coke', Jim felt it was probably a good idea to choose a different title if he was going to hand it over to his kid sister to sing.

Jim says: 'I was supposed to sing it, but she was just there, so I said, "Do you want a go?" Then I thought the title was rather inappropriate, so she made up the title. "Maureen Tucker". Perfect.' Linda came up with the name when it became apparent that her no-frills, slightly child-like vocal was not dissimilar to that of Tucker's own voice, as heard on Velvet Underground songs such as 'I'm Sticking With You'.

Although the brothers were recording separately, William wanted to watch Linda sing, but it wasn't to be. 'William called and asked if he and Hope could come,' Linda says. 'I was too nervous to sing in front of Hope, so I asked them not to.'

Later that year, however, the Reids invited Linda to sing 'Moe Tucker' during their show at Benicassim in Spain. Not only did she agree, she felt totally at ease, even in front of 20,000 fans, and with her favourite band The Stone Roses watching from the wings.

'I'd been watching William and Jim downing their whisky to take away their nerves,' remembers Linda, 'and I was sitting sipping my water, being so calm. They'd just laugh at me.'

Munki was completed in the summer of 1997, but the label was still not happy. Rob Dickins told the Reids he would release it if they wanted him to, but warned Jim that 'nobody's into it in this building'. He followed this up by gently suggesting the Reids find someone else to put it out.

It was a cruel blow after over a decade with the same label, but after years of feeling Warners were never 100 per cent behind them, they were ready to find someone passionate and likeminded; someone who would put as much energy into promoting *Munki* as they had making it. Someone like Alan McGee, perhaps.

After a difficult period in the early 1990s, which saw Creation in debt and McGee on drugs, the label's fortunes had turned around. After selling half of the company to Sony, Alan signed Oasis, and in 1995 he was hailed by *NME* as a 'Godlike Genius'. Creation was now seen as one of the best independent labels of its time.

The Mary Chain at this point were kicking their heels. William was using the downtime to record tracks of his own for his EP 'Tired Of Fucking', credited on release simply to 'William', before working on further songs for his side project, Lazycame. Jim and Ben continued jamming in the Drugstore, recording a handful of demos under the name TV69. But the Mary Chain/Creation story was about to come full circle.

Jim, who had long since patched up his differences with McGee, didn't approach Creation directly, perhaps concerned that McGee would feel obliged to take them on, but *Munki* reached his ears via mutual associates. Jim admits that, while he strongly believes *Munki* is 'one of our best', he wasn't sure whether McGee had just stepped in to do the Mary Chain a favour. McGee's recollection of what happened confirms otherwise.

'Simon Esplen – the husband of Oasis's marketing manager Emma Greengrass – gave me the Mary Chain record,' McGee explains. '"Cracking Up" was on it. It was fucking great. Me and Bobby Gillespie were listening to it, and we looked at each other and Bobby said, "You've got to do it." We phoned up the lawyer and signed them.' The Mary Chain had come home.

27

Cracking Up

*We were like a weird married couple who had a baby called The
Jesus and Mary Chain. By* Munki, *it was obvious we were going to
be divorced.*
William Reid to Nick Hasted in *Uncut*

It had been some time since the Mary Chain had emerged blinking into
the live arena, so a run of promotional dates was arranged in the early
months of 1998 to create a buzz around *Munki* in the US. The band's
New York date proved eventful from the off: the night before the show
at The Fez, William was arrested for 'abusing a policeman', according to
the *NME*. As the gig was about to start the following day (4 March)
William merrily told the assembled crowd of journalists and record
executives: 'If anyone wants to suck my cock, come backstage afterwards.' 'That'll be the shortest queue in living memory,' muttered Jim.
After briefly tearing a strip off the invited audience for probably never
buying a record, William thundered into the opening riff of 'Cracking
Up' and they were off.

The following day, after a handful of interviews that William
managed to avoid (*Q* magazine was informed that speaking to the press
'fucked with his head'), the Mary Chain boarded the plane home.

It was time for the Reids to consider bringing in some new blood for
the forthcoming UK tour – Ben Lurie had taken care of bass duties in
the studio, but a new bass player was needed for the upcoming dates as
Ben would be moving back to guitar. One name that lingered in the
Mary Chain's mental Rolodex was Lush's Philip King, who had auditioned to play guitar with the group years earlier.

Lush had recently split after the tragic suicide of their drummer Chris Acland in 1996, leaving the remaining band members in a state of shock and grief. Philip wasn't sure he even wanted to play at all when the call from the Reids came. 'It was awful,' he says. 'Initially I thought I didn't want to do it, but then I thought, Come on, it's the Mary Chain.'

The first gig they played together was at Reading's Alleycat as a warm-up before an industry gig at the Water Rats in King's Cross. Philip recalls being unsettled by the occasional false starts during the shows. 'There were, and still are today, quite a few songs where you get into it and someone makes a mistake, Jim goes, "Stop!" and you have to start again. I'm used to it now.'

The Jesus and Mary Chain were plunged straight back into life on the road for the promotional tour for *Munki* in June 1998 to coincide with the album's release that month. Touring was something William still hated, and considering that the previous two years had been spent recording and tinkering about in the Drugstore or at home, this would most likely have been something of a shock to the collective system. It is impressive that they managed to tour as much as they did that year, considering how fraught things were behind the scenes.

It was soon time to go back to the US to play Chicago, Seattle, San Francisco and Los Angeles' Garage venue. This final date in LA would be marked by another William-insults-police-officer incident and a night in the cells. It was also notable because the Mary Chain played a bizarre gig at the Garage's Club Sucker, hosted by Dr Vaginal Davis – a large, black, pre-op transgender woman who enhanced the Mary Chain's set by mounting the stage in a tiny dress and announcing her intention to give them all blow-jobs. The show reportedly ended when the DJ played the 12-inch of the Ashford And Simpson pop hit 'Solid (As A Rock)', with the audience happily bellowing the words 'Solid as my cock' along with it. The Reids and co. didn't stay to sign autographs that night.

After returning to Europe and playing a selection of summer festivals including Roskilde and Glastonbury, the Mary Chain headed back to London to appear at the South Bank's Meltdown festival alongside New York proto-punk duo Suicide. This Meltdown was curated by John Peel, an early supporter of the Mary Chain, and there were guest appearances from Bobby Gillespie (singing Hope Sandoval's part on 'Sometimes

Always'), My Bloody Valentine's Kevin Shields, Primal Scream's Andrew Innes and Emma Anderson of Lush.

Terry Edwards also joined the band for this live performance, but it was, as he recalls, 'a bit of a splitting-up gig', which concluded with William venting his spleen into the microphone long after the rest of the group had left the stage. Philip King says: 'He started ranting about how John Peel never played them on the radio or something. It was kind of par for the course though.'

By this point, Jim admits, the Reids' relationship had completely disintegrated after several years of dwindling communication between the pair. If there was any hope of a reconciliation in the near future, the brothers would need to have some space from each other – not in the studio, not on the road, just living their own lives and trying to find their own equilibrium. The last thing they needed was to pack their suitcases, grab their passports and hit the road again, least of all for six weeks in America. But that, unfortunately, is exactly what they had committed to.

'If someone had looked at it who gave a shit,' says Jim, 'they'd have said, "They need to not see each other for a year, then the band might be able to continue." But no, we were booked on this tour. It started with a festival in San Diego, and we were driving to Los Angeles when we had a big row.'

Ben Lurie remembers: 'There'd been all sorts of fraught moments on the *Munki* tour. Everything had become magnified. You've only got certain ways to flex your muscles, so if that's always turning up half an hour late when everyone's waiting to leave the hotel, that's one of the things you can do, and that irritates the shit out of everybody. Things like that develop.'

The San Diego show had not gone well, and, in Ben Lurie's opinion, it was William who had 'screwed up'. The journey to LA was tense even by Mary Chain standards, but the atmosphere took a nose-dive when a very stoned William started insisting that he wanted to drive the van. 'I thought, Maybe if I punched him he'd just shut the fuck up,' Ben remembers. 'I'm not really a punching kind of person, but I thought, Maybe it will just startle him.'

Jim was sitting between Ben and William when the argument kicked off. He'd threatened to punch William himself, but then decided it wasn't worth it and lay back down for a nap. 'The next thing I know, Ben hit William and both of them started fighting on top of me,' Jim says. 'I was getting trampled.'

At one point the tour manager pulled the van over to try to break up the scrap. 'It was like a schoolteacher with naughty children,' says Philip King. 'I remember the lighting guy was actually on the phone after it all went off, trying to get another job.'

This was the point at which, after so many years and so many fights, Jim knew it really was the end of the Mary Chain. This was at least something he and William weren't going to argue about. William declared that the LA show at the House of Blues would be his final gig. 'It was rather distressing,' says Jim. 'What I should have done then was have a good night's sleep and then review the situation in the morning, but what I actually did was stay up all night snorting cocaine with Ben.'

Jim and Ben lounged in the hotel's hot tub downing champagne in a bid to numb their shock and anger and, to be fair, they didn't believe they were actually going to play the gig the next day at all. By the time they realised it would be going ahead, they were 'obliterated' and, as a result, saw no point in stopping. When the band were due on stage, Jim admits, 'I was not in any fit state to be in public. I remember going on and screaming at William and then thinking, Oh fuck. I'm on stage.'

What happened next would go down in rock 'n'roll history. Philip King remembers: 'We'd start a song, and then Jim would just start going, "Baby, baby, baby, baby, baby . . ." You're playing and thinking, OK, so . . . when do we change for the chorus? William just had his head down. Every song we started collapsed.'

William remembers yelling at Jim to 'get his shit together', feeling that, while he too was relatively wasted, he had the upper hand because at least he was playing the same song as the rest of the band.

'William used to annoy Jim all the time onstage by tinkering with his guitar between songs,' says Ben, 'and I think Jim thought, I'm going to teach him a lesson, I'm going to annoy him. Anyway, it worked. Everyone just got so annoyed . . . I was looking down, and when I looked up everyone had just walked off stage.'

'Jim was trying to pull the amp over,' Philip adds. 'He was swearing at Nick, and Nick was like, "Fuck off!" It was Nick and I who walked off first . . . When the fifth or sixth song collapsed, we just looked at each other . . . we'd had enough and walked off. Then everyone else left.'

After severally storming into the dressing room, the band had never needed a drink more, but the fridge had been locked. Meanwhile, they watched the backstage CCTV screens in horror; ugly scenes were erupting in the audience. 'There were people trying to pull down the curtains, throwing stuff,' says Philip. 'The worst bit was that we couldn't get a drink, though.'

The promoter was furious, and it was, as Jim recalls, the only Mary Chain show that ended with the audience having their money refunded. 'And quite rightly so,' he says. 'It was totally non-musical. I'm just glad it was before the days when everything went on YouTube. That would have been fairly humiliating.'

The Mary Chain were no more, but the reality was that they still had tour dates to honour and stood to lose a fortune if they pulled out. They had no choice but to fulfil their commitments without William, although beyond that point, that was it. 'There was never any thought of the band continuing,' says Jim. 'The band is me and my brother. It's not me, it's not my brother, it's me and my brother.'

William was understandably in shock and not wanting to be alone, he decided to travel to Seattle to be with his girlfriend (and future wife) Dawn. At William's request, tour manager Laurie Small booked a plane ticket for the next day and, when he went to deliver the ticket to William's hotel room, he asked him one last time whether he really wanted to leave. After a moment's hesitation, William grabbed the ticket. No more Mary Chain.

*

William was so traumatised by the split that he could barely speak for days. He had obviously known the writing was on the wall – they all had – but he thought the band would complete the tour and then dwindle away, rather than having to make an announcement to the media. 'It was a violent end, like somebody took a gun and shot the Mary Chain,' he said. The brothers didn't speak again for 'a year, maybe more', says Jim. 'We completely went our separate ways.'

The night after William left, the Mary Chain played their first date without him in a supper club in San Juan Capistrano. Poignantly, they had set up William's amp just in case he turned up after all. The band's set was cut short, as William sang "Cracking Up" and "I Hate Rock'n'Roll", but, as the promoter readily reminded them the moment they left the stage, they were under contract to play for a certain amount of time. They had to go back on and play 'Reverence', extending it for fifteen minutes to fulfil their obligation.

The Mary Chain had to cope with cancellations and pulled fees by promoters who wouldn't go ahead without William. Laurie Small was instrumental in ensuring they minimised their financial losses, but the emotional loss was considerable. 'It was bloody awful,' Jim admitted to *Uncut*'s Simon Goddard in 2001. 'We were standing on stage as the Mary Chain, but I looked to my left and that big mop-top wasn't there.'

The final date of the US tour was supposed to be in Providence, Rhode Island, but it all fell apart when the promoter disappeared. Providence indeed that night, Philip decided to get some much-needed space from the rest of the band and get away, while the others, he discovered later, rather surreally 'almost got into a punch-up with the cast and crew of *Riverdance* at the hotel bar'.

*

After the tour was finally over, the band staggered back to London to lick their wounds. The period that unfolded post-Mary Chain was, as Douglas Hart observed, 'a real struggle', and it would be nearly a decade until the brothers would play live together again. Jim sank into 'an ocean of booze' and was soon broke after 'chucking money about like an idiot'. His solution was to take in lodgers to bring in some cash. However, his lodgers included Ben Lurie and other friends, and Jim's Kentish Town home soon became a bit of a party house, much to the chagrin of the neighbours. 'It was very bad for my health,' Jim admits. 'Every night was drink and drug hell. Or heaven, depending on which way you look at it. I got pretty fucked up.' Jim, understandably, was so scorched by the last Jesus and Mary Chain tour and the incidents that had led to the split that he couldn't bear to even go near a guitar, he didn't play music at home and he certainly didn't want to step out onto a stage any time soon.

William, meanwhile, had plunged into work mode, developing his solo project Lazycame. He released the 'Taster' EP and the *Finbegin* LP in 1999, while *Yawn!* and *Saturday The Fourteenth* came out the following year. The work is pure, unfettered William, but a William evidently at a singularly difficult point in his life. Musically, while often beautiful, whimsical and Syd Barrett-surreal, lyrically William occasionally veers into disturbing territory ('She's been fucking since the age of ten . . .' he croaks on '510 Lovers') and *Saturday The Fourteenth* is cathartic to the point that, when William listened to the album sober, he didn't want to release it. The songs also have a loose, disjointed feeling, as though some of them were being worked out for the first time in an unaired bedroom, curtains closed and, as with 'Tired Of Fucking', released in the same year as *Munki* on Creation Records, there is a spatial oddness that ventures into free improvisation.

William also wanted to play live, with Philip King and Nick Sanderson as his backing band, but 'rehearsals' usually ended up in the pub and eventually the project was shelved. It wouldn't be long until William decided to leave his former life behind altogether and move to LA.

Perhaps William's adoption of Los Angeles as home isn't such a surprise; William's then partner was American after all, and psychologically it was important to put some miles between himself and the Drugstore, London, everything that had such strong associations with the Mary Chain. Also, while the Reids had always appreciated the UK's musical broadmindedness, William increasingly found that looking at Britain from the outside, that is, from the US, left him feeling 'embarrassed'.

He didn't miss Britain much; indeed, he managed to make himself feel he was still there, just with nicer weather, because of his Slingbox, a device connected to his mother's TV back in East Kilbride. The Slingbox allowed him to watch British programmes and, according to John Moore, 'change her channels from LA, which infuriated her, but also reminded her she was not watching alone'.

Slingbox aside, was William changed by the hard-boiled showbiz glitter of Los Angeles? 'No,' Jim insists. 'He stumbles around Beverly Hills like Rab C. Nesbitt.'

28

Changes

*My three wishes? That little alien blokes would come and govern
the planet and make everybody be nice to each other. And that
they would bring many drugs with no ill effects. And that I would
be given a licence to kill.*
Jim Reid to Kitty Empire in *NME*, 1998

As the new millenium dawned, Jim Reid decided to pull together a band
of his own, although, as he admits himself, 'band' might not be quite
the right term. 'Drinking club' would probably be a more accurate
description. 'If the truth be told it was an excuse to go to far-flung
locations and get wasted,' says Jim. Fair enough.

It was time to have some fun and also experience life on the road
without William by his side – of course, Jim had already experienced
the latter at the end of the last Mary Chain tour, but this time it was
actually supposed to be this way. Jim already had the right mix of musicians around him – Nick Sanderson and his wife Romi Mori, who
played bass in The Gun Club, and Ben Lurie, who became very much
the driving force of the group that would become Freeheat. After a nervous debut at Camden's intimate Barfly venue, the alcohol-fuelled
Freeheat roadshow began.

'We did two tours of America, and it was insanity,' Jim says. 'We just
drifted into these psychotic situations. It was like your life had fallen
through the cracks. I'd be thinking, Not long ago I was playing at the
Hollywood Palladium, and now I'm in this motel in the middle of
nowhere, and there are crack dealers, curtains twitching, how did this
happen?'

Ben Lurie recalls: 'A woman in America told us she could sort out a tour but we could only do it if it paid for itself, as we didn't have any money to put into it. The first warning sign should have been being picked up by a limousine at Boston Airport and then being driven to a Holiday Inn. I think we were the only people who were driven to the Holiday Inn Express in a limo.'

The promoter of the tour ended up losing a considerable amount of money, and Freeheat would hand over the EP 'Don't Worry Be Happy' to help cover the losses. 'It's all exciting, though,' says Jim. 'Great, but surreal. If William Burroughs had written a story about a rock'n'roll band, it would have been Freeheat.'

The year 2000 also saw William Reid striking out on his own and playing live without his brother for the first time in his life. His acoustic solo debut took place at the intimate 12 Bar Club in London's Denmark Street in March, eighteen months after the Mary Chain's split, in front of his wife Dawn and a collection of Mary Chain super-fans. He was clearly nervous, but 'he strikes a chord' wrote *Uncut*'s Nick Hasted, also lurking in the crowd, 'and he's back'. He even played a handful of Mary Chain songs, including the poignant 'Never Understood' ('I think I'm going out of style/I think I've known it for a while . . .') and 'Reverence'.

William had recently experienced something of a turnaround in his health, thanks to a new era of domesticity (and detachment from everything that connected him to the past). Family life with Dawn, her child and eventually a baby of their own would, temporarily at least, help him to break away from alcohol and drugs. The idea of making music sober excited him, and the thought of being able to turn up for an interview, and not have to conduct it in a pub, was liberating too. 'Small achievements,' he admitted, 'but for me, it's like the clouds parting.' At this point in time, however, William was still adamant there would be no more Mary Chain – there had been too much hurt, and he had only just started to feel that he had his life back.

It would still take some years for the psychic wounds to heal on each side of the Reid fence after The Jesus and Mary Chain's breakup, but another (temporary) casualty of the split would be Sister Vanilla's debut album *Little Pop Rock*. Linda had always been supportive, visiting her brothers in the studio over the years and giving her honest opinions, and William in turn wanted to help Linda make an album of her own. The idea was, originally, that this would be an enjoyable family Reid production, germinating as it had during happier (but not that happy) times. Work on *Little Pop Rock* started in 1996. By the mid-2000s it still wasn't complete.

'After every tour we wanted to kill each other, and after the last one we nearly succeeded,' Jim had said grimly after the final sputtering flames of the Mary Chain were forcibly extinguished – obviously the idea of getting together to work on anything at all was something they were not keen on. All the same, over the years to come, *Little Pop Rock* became a vital part of the healing process for the brothers' scorched relationship. 'It was the thing we all had in common,' says Jim.

Linda was understandably put out that the album William had promised would be out in two weeks took almost a decade to complete. Geography didn't help, nor did the Cold War between the brothers, which meant that much of the album had to be recorded in separate parts. Linda says: 'We recorded it in William's house in Muswell Hill, Jim's house in Kentish Town, the Drugstore, William's house in LA and the Glasgow flat of a friend of Stephen Pastel. It was difficult when William and his family moved to LA. I started thinking it was never going to get finished.'

However, via *Little Pop Rock*, Jim and William did, inevitably, have to talk to each other occasionally, and they reunited in the studio with Linda during a family trip to LA. 'That was one of the few times on the album when William and Jim and I worked on the record together,' says Linda. 'It was good to work with William and Jim. They are very different, but both are so talented and such good people. To be able to make my own record but with their help was such a privilege.'

The melodic, sometimes dreamy *Little Pop Rock* would finally be released in March 2007 to be greeted with hearty enthusiasm by Mary Chain fans, delighted to hear the family-affair album that had played its part in bridging the chasm between the brothers. Sadly there would be no more forays into music for Linda, however. 'We knocked that out of her,' Jim laughs.

Jim, meanwhile, had been playing solo shows, accompanied by Philip King on guitar. If Jim felt exposed in Freeheat with no brother by his side, this would be even tougher. He would still muster up artificial courage thanks to the booze, but the time soon came when, after years of living in the grip of alcoholism, he chose to stop completely, which was no mean feat.

'I stopped drinking because I played a fairly disastrous show,' Jim explains. 'My wife Julie and Phil King set it up. It was a good opportunity for me. But I met Duffy from Primal Scream, late morning or early afternoon, and we went to the pub. I showed up at the sound-check, already wobbling, and Julie said, "You've got to stop drinking." I said, "I know what I'm doing, I've been doing this for years." By the time of the gig I couldn't remember where I was.'

This solo show was a watershed moment for Jim. The following day, Jim's wife Julie gave him an ultimatum: family or the bottle. 'I chose family.'

Many Mary Chain fans will know that Julie and Jim recorded a duet together, 'Song For A Secret', released as a 7-inch in 2005. 'It was a good single,' says Jim. 'If we do an album I'm going to re-record it. I don't want it to be forgotten.'

It was a stack of 'Song For A Secret' 7-inches that caught the attention of guitarist Mark Crozer, who was running a booking agency and who would soon, little did he know it at the time, be playing with Jim himself. Mark was intrigued to hear the duet, and to learn of Jim's solo project. 'I ended up booking some shows for Jim in the UK,' says Mark. 'Then, backstage at a gig in Brighton, we started talking about having a band. I said, "I'll play bass for you," kind of volunteering.

'I'd never really been a bass player until I'd offered my services. Then I said, "I know this drummer . . ." I'd just met [former Ride drummer] Loz Colbert a few weeks before and I thought Loz would be great for the band, because I knew Ride were influenced by the Mary Chain.'

Before long Jim, Philip, Mark and Loz met in a rehearsal room in Oxford, near where Mark and Loz were based, and, as Mark recalls, 'it gelled'. Jim had only just quit alcohol when they started rehearsing, and the quiet but heavy significance with which he turned down a casual drink is something Loz has never forgotten. 'When he looked at me and said, "No . . ." it seemed important. Then he said, "When I drink, I tend to drink an awful lot."'

For someone who would automatically reach for the bottle to quell his nerves, this was a brave new period for Jim, and he staunchly stuck to his new routine for years. It wasn't easy – he had no alcohol in his system to embolden him, and no brother by his side on stage. After gigs, Jim would simply go straight back to the hotel to avoid the usual flow of alcohol.

One thing Jim might have found hard to contemplate was the idea of performing a Mary Chain show while sober – not that that was something he had to worry about, or so he thought. The band had dissolved almost a decade earlier and there had been no conversations about reforming. However, in 2007 the organisers of California's Coachella Valley Music and Arts Festival came calling. Originally it had been suggested that Jim's solo band play a slot, but the conversation soon developed into a plea for the Mary Chain to reform at the festival.

'Coachella came to us with an offer and I thought it was a good one,' Jim recalls, 'but it hadn't occurred to me that we would ever get back together. When I said, "I'm never going to do this again," I meant it.

'But it was nine years later, you think, "Maybe things will be different." I'd assumed William wouldn't be into the idea, and he assumed I wouldn't be. But we got on the phone one night and I said, "I'd probably do it." And he said, "Me too." Just as we'd decided that, Coachella doubled their offer, so it was, "Woohoo!"'

If reports of a Mary Chain reunion were hard for the public to believe after the years of pain, pugilism and piss-artistry that had led to their messy demise, it was even harder for Philip, Mark and Loz to fathom. On hearing about the upcoming show, Mark thought it was a joke at first, while Phil brushed it off as a rumour. But no, it was happening. Hell had indeed frozen over.

The Reids allowed themselves to be cautiously excited. It seemed like a resolution, and, as John Moore has observed, the fact that their father had sadly passed away the year before made them look at their situation in a different light. Life was just too short. Rehearsals were booked for two weeks in a studio in Shepherd's Bush and William flew from LA to meet the latest Mary Chain line-up.

The sense of anticipation was almost tangible, and Mark and Loz weren't sure what to expect, but when William turned up he was affable and positive, which immediately made the new members of the band relax. The first few minutes were civilised. Too civilised. Within seconds of launching into the first song, a jet-lagged William and a keyed-up

Jim were at each other's throats. 'It was a massive bust-up,' says Jim, 'But it was more to do with getting something out of our systems. We'd kind of made up, but there was still all this background resentment. It was a boil that needed to be lanced.'

Once they had cleared the air, the band could get to grips with the set, and it was fascinating for Loz and Mark to witness the symbiotic nature of the Reids' songs. 'Jim's songs made sense when William added his parts to them,' Loz explains, 'but William's songs really fell into place when Jim started singing. They just became the right song as soon as Jim opened his mouth, and as soon as William started playing, it just felt like we were ready to take off.'

29

Fear, Film-Stars and the Future

*You're up there on stage at Coachella, and all you can think about
is how awful it would be if your trousers fell down.*
Mark Crozer

April 2007: the time had come for the newly reformed Jesus and Mary
Chain to fly to California. No one knew whether to view it as a one-
off at this stage, but Jim's mantra was, quite wisely, to see how it goes
and take each moment as it comes. They had a major hurdle to get
over first – it would be the first time Jim had ever played sober with
the Mary Chain, and also the first time he'd played live with his
brother for nearly a decade. To make it even more daunting, it had
been decided that Hollywood film-star Scarlett Johansson would
provide backing vocals on 'Just Like Honey'. The song had featured
on the soundtrack of the movie *Lost In Translation*, which starred
Johansson and Bill Murray, and Johansson had proclaimed herself a
great admirer of the Mary Chain.

Flattering as this was, Jim was 'terrified. Absolutely terrified,' he
shudders. 'We did a show the night before in Anaheim, California, and
that went well, but me being a glass-half-empty type of a bloke, I thought,
Fuck it, the first show was bound to be the best! Then you've got this
starlet there . . . it was scary, I just didn't know how to deal with the situation. I would have if I was drunk, but sober I just don't know what to
do.' Scarlett and her entourage ventured into the Mary Chain's dressing
room – a nerve-racking experience in itself – but after a few silent,
awkward moments, William 'piped up, probably about something drug-
related,' remembers Loz Colbert, and the ice was broken.

The Jesus and Mary Chain finally ambled on to the stage as the sun was setting behind the mountains, a glorious setting for a comeback. The rumour that Scarlett Johansson was going to join the band on stage had long been circulating the site, and when she finally walked on, a huge cheer erupted and every camera-phone in the place was held aloft. John Moore thought it hilarious that, 'in true Mary Chain style, they didn't even bother to introduce her'.

The show was a success, the Mary Chain were back, and there was no reason why they should stop at Coachella. A healthy run of tour dates would follow, including an appearance alongside their long-time compadres The Pastels at Jarvis Cocker's Meltdown on the South Bank (with Duke Spirit's Liela Moss on backing vocals for 'Just Like Honey'). They also played a show at the Brixton Academy, a venue that had hosted many Mary Chain concerts over the years. The Academy was packed, but unlike the early days, instead of delivering put-downs to their audience, Jim made a self-deprecating joke that, 'misheard' by the press, was interpreted as though the comeback kings had insulted their loyal fans. In response Jim wrote this statement, which appeared on the *April Skies* fan site.

'It's been reported in a couple of reviews [the *NME* and the *Independent*] that at our Brixton Academy show I made a comment to the audience, "You are a bunch of miserable bastards". Some people might think it's no big deal, but I think it's important to point out that I did in fact say "*We* are a bunch of miserable bastards", which seemed appropriate at the time, as it was just after the song "Happy When It Rains".

'I've asked both these publications to print a retraction, but I'd have more chance of the editors coming round cleaning my toilets . . . But for what it's worth, it amazes me that we can still play in venues such as the Brixton Academy, and that anyone cares enough to come. I certainly don't take a Jesus and Mary Chain audience for granted.'

So in case you missed that statement the first time around and had been feeling aggrieved about the whole 'miserable bastards' debacle, now you know.

★

The Mary Chain had a busy year of international touring ahead, with William seemingly feeling better about hitting the road than ever (Jim, conversely, now prefers to stay at home). The fans were in their element, particularly those who thought their chance to see the Mary Chain had long since passed. Chilean Mary Chain devotee Carlos Benavides remembers that when the band announced they would be playing a show in his country, he 'almost jumped out of the window' (in euphoria, I hasten to add). 'It was like Jesus Christ's second coming.'

While the live dates were going well, taking them through to the end of summer 2008, Jim still baulked at William's enthusiasm for making a new album. He was keen to book a studio in LA for the sessions, but Jim had to put the brakes on. It just didn't make sense to him to haemhorrage money when it was now easier than ever to make a perfectly decent record by recording at home. However, this was not the only reason Jim felt unsure. 'I just couldn't see that things had moved along enough from the break-up,' he says. 'At that time I was on the wagon, and I found it difficult to deal with William because he was very much not on the wagon. We did do a couple of sessions in LA, and he would get very stoned. I just didn't want to make an album under those circumstances.'

All the same, the appetite for a new album from the Reids was strong, and the following year Kevin Oberlin, an associate of William's and now the Mary Chain's manager, collated an album's worth of demos from both Reids. It remains unreleased, but as guitarist Mark Crozer recalls, 'It almost looked like it was going to come out. It might not have been exactly as they'd wanted it, but it was really good.'

The mock-up album included 'All Things Must Pass', a song of William's originally intended for one of his solo records. The track, a contemplative song about getting older, remains a live favourite, and was included on the soundtrack to the hit US TV series *Heroes*. 'That song just makes so much sense,' says John Moore. '*Each drug I take is gonna be my last . . . each girl I touch is gonna be my last . . .* We'll probably have a heart attack on the job . . . Oh dear. Coitus interruptus. Good idea for a song: every little thrill that you have, you might not get away with it this time.'

The title of this song was tragically prescient for the news that was about to hit the Mary Chain, and the next time they would play live together would be under extremely sad circumstances. On 8 June 2008, former Mary Chain and Freeheat drummer Nick Sanderson died of lung cancer, aged just 47, news that sent the Reids reeling. The brothers wanted to do something to commemorate the life of their friend and former bandmate, and, on 27 October the Mary Chain, British Sea Power and Black Box Recorder (John Moore's group with Luke Haines and Sarah Nixey) performed at a tribute show for Sanderson at the Forum in Kentish Town, North London, organised by the Reids themselves. Sanderson had been working as a train driver on the Brighton-London line, a job that inspired the Earl Brutus song 'Train Driver In Eyeliner', in turn providing the title of his tribute concert. (There is an excellent and moving account of this evening on Andy Von Pip's website www.thevpme.com.)

'Nick was such a great bloke,' Jim says. 'A bloody star. That was a sad old occasion, but it was good to do it. I was on the wagon at that time and I don't think I've ever wanted a drink so much in all of my life.'

*

After a smattering of gigs, a good two years would pass before the Mary Chain would tour again, with Jim moving his family down to Sidmouth in Devon, away from the grime and neurosis of London. The ghost of the Reids' mutual fury had been exorcised (mostly) and the Reids were communicating, but Jim was still wary of how that might change if they threw themselves fully into the Mary Chain and all that came with it. However, after being pulled back into the limelight, a tour of the US beckoned, and Philip King, who had been playing in John Moore's Rock'n'Roll Trio with Loz Colbert on drums, suggested the Reids bring John back into the fold.

'It seemed natural,' says Jim. 'Although it was weird having John in the band: he's like a cross between Mr Kipling and Iggy Pop. Give him a shandy too many and he'll tear the place apart, but then he's walking about in his linen suit and lime-green sandals, Panama hat. God bless him.'

John remembers suddenly being deluged with phone-calls from Jim one evening – not a typical occurrence. 'He even tried to Skype me,' John says. 'I thought, Oh shit, William's died. But he asked me what I was doing next month, would I like to come to America and China? "Hmm, suppose so . . .!"'

From the point of view of Mark and Loz, nothing had been said other than a cheery 'See you next year!' at the end of 2008. 'But it makes sense to me why they did it with a new incarnation,' says Mark. 'John and Jim are really good friends. And I always felt like one of those red-shirt *Star Trek* characters, you know at some point they're going to get killed."

Replacing Loz on drums would be Brian Young from Fountains Of Wayne, and he and William flew over to the UK in early 2012 to rehearse at John Henry's, in a ramshackle part of King's Cross, near Pentonville Prison. There were, as John recalls, 'no major incidents' and they were soon ready to fly to Texas for the South By South West festival on 15 March, a date notable for being the anniversary of the North London Poly 'riot'.

'It was a testing ground,' says John. 'A lot of promoters came to see if we were still bookable, and apparently we are, so it went from there. Then we went to China, which was fabulous. Beijing was just so overpowering. And it's nice to go to a place like Hong Kong where you can get a bunch of suits made fairly cheaply.'

John also had his heart set on going to Raffles, the stunning colonial hotel named after Stamford Raffles, founder of modern Singapore. John was sufficiently attired to swan into the bar and cast his peanut shells upon the floor (not a euphemism) as tradition dictates. But despite John's suggestion that the rest of the Mary Chain leave their jeans at the hotel in favour of smart trousers, they did not.

'I'm a bit of a bastard, really,' John admits. 'I had my suit on and I was saying, "We've got to go to Raffles! Smarten yourself up a bit." They were going, "We'll be all right." And I said, "But I want to go to the Writers' Bar. I want to see where Somerset Maugham and Noel Coward used to hang out." They couldn't get in because they weren't wearing suits. I think Jim was upset that I went in without them.'

*

Controversially, two gigs were booked for October in Tel Aviv. This caused something of a backlash on social media and prompted the departure of John Moore. In response, Jim made a public statement

---

*And yet, Lazarus-like (not that Lazarus was in a band, as far as we know), Mark is back in the Mary Chain line-up at the time of writing

explaining the Mary Chain's apolitical stance, and their wish to play for Mary Chain fans wherever they are, and he clarifies this here:

'I despise the Israeli government, but I despise the British government,' Jim explains. 'Tony Blair took this country to war in Iraq based on a lie. What am I going to do, leave Britain? No, I'll play in front of Mary Chain fans wherever I find them, and if I find them in Israel I'll play there. I didn't play to the Israeli government, I played to Israeli kids who love my band. When we went to Tallinn it was still part of the USSR, and it was the same: kids who'd never seen stuff like this and were just in awe. But the state was rotten to the core.

'We had two girls singing on "Just Like Honey" – on the first night it was an Israeli girl and on the second it was a Palestinian girl. What did I do wrong? Sod all. The Palestinians are being treated badly out there, but not by the kids who came to our gig.'

It's been said that if something happens once, there's only a slim possibility it will happen a second time. But if it does happen a second time, it will definitely happen a third. Or something like that, anyway. And so we come to the Mary Chain and McGee. Within days of the first edition of this book being published in May 2014, Alan McGee told the world that not only was he reviving Creation as a management company with business partner Simon Fletcher, he had signed up the Mary Chain as his first clients – another neat full circle. McGee also announced that the Reids would reunite with recent JAMC alumni Mark Crozer, Philip King and Brian Young in November 2014 to perform a run of shows during which they would play *Psychocandy* in its entirety, in advance celebration of its thirtieth anniversary.*

The shows would be reliably disorientating and luminous – between the glaring lights, practically used as weapons, literally stunning the audience into a daze of confusion, and the overwhelming tides of distorted sound (punctuated halfway through with an antique public information film about East Kilbride), the Mary Chain, five black

---

* Naturally, a veritable who's who of Mary Chain history could be seen backstage after the shows at London's Troxy and at the much-anticipated Glasgow gig – at Barrowland, of course. The latter show was supported by Strawberry Switchblade's Rose McDowall, and also marked the first time Jim and Murray Dalglish had met since the release of 'Upside Down', which the Mary Chain played onstage during the *Psychocandy* show – an 'emotional' moment for Murray.

silhouettes against a hell-fire crimson background, had successfully hypnotised everyone yet again. McGee had insisted on using the same mix on the sound desk, at the first London show at least, that the Mary Chain had had at their first ever shows thirty years earlier – a deafening decision, practically a declaration of sonic warfare, and a gleeful juxtaposition against the genteel elegance of London's Troxy. At the time of writing, more dates are being planned as the united force of Creation and the JAMC steam into the future. New releases are also mooted – 'when' rather than 'if'.

And there has been talk of a new album – there's more than enough material, and Jim asserts it would be 'as good a Mary Chain album as there's ever been'. The fact remains that, creatively, whatever the Reids do separately, something magical always occurs when they join forces.

'I don't think either Reid has managed to top being in the Mary Chain,' observes their former press officer Mick Houghton. 'That must be hard for them, but that in itself is also a measure of how successful they were and what an impact they made.'

Finally, it seems, The Jesus and Mary Chain are receiving more widespread respect for the uniquely powerful and affecting quality the Reids brought to pop music, cutting through the bland, the anodyne and the manufactured just when the laser-like energy of punk seemed all too far away. But the Mary Chain's music, lyrics and attitude continue to endure because they are every bit as relevant and necessary today. As Alan McGee put it, 'For the benefit of music, God, did Britain, and the world, need The Jesus and Mary Chain.' And, in this current culture of disposability, short attention spans and cynical TV 'talent' shows, it's arguable we need them even more. The Mary Chain have stayed true to themselves throughout decades of change, although that is not to say that they've stayed the same – far from it. But it is that fierce sense of integrity, combined with the courageous and often transcendent quality of their music, that has seen them through the turbulence, the wilderness and the facile nature of fame.

'We have an ability to keep our distance from the business itself,' Jim Reid told *Melody Maker*'s Kevin Westerberg. 'If you don't, you're liable to be chewed up and spat out. Everything to do with The Jesus and Mary Chain we oversee. We're just ourselves.'

'After the split, it would be once in a blue moon anyone would say, "Wow, the Mary Chain,"' Douglas adds. 'But even when we were at our peak, we knew there was a fickleness to it all. The most important thing is when someone says, "We started a band because of you." It all comes down to that. The only thing that matters is having an impact on some kid. And things come back round, don't they?'

Timeline

This timeline takes us from the year of The Jesus and Mary Chain's inception to their split, and ultimately their reunion in 2007. (Note: it is not an exhaustive timeline of the Mary Chain's every move; rather it is a tool to put their story into a broader cultural context.)

1983

In East Kilbride, Scotland, brothers William and Jim Reid start to write songs and record demos on a Portastudio bought with their father's redundancy money. Meanwhile in London, Alan McGee starts Creation Records with Dick Green and Joe Foster. Also this year, The Birthday Party break up, with singer Nick Cave forming The Bad Seeds soon after the split. My Bloody Valentine, later to join the Creation family also form this year in Dublin.

January: Trevor Horn, Jill Sinclair and Paul Morley start the label ZTT (Zang Tuum Tumb).

1 February: Long-running breakfast television programme *TV-AM* is launched.

26 February: Michael Jackson tops the US charts with the album *Thriller*. On the same day, The Cramps, a favourite band of the nascent Jesus and Mary Chain, release their first live album, *Smell Of Female*.

2 March: Compact discs go on sale to the general public.

July: Glaswegian goth-pop duo Strawberry Switchblade release their debut single 'Trees And Flowers' through 92 Happy Customers, a label run by Will Sergeant (Echo and the Bunnymen). It sells 10,000 copies.

1 September: Joe Strummer and Paul Simonon announce the dismissal of Mick Jones from The Clash.

24 October: ZTT releases the provocative debut single by Frankie Goes To Hollywood, 'Relax'.

2 December: Michael Jackson's fourteen-minute video for 'Thriller' is premiered on MTV.

The Flying Pickets are at number 1 on Christmas Day in the UK with 'Only You'.

1984

The first line-up of The Jesus and Mary Chain is formed: Jim Reid on vocals, William Reid on guitar, Douglas Hart on bass and Murray Dalglish on drums. This year, their demo tape reaches the ears of Alan McGee via the band's new ally Bobby Gillespie, and this leads to a gig at McGee's London club night the Living Room and ultimately a record deal with Creation Records. The Jesus and Mary Chain record their first single, 'Upside Down', in the autumn of 1984 before embarking on their first tour. This is the year that The Jesus and Mary Chain rocket from obscurity to acclaim within a startlingly short space of time.

11 January: BBC Radio 1 DJ Mike Read announces live on air that he refuses to play Frankie Goes To Hollywood's single 'Relax', on account of its suggestive lyrics. The BBC bans the single, which subsequently goes to the top of the UK charts, where it stays for five weeks.

20 February: The Smiths release their eponymous debut album via Geoff Travis's label Rough Trade.

1 April: Marvin Gaye is shot dead by his father in Los Angeles.

8 June: The Jesus and Mary Chain play their first gig at Alan McGee's Living Room club on Tottenham Court Road. McGee falls in love with them instantly and signs them to Creation. Two days later, the Mary Chain play at Glasgow club Night Moves. The reception is not so positive and the band are unceremoniously thrown out of the venue mid-set.

25 June: Prince releases *Purple Rain*.

17 September: The Mary Chain play an inebriated show at Alice In Wonderland – a psychedelic club night in Soho co-run by Clive 'The Doctor' Jackson from Doctor and the Medics, and one of a handful of London dates organised by Alan McGee. They are physically hauled off stage by the promoters and told never to return.

11 October: The Mary Chain and Bobby Gillespie's band Primal Scream play their first gig together in Glasgow. Bobby has also just joined the Mary Chain, replacing drummer Murray Dalglish, and this is his first gig with the Reids and Douglas.

23 October: The UK sees for the first time the scale of the famine in Ethiopia, thanks to a news report by the BBC newsreader Michael Buerk. Bob Geldof is one of the millions watching and he is subse-quently inspired to organise Band Aid, and later Live Aid.

24 October: The Jesus and Mary Chain play London's Three Johns pub. In the audience is *NME* journalist Neil Taylor, who subsequently proclaims the band to be 'the best thing since the Sex Pistols'.

26 October: The Jesus and Mary Chain, Biff Bang Pow! and Jasmine Minks set off for the Creation package tour of Germany. When they return on 4 November, the Mary Chain discover they are all over the music press, thanks to their debut single 'Upside Down' (released to the public in November) and their incendiary Three Johns gig.

29 October: Frankie Goes To Hollywood release their debut album *Welcome To The Pleasuredome*. It goes straight to number 1.

9 November: 'Upside Down' is released, with the Mary Chain's Syd Barrett cover 'Vegetable Man' on the B-side. This single is The Jesus and Mary Chain's first release on Creation Records.

25 November: The Mary Chain play the Ambulance Station in Old Kent Road – a heavy gig but also the night Rough Trade boss Geoff Travis, also running Warners imprint Blanco Y Negro, sees them for the first time.

3 December: The Band Aid charity single 'Do They Know It's Christmas?' is released, becoming the fastest-selling UK single of all time.

29 December: The Jesus and Mary Chain play ICA Rock Week on Jim's twenty-third birthday.

1985

In January, the Reid brothers and Douglas Hart move to London after signing with Blanco Y Negro. They record their second single 'Never Understand' with the late John Loder at Southern Studios, and work soon begins in earnest on debut album *Psychocandy*. The album is released in November.

2 February: The Jesus and Mary Chain appear on *The Old Grey Whistle Test*, performing 'In A Hole'. 'Never Understand', the first single from the album *Psychocandy*, is released on Blanco Y Negro this month.

22 February: 'Never Understand', The Jesus and Mary Chain's first release on Blanco Y Negro, comes out, with 'Suck' on the B-side.

15 March: The Jesus and Mary Chain's show at the North London Polytechnic descends into violent chaos.

5 April: The Jesus and Mary Chain play New York's Danceteria. This is their first trip to the US, organised by the late promoter Ruth Polsky.

7 April: Wham! become the first Western pop group to play in China.

27 May: The Jesus and Mary Chain release the single 'You Trip Me Up'. 'Just Out Of Reach' is the B-side.

25 June: The Jesus and Mary Chain play Manchester's Hacienda with Primal Scream – Bobby Gillespie's then girlfriend Karen Parker (who provides backing vocals on 'Just Like Honey') plays drums instead of Bobby.

13 July: The Live Aid pop concerts, organised by Bob Geldof and Midge Ure, raise over £50 million for Ethiopian famine relief.

9 September: The Jesus and Mary Chain play London's Electric Ballroom – a gig now legendary for its riotous scenes. They play, or attempt to play, 'Just Like Honey' live for the first time.

30 September: 'Just Like Honey', the third single from *Psychocandy*, is released. 'Head' is the B-side.

November sees the release of The Jesus and Mary Chain's debut album *Psychocandy*. It receives glowing reviews and continues to be listed in 'best album' lists to this day, including *Rolling Stone* magazine's '500 Greatest Albums of All Time'.

25 December: The charity Comic Relief is founded. Shakin' Stevens' single 'Merry Christmas Everyone' takes the Christmas number 1 spot on the UK single charts.

26 December: Thin Lizzy front man Phil Lynott is rushed to hospital after a suspected heroin overdose. He dies on 4 January 1986.

1986

This year, Bobby Gillespie leaves the group to concentrate on Primal Scream. He is replaced by John Moore. The Jesus and Mary Chain release 'Some Candy Talking' and part ways with Alan McGee.

5 January: The Pet Shop Boys' single 'West End Girls' is the first number 1 UK single of 1986.

21 February: The Dead Kennedys play their final concert at UC Davis in California.

8 March: The Jesus and Mary Chain return to the US, this time with new drummer John Moore in tow after the departure of Bobby Gillespie.

2 May: Country superstar Dolly Parton opens her theme park, Dollywood, in Tennessee.

14 July: The Jesus and Mary Chain release the 'Some Candy Talking' EP.

September: The Mary Chain decide to part ways with manager Alan McGee.

15 November: The Beastie Boys' *Licensed To Ill* becomes the first hip-hop album to reach number 1 in the USA.

Jackie Wilson's 'Reet Petite' claims the Christmas number 1 spot.

1987

The Jesus and Mary Chain release *Darklands* this year, but extensive touring and external pressures are taking their toll. John Moore has moved to guitar and the Reids decide to use programmed drums instead of a live drummer, which attracts mixed reviews in the US.

25 January: Steve 'Silk' Hurley goes to number 1 with the single 'Jack Your Body' – the first house music track to top the UK charts.

7 April: Alice Cooper almost dies on stage when his 'gallows' prop malfunctions.

20 April: The Jesus and Mary Chain release 'April Skies', the first single from their second album *Darklands*.

May: Whitney Houston's song 'I Wanna Dance With Somebody' is the first number 1 to be released as a CD single.

3 August: The Jesus and Mary Chain release 'Happy When It Rains', the second single from *Darklands*.

September: The Jesus and Mary Chain release *Darklands*. On 4 September the band embarks on an extensive UK tour promoting the album.

4 October: Electronic data gathering replaces the sales diary technique for collating the UK charts. The chart publication date is also moved from Tuesday to Sunday.

26 October: The Jesus and Mary Chain release 'Darklands', the title track from the album.

3 November: After a handful of European dates, The Jesus and Mary Chain take the *Darklands* tour to the US.

15 November: The Jesus and Mary Chain play Toronto's RPM Club. During the show, Jim Reid, provoked by a verbally abusive audience member, lashes out and strikes the punter with his mic-stand. Reid is arrested.

By the end of November, the first acid house raves have started to spring up.

25 December: The Pet Shop Boys are at number 1 on Christmas Day with their cover of Elvis Presley's 'Always On My Mind'.

29 December: The nineteen-year-old Kylie Minogue releases her debut single, 'I Should Be So Lucky', via Stock Aitken and Waterman, just in time for Jim Reid's birthday. The single climbs to number 1 the following February, where it remains for five weeks.

1988

John Moore leaves The Jesus and Mary Chain to concentrate on his solo career. The Mary Chain release stand-alone single 'Sidewalking', inspired by the hip-hop they'd heard during trips to New York, and the popular compilation album *Barbed Wire Kisses: B Sides & More*.

21 March: The Pixies release their debut album *Surfer Rosa* on UK label 4AD.

28 March: The Jesus and Mary Chain release the stand-alone single 'Sidewalking'.

April: The Jesus and Mary Chain release *Barbed Wire Kisses: B Sides & More*.

12 August: Public Enemy stage a concert at Riker's Island for 250 prisoners.

9 September: The Jesus and Mary Chain embark on a tour of Australia with their former roadie David Evans on guitar as John Moore's replacement.

November: Madchester band The Happy Mondays release the album *Bummed*.

4 December: Roy Orbison gives his final concert in Akron, Ohio, before suffering a fatal heart attack two days later.

25 December: Cliff Richard's 'Mistletoe And Wine' is Christmas number 1, the biggest-selling single of the year, keeping Kylie Minogue and Jason Donovan's single 'Especially For You' from the top spot. The entire top ten over the festive period is a veritable pop cheeseboard.

1989

The Jesus and Mary Chain tour 'Sidewalking', and also 'co-headline' with Iggy Pop, with disastrous results. A heavy year of touring, 1989 also takes the band on a bizarre trip behind the Iron Curtain to Estonia, amongst other places. The album *Automatic* is released in September.

21 March: Madonna's video for 'Like A Prayer' causes controversy due to its use of religious imagery.

May: The Stone Roses release their debut album *The Stone Roses*.

14 May: A pop supergroup, including Holly Johnson, Paul McCartney, The Christians and Gerry Marsden, go to number 1 in the UK charts with a new version of 'Ferry 'Cross The Mersey', in honour of the victims of the Hillsborough disaster.

June: Nirvana release their debut album *Bleach*.

September: The Jesus and Mary Chain unveil their 'driving across America album' *Automatic*, and first single 'Blues From A Gun'.

22 October: Folk singer Ewan MacColl dies.

30 October: The Jesus and Mary Chain embark on an extensive tour of the UK and Europe.

6 November: The Jesus and Mary Chain release 'Head On', from the album *Automatic*, with 'In The Black' on the B-side.

13 November: The Jesus and Mary Chain release two more single versions of 'Head On' with different B-sides – one with 'Deviant Slice' and the other, 'I'm Glad I Never'.

25 December: The Christmas number 1 spot is claimed by Band Aid II, 'Do They Know It's Christmas?'

1990

The Jesus and Mary Chain tour *Automatic*, and are joined in June by Nine Inch Nails. Ben Lurie is now in the Mary Chain line-up on guitar. A major bust-up between the Reid brothers in Tokyo causes the Mary Chain to split up – although they don't tell anybody outside the inner circle, and patch things up by Christmas. Meanwhile this year, vinyl is declining and the boy band phenomenon is rising.

7 January: New Kids on the Block single 'Hangin' Tough' is the first UK number 1 of 1990.

21 January: MTV's *Unplugged* series is aired for the first time, starting with British group Squeeze.

25 January: The Jesus and Mary Chain head off on the *Automatic* tour, starting in Vancouver.

26 January: Emerging band Nine Inch Nails join the *Automatic* tour in Chicago.

12 February: The Cramps release their fourth studio album, *Stay Sick!*, produced by Poison Ivy.

4 April: The North American *Automatic* tour ends in New York at the Ritz venue.

27 May: The Stone Roses stage their now legendary show at Spike Island ('the birthplace of the British chemical industry') in Cheshire.

27 August: The Jesus and Mary Chain release the 'Rollercoaster' EP.

15 October: British shoegazing group Ride (with future Mary Chain member Loz Colbert on drums) release their debut album *Nowhere* on Creation Records.

27 November: 'Vocal' pop duo Milli Vanilli admit to miming on their hits, such as 'Girl You Know It's True'. Their Grammy award is revoked. On the same day, The Happy Mondays release their hit album *Pills 'n' Thrills And Bellyaches*.

25 December: Cliff Richard claims the Christmas number 1 in the UK once more, this time with 'Saviour's Day'.

1991

With the Reids communicating with each other again, work begins on a new LP, *Honey's Dead*, the 'last sober album', as Jim refers to it. Founding member and bass player Douglas Hart leaves the band. The Reids buy their own studio in Elephant and Castle, South London. They call it The Drugstore.

15 January: Yoko Ono brings together a 'Peace Choir' – featuring Tom Petty, Bonnie Raitt, Peter Gabriel and Lenny Kravitz among others – to record and release a version of 'Give Peace A Chance' in reaction to news of the imminent Gulf War.

May: The Smashing Pumpkins release their debut album *Gish*.

June: Bryan Adams' single '(Everything I Do) I Do It For You', featured in the hit movie *Robin Hood: Prince Of Thieves*, is released. It spends sixteen weeks at number 1 in the UK.

18 July: Perry Farrell launches the first Lollapalooza tour, intended as a send-off for his dissolved band Jane's Addiction. Acts on the bill included Nine Inch Nails, Siouxsie and the Banshees and Rage against the Machine.

August: Blur release their debut album *Leisure*, which peaks at number 7 in the UK chart.

September: Nirvana release their second album, *Nevermind*. In the same month, the Pixies release the album *Trompe le Monde*, which includes their cover of the Jesus and Mary Chain single 'Head On'.

27 October: U2's single 'The Fly' replaces Bryan Adams' '(Everything I Do) I Do It For You' at the top of the UK chart.

November: Michael Jackson releases *Dangerous*, which goes on to be the best-selling album of the decade.

4 November: My Bloody Valentine release *Loveless*, their third album. The recording process has taken two years and reportedly cost £250,000, a figure that nearly bankrupts Creation Records.

24 November: Queen frontman Freddie Mercury dies just 24 hours after formally announcing that he is suffering from AIDS.

25 December: Queen are at number 1 for Christmas in the UK with the double A-side 'Bohemian Rhapsody'/'These Are The Days Of Our Lives'. Proceeds go to the Terence Higgins Trust.

1992

The Mary Chain embark on the Rollercoaster tour, release the single 'Reverence' (which becomes a top ten hit, much to the surprise of the Reids themselves) and take part in the 'unbearable' touring festival Lollapalooza. Also this year, Alan McGee sells half of Creation Records to Sony after struggling with debt.

27 January: British band Lush release their album *Spooky*, reaching number 7 in the UK album chart.

3 February: The Jesus and Mary Chain release the controversial 'Reverence', which unexpectedly goes to number 10 in the UK single charts.

2 March: The Jesus and Mary Chain release 'Far Gone And Out', with B-side 'Why Do You Want Me?'

9 March: The KLF famously appear on the Brit Awards, firing blanks over the audience from an automatic weapon.

23 March: The Jesus and Mary Chain release *Honey's Dead* and embark on the first leg of their Rollercoaster tour, with Dinosaur Jr, My Bloody Valentine and Blur, before touring Europe through April and May.

April: The Jesus and Mary Chain release 'Far Gone And Out', the second single from *Honey's Dead*.

22 June: The Jesus and Mary Chain release 'Almost Gold', the third single from *Honey's Dead*. The B-side is 'Teenage Lust' (Acoustic Version).

18 July: The Jesus and Mary Chain travel to San Francisco to be part of the Lollapalooza tour with Pearl Jam, Soundgarden, Red Hot Chili Peppers and others. The tour lasts until 28 August and is not an enjoyable experience for the Mary Chain.

September: The Shamen's single 'Ebeneezer Goode' causes a stir because of its purported endorsement of Ecstasy. It shoots to number 1 in the UK, and becomes one of the most controversial number ones of the 1990s.

23 October: The Jesus and Mary Chain's Rollercoaster tour resumes in the US, this time with Spiritualised and Curve.

25 December: Whitney Houston's cover of Dolly Parton's 'I Will Always Love You', as featured in the film *The Bodyguard*, is the Christmas number 1 for 1992. It has been firmly at the top of the charts since 29 November and remains there until the end of the year.

The Reids start working on material for new album *Stoned & Dethroned*, collaborating with Mazzy Star singer Hope Sandoval and Shane MacGowan. The Jesus and Mary Chain also release their second compilation album, *The Sound Of Speed*, in August.

22 March: Depeche Mode become the first alternative British band to get to number 1 in the USA on the Billboard 200, with the album *Songs Of Faith And Devotion*.

29 March: Suede release their eponymous debut album. It enters the chart at number 1, and sets a new record for the fastest-selling debut LP by a UK act in Britain.

May: Blur release *Modern Life Is Rubbish*.

31 May: Oasis play King Tut's Wah Wah Hut in Glasgow. Creation Records boss Alan McGee is in the audience. He offers them a recording contract.

7 June: Prince announces he is changing his name to an unpronounceable symbol; for ease, he becomes 'the artist formerly known as Prince' until presumably even he gets tired of it and reverts to 'Prince' in 2000.

28 June: The Mary Chain release the 'Sound Of Speed' EP.

August: The Jesus and Mary Chain release the compilation album *The Sound Of Speed*.

18 November: Nirvana play *MTV Unplugged*.

25 December: The UK's Christmas number 1 is claimed by Mr Blobby (a character from the UK TV show *Noel's House Party*, whose vocabulary is limited, side-splittingly, to the word 'blobby') with the song 'Mr Blobby'. The single knocks Meatloaf's 'I Would Do Anything For Love (But I Won't Do That)' off the chart top spot after seven long weeks.

The Jesus and Mary Chain, now with Curve drummer Steve Monti in the group, release *Stoned & Dethroned* in August. A fractious promotional tour ensues.

16 January: D:Ream's 'Things Can Only Get Better' is the first UK number 1 single of 1994, later becoming the 'theme song' for Tony Blair's New Labour.

11 February: The three surviving Beatles reunite in secret to record additional music for some of John Lennon's unfinished demos. The track 'Free As A Bird' is released the following year as part of the *Beatles Anthology*.

7 April: Dr Feelgood singer and proto-punk figurehead Lee Brilleaux dies after battling lymphoma.

8 April: Nirvana frontman Kurt Cobain is found dead. His death, three days earlier, is declared suicide from a self-inflicted gun-shot.

29 May: Scottish pop band Wet Wet Wet's single 'Love Is All Around' goes to number 1 in the UK, staying at the top of the charts until 4 September.

18 July: The Jesus and Mary Chain release 'Sometimes Always' (B-side: 'The Perfect Crime'), the first single from their album *Stoned & Dethroned*. The duet between Jim Reid and Mazzy Star singer Hope Sandoval reaches number 22 in the UK charts.

August: The Jesus and Mary Chain release *Stoned & Dethroned*. Oasis unleash *Definitely Maybe*, which becomes the fastest-selling debut album in the UK. The record is broken in 2006 by Arctic Monkeys' catchily titled *Whatever People Say I Am, That's What I'm Not*.

23 August: Jeff Buckley releases the album *Grace*.

10 October: The Jesus and Mary Chain release 'Come On', the second single from *Stoned & Dethroned*. The B-side is 'I'm In With The Out Crowd'. The band also head out on their first tour since 1992, with Mazzy Star in support. They tour the US, concluding on 28 November in San Diego.

25 December: East 17 claim the Christmas number 1 with 'Stay Another Day', not a particularly festive song; in fact it's totally miserable. Still, it does have church-bells on it.

1995

Ever prolific, William and Jim Reid have already started working on material for their sixth studio album *Munki*. They also release the 'Hate Rock'n'Roll' EP and William's song 'I Hate Rock'n'Roll'.

1 February: Manic Street Preachers member Richey Edwards goes missing.

May: The Jesus and Mary Chain release the 'Hate Rock'n'Roll' EP and also the single, 'I Hate Rock'n'Roll'. They then embark on a short tour of Australia and Japan before returning to Europe for a stint of summer festivals.

September: Blur release *The Great Escape*, which tops the album charts. The single 'Country House' from this album also becomes the band's first number 1, crucially beating Britpop rivals Oasis and their single 'Roll With It' to the top.

October: Oasis release their second album *What's The Story, Morning Glory?* It becomes the third best-selling album in the UK ever.

December: The Beatles release 'Free As A Bird', their first single in over twenty years.

25 December: Michael Jackson is at number 1 on Christmas Day in the UK with 'Earth Song'.

1996

Munki, the Jesus and Mary Chain's final studio album to date, is under-way at The Drugstore. Work also begins on *Little Pop Rock*, the Reids' sister Linda's own album.

13 February: Take That announce they will be splitting up. The news causes such despair that a telephone helpline has to be set up to deal with the hysteria.

19 February: Pulp singer Jarvis Cocker disrupts Michael Jackson's performance of 'Earth Song' at the Brit Awards by mounting the stage, lifting his shirt and waggling his bottom in Jackson's direction. Cocker later states that his actions are 'a protest at the way Michael Jackson sees himself as some kind of Christ-like figure with the power of heal-ing'. The now defunct music paper *Melody Maker* suggests Cocker should be knighted for the stunt.

18 March: The Sex Pistols announce they are to reform for a twentieth-anniversary tour.

30 May: Depeche Mode singer Dave Gahan is arrested upon release from hospital, having overdosed on a heroin and cocaine 'speedball' in a Los Angeles hotel room and been pronounced clinically dead for two minutes.

8 July: The Spice Girls release their debut single, 'Wannabe'. It tops the British chart for seven weeks and is also number 1 in thirty-one coun-tries, becoming the biggest-selling debut single by an all-female group of all time.

6 August: The Ramones play their final show at the Palace in Hollywood.

17 October: Lush drummer Chris Acland commits suicide.

8 November: The film *Hype!*, about the Seattle grunge scene, goes on general release after premiering at the Sundance Film Festival.

25 December: The Spice Girls' '2 Become 1' is the UK's Christmas number 1. Merry Christmas, music-lovers.

1997

The Jesus and Mary Chain complete work on *Munki* at the Drugstore, and part ways with Blanco Y Negro, who choose not to release the album.

12 February: David Bowie receives a star on the Hollywood Walk of Fame.

21 May: Radiohead release *OK Computer*, which tops the album chart for two weeks and is widely hailed as one of the greatest albums of all time.

4 August: Afrobeat pioneer Fela Kuti dies.

21 August: Oasis release the album *Be Here Now*, which sells 695,761 units in its first three days, becoming the fastest-selling album in UK history.

29 September: The Verve release *Urban Hymns*. The majority of their royalties for the hit single 'Bittersweet Symphony' go to the Rolling Stones after a legal dispute over a sample of the Stones' song 'The Last Time'.

17 November: The Prodigy release 'Smack My Bitch Up', which garners widespread media attention not least because it was presumed to glorify misogyny and violence against women. The band deny the claims.

19 November: Gary Glitter is arrested after images of child pornography are found on his computer.

22 November: INXS singer Michael Hutchence is found dead.

25 December: The Spice Girls once again claim the Christmas number 1 spot in the UK, this time with the perhaps appropriately titled 'Too Much'.

1998

The Jesus and Mary Chain reunite with Alan McGee's Creation Records, releasing *Munki* in June and embarking on an extensive promotional tour with Philip King (Lush) on bass. Tensions and personality clashes finally tip the band over the edge and William Reid leaves the US leg of the tour in September.

4 January: BBC charity single 'Perfect Day' pushes the Spice Girls off the top of the UK singles chart, becoming the first British number 1 single of 1998.

19 January: Rockabilly guitarist Carl Perkins dies.

6 April: The Jesus and Mary Chain release the first single from *Munki*, 'Cracking Up', via Creation Records.

7 April: Singer George Michael is arrested for 'lewd conduct' in a public toilet in Beverly Hills.

14 May: Frank Sinatra dies.

18 May: The Jesus and Mary Chain release 'I Love Rock'n'Roll', the second single from the album *Munki*.

1 June: The Jesus and Mary Chain release *Munki* on Creation Records.

12 June: The Jesus and Mary Chain tour *Munki*, starting at Chicago's Metro venue.

4 July: The Jesus and Mary Chain appear at the Meltdown Festival, curated by late broadcaster John Peel, on London's South Bank.

5 July: Teenage pop singer Billie Piper becomes the youngest British solo artist to debut at number 1 in the UK singles charts with 'Because We Want To'.

24 July: The Jesus and Mary Chain appear at Glasgow's Barrowland venue for the last time. Primal Scream also perform. Douglas Hart, perhaps presciently given the circumstances to come, films the show.

25 August: Singer Lauryn Hill releases her debut solo album *The Miseducation Of Lauryn Hill*. It sells nineteen million copies worldwide and is certified 7x Platinum.

9 September: The Jesus and Mary Chain return to the US to tour, with Mercury Rev in support. Within two days, the band split up, with William leaving the tour.

23 October: Britney Spears' debut single '. . . Baby One More Time' is released, going on to become the top-selling single of 1999.

8 November: The Jesus and Mary Chain – without William – play their final show in Thessaloniki, Greece.

25 December: The Spice Girls are at number 1 for the third Christmas in a row, this time with the song 'Goodbye' (as Geri Halliwell has just left the band). This song is soon displaced by the rather less sentimental 'Chocolate Salty Balls' by *South Park* character Chef.

2007

After a hiatus of nearly ten years, the Reids reunite for the Coachella Festival in April, and a year of touring ensues for The Jesus and Mary Chain, this time featuring Mark Crozer on guitar and Loz Colbert (Ride) on drums, with former members John Moore and Philip King later joining the line-up. (The current line-up includes Philip King and

Fountains of Wayne drummer Brian Young.) The year 2007 also sees the eventual release of Sister Vanilla's *Little Pop Rock*, the album the Reids made with their younger sister Linda.

7 January: The first number 1 of the year is claimed by *X Factor* star Leona Lewis, with the single 'A Moment Like This'. In October, her song 'Bleeding Love' becomes the biggest single of the year, remaining at the top of the charts for six weeks. (The video, incidentally, features the singer crouching by a radiator while singing 'Keep bleeding . . .' Either this is a happy accident or the director had a sense of humour.)

12 January: American jazz artist Alice Coltrane dies.

22 June: The Jesus and Mary Chain appear at the Meltdown Festival, curated by Jarvis Cocker, on London's South Bank. The Pastels are in support.

4 August: US singer-songwriter and producer Lee Hazlewood dies.

7 September: After playing a clutch of summer festivals, The Jesus and Mary Chain play London's Brixton Academy.

10 October: Radiohead release *In Rainbows* themselves. It is made available as a download and fans are invited to pay what they want for it.

22 October: The Jesus and Mary Chain embark on a short US tour.

10 December: Led Zeppelin reunite in London after twenty-five years. John Bonham's son Jason plays drums.

25 December: *X Factor* singer Leon Jackson is at number 1 on Christmas Day with 'When You Believe'. The domination of *X Factor* over our charts is now very much in place and remains so in the coming years. Not that it needs to affect us, of course.

Sources

The main voices in this book belong to:

Jim Reid
Founding member and lead singer of The Jesus and Mary Chain from 1983 to date. Solo projects include the group Freeheat.

William Reid
Founding member and lead guitarist of The Jesus and Mary Chain from 1983 to date. Solo projects include Lazycame and William.

Douglas Hart
Founding member of The Jesus and Mary Chain and bass player from 1983 to 1991. Other projects have included Acid Angels and Cristine. Now a film-maker, Douglas Hart has made music videos for artists including My Bloody Valentine, The Horrors and Paul Weller and films including the award-winning *Long Distance Information*.

Bobby Gillespie
Drummer in The Jesus and Mary Chain from 1984 to 1986. Frontman, founding member and songwriter in Primal Scream.

Alan McGee
Founder of Creation Records. First manager of The Jesus and Mary Chain and Primal Scream. After parting ways with The Jesus and Mary Chain he went on to manage My Bloody Valentine, Oasis and The Libertines among others. He retired from music management in 2008, but in 2013 announced he would be launching a new record label, 359 Music. He has also made the movie *Kubricks* with director/writer Dean Cavanagh.

Murray Dalglish

First drummer in The Jesus and Mary Chain. Murray Dalglish left the band in 1984, going on to play drums in Baby's Got A Gun and, latterly, Trixie's Big Red Motorbike. He also owns a hairdressing salon in East Kilbride.

Linda Fox

Linda Fox (née Reid) is William and Jim Reid's younger sister. She is also known as the recording artist Sister Vanilla, and made an album, *Little Pop Rock*, with her brothers. The album was released in 2007.

John Moore

Drummer and later guitarist in The Jesus and Mary Chain after the departure of Bobby Gillespie. Also a writer, he enjoyed success with solo projects including John Moore and the Expressway after leaving the Mary Chain, and later with Black Box Recorder alongside Luke Haines and Sarah Nixey. He joined The Jesus and Mary Chain again in 2012.

Neil Taylor

Former *NME* journalist, C86 pioneer and founder of digital publishing imprint Ink Monkey Books.

Clive 'The Doctor' Jackson

Lead singer in Doctor and the Medics. Jackson also ran the club night Alice in Wonderland in central London in the 1980s. Clive Jackson continues to tour and DJ.

Joe Foster

Also known as 'Slaughter Joe', Foster, a producer and former member of the Television Personalities and Biff Bang Pow!, co-founded Creation with Alan McGee and Dick Green. He also runs the PoppyDisc label, which has artists including BMX Bandits and Norman Blake on its roster.

Stephen Pastel

The professional name of Stephen McRobbie, lead singer and guitarist in The Pastels since their formation in Glasgow in 1981. In May 2013 the Pastels released *Slow Summits*, their first album since *Illumination* in 1997.

Pat Collier
Engineer/producer, former owner of Alaska Studios, where The Jesus and Mary Chain recorded 'Upside Down', engineered by Collier. He also mixed 'You Trip Me Up'. Pat Collier now works from Perry Vale Studios in Forest Hill, south-east London.

Geoff Travis
Founder of Rough Trade Records and the Rough Trade chain of record shops. Also founder of Blanco Y Negro (a subsidiary of Warners), who signed The Jesus and Mary Chain in 1985.

Jeannette Lee
Co-owner of Rough Trade Records with Geoff Travis, Jeannette Lee also worked with The Jesus and Mary Chain during their time with Blanco Y Negro.

Mick Houghton
Former press officer for The Jesus and Mary Chain, Echo and the Bunnymen and many others during his time working with Warners before setting up his own PR company, Brassneck Publicity. Mick Houghton is also a prolific writer, and at the time of writing he is working on a biography of Sandy Denny.

Laurence Verfaillie
After working with Alan McGee at Creation Records, Laurence Verfaillie went on to be a leading music PR and was the managing director of drum-and-bass PR company Electric. She now runs a successful French delicatessen called Degustation in south London.

Chris Morrison
Chris Morrison, founder of CMO Management, managed The Jesus and Mary Chain from 1987. He is also famous for having managed Blur and Damon Albarn, and currently manages artists including Grace Jones, Mutya Keisha Siobhan and Morcheeba.

Jerry Jaffe
Former senior vice-president of A&R at PolyGram Records, Jerry Jaffe worked with Chris Morrison and managed The Jesus and Mary Chain's career in the US. He set up Management By Jaffe and managed the careers of artists including St Etienne, Dead or Alive and Midge Ure. Jerry Jaffe also ran the US operations for Creation Records until 1995.

David Evans
A one-time roadie for The Jesus and Mary Chain, David Evans stepped in to play guitar when John Moore first left the group. He now works as a designer.

James Pinker
New Zealand-based drummer, percussionist and engineer James Pinker joined The Jesus and Mary Chain briefly at the end of 1987 and appears on the compilation album *The Power Of Negative Thinking*. He has also worked with Dead Can Dance, The Pogues and Nusrat Fateh Ali Khan.

Philip King
Bass player for UK shoegaze legends Lush and later for The Jesus and Mary Chain, Philip King is in the current line-up of the band, now playing guitar two decades after failing an audition to be their guitarist. Philip is also a picture researcher, working with publications such as *Uncut*.

Ben Lurie
London-born Australian musician Ben Lurie was working on reception at Rough Trade before joining The Jesus and Mary Chain, at first to play guitar and later, replacing Douglas Hart on bass. Ben Lurie was also in Jim Reid's group Freeheat, and is now a graphic designer.

Steve Monti
Drummer for Curve, Ian Dury and the Blockheads and later the Wilko Johnson Band, Steve Monti joined The Jesus and Mary Chain in 1992. Monti has also worked with the Cocteau Twins among others.

Lincoln Fong
Engineer and bass player Lincoln Fong joined The Jesus and Mary Chain initially as a technician, and later post-*Stoned And Dethroned* (1994) on bass. As an engineer Fong has also worked with artists including the Cocteau Twins and Pete Townshend.

Alan Moulder
Closely connected with the UK shoegaze movement (and married to Curve frontwoman Toni Halliday), engineer and producer Alan Moulder first worked with The Jesus and Mary Chain as an assistant engineer on sessions with the engineer Flood. He is considered to be one of the UK's best engineers and has worked with Nine Inch Nails, My Bloody Valentine, Foals, Arctic Monkeys and others.

Loz Colbert
Founding member and drummer in Oxford-based shoegaze group Ride, Loz Colbert would eventually join The Jesus and Mary Chain after working with Jim Reid on his solo project prior to the band's reunion at Coachella in 2007. More recently he has been working with Gaz Coombes of Supergrass.

Mark Crozer
Guitarist/bass player who joined The Jesus and Mary Chain in 2007 for the reunion appearance at Coachella, after being in Jim Reid's solo band up to that point. Other projects include The International Jetsetters and Mark Crozer and the Rels.

John Robb
Musician and writer John Robb (formerly of The Membranes) conducted The Jesus and Mary Chain's first interview in 1984, for the magazine *ZigZag*. Robb has written a number of books including *Punk Rock: An Oral History* and is the frontman with the group Goldblade. He also runs the rock journalism website *Louder Than War*.

Discography

STUDIO ALBUMS

Psychocandy
Released: November 1985
Labels: Blanco Y Negro, Warner Bros
Peak chart position: UK 31; US 188
Certification: Gold (UK)

Personnel according to sleevenotes:
The Jesus and Mary Chain/Jim Reid – vocals, guitar/William Reid – vocals, guitar/Douglas Hart – bass/Bobby Gillespie – drums

Additional musicians:
Karen Parker – backing vocals/Laurence Verfaillie – backing vocals

Technical personnel:
The Jesus and Mary Chain – production/John Loder – engineering

Design personnel:
Greg Allen – art direction/Alastair Indge – sleeve photography/Bleddyn Butcher – sleeve photography/Chris Clown – sleeve photography/Mike Laye – sleeve photography/Rona McIntyre – sleeve photography/Stuart Cassidy – sleeve photography

Track listing:
'Just Like Honey'/'The Living End'/'Taste The Floor'/'The Hardest Walk'/'Cut Dead'/'In A Hole'/'Taste Of Cindy'/'Never Understand'/

'Inside Me'/'Sowing Seeds'/'My Little Underground'/'You Trip Me Up'/
'Something's Wrong'/'It's So Hard'

The 1986 CD release also contains the track 'Some Candy Talking'.

The 2011 reissue included the following extra CD/DVD:

'Upside Down'/'Vegetable Man'/'In A Hole' (John Peel radio session, 23 October 1984)/'You Trip Me Up' (John Peel radio session, 23 October 1984)/'Never Understand' (John Peel radio session, 23 October 1984)/'Taste The Floor' (John Peel radio session, 23 October 1984)/'The Living End' (John Peel radio session, 3 February 1985)/'Inside Me' (John Peel radio session, 3 February 1985)/'Just Like Honey' (John Peel radio session, 3 February 1985)/'Some Candy Talking' (John Peel radio session, 29 October 1985)/'Psychocandy' (John Peel radio session, 29 October 1985)/'You Trip Me Up' (John Peel radio session, 29 October 1985)/'Cut Dead' (John Peel radio session, 29 October 1985)/'Up Too High' (Portastudio demo, 1984/85)/'Upside Down' (Portastudio demo, 1984/85)/'Never Understand' (Portastudio demo, 1984/85)/'Taste the Floor' (Portastudio demo, 1984/85)/'In A Hole' (Portastudio demo, 1984/85)/'Something's Wrong' (Portastudio demo, 1984/85)/'Just Like Honey' (demo version, October 1984)/'The Living End' (Alaska Studios demo, June 1985)/'My Little Underground'/'Never Understand (Alternate Version)'/'Jesus Fuck'

DVD:

'Never Understand' (music video)/'You Trip Me Up' (music video)/'Just Like Honey' (music video)/'In A Hole' (*Old Grey Whistle Test*, 12 March 1985)/'Riot At North London Polytechnic – Interview And Live Clips' (The New Music, 15 March 1985)/'Interview' (VRT, Belgium, 17 March 1985)/'Never Understand' (VRT, Belgium, 17 March 1985)/'Just Like Honey' (*The Tube*, 11 November 1985)/'Inside Me' (*The Tube*, 11 November 1985)

Darklands
Released: August 1987
Labels: Blanco Y Negro, Warner Bros
Peak chart position: UK 5; US 161
Certification: Gold (UK)

Personnel:
Jim Reid – vocals (tracks 2–4, 6–8, 10), guitar, bass, drum machine programming/William Reid – vocals (tracks 1, 5, 9), guitar, bass, drum machine programming, production

Additional personnel:
Bill Price – production (tracks 1, 3, 4, 6, 8, 9)/John Loder – production (tracks 5, 7, 10)/Helen Backhouse – design/Andrew Catlin – photography/John Maybury – photography/Tim Broad – photography

Track listing:
'Darklands'/'Deep One Perfect Morning'/'Happy When It Rains'/'Down On Me'/'Nine Million Rainy Days'/'April Skies'/'Fall'/'Cherry Came Too'/'On The Wall'/'About You'

Automatic
Released: September 1989
Labels: Blanco Y Negro, Warner Bros
Peak chart position: UK 11; US 105
Certification: Silver (UK)

Personnel:
The Jesus and Mary Chain/Jim Reid – vocals (tracks 2, 4–10), guitar, synthesizer, drum programming, production/William Reid – vocals (tracks 1, 3, 11), guitar, synthesizer, drum programming, production

Additional personnel:
Alan Moulder – engineer/Jamie Harley – recording assistant/Lee Curle – recording assistant/Dick Meaney – mixing assistant/Richard Thomas – drums on 'Gimme Hell'/Ryan Art – design/Steve Mitchell – photography/Andrew Catlin – photography

Track listing:
'Here Comes Alice'/'Coast To Coast'/'Blues From A Gun'/'Between Planets'/'UV Ray'/'Her Way Of Praying'/'Head On'/'Take It'/'Halfway To Crazy'/'Gimme Hell'/'Drop' (not on original vinyl release)

Honey's Dead
Released: March 1992
Labels: Blanco Y Negro, Def American
Peak chart position: UK 14; US 158

Personnel:
Jim Reid – vocals (tracks 1–3, 5–6, 8), guitar, producer/William Reid – vocals (tracks 4, 7, 9–12), guitar, producer/Steve Monti – drums, percussion

Additional personnel:
Alan Moulder – engineer (except track 9), mixing/Flood – engineer (track 9)/Andy Catlin – photography

Track listing:
'Reverence'/'Teenage Lust'/'Far Gone And Out'/'Almost Gold'/'Sugar Ray'/'Tumbledown'/'Catchfire'/'Good For My Soul'/'Rollercoaster'/'I Can't Get Enough'/'Sundown'/'Frequency'

Stoned & Dethroned
Released: 23 August 1994
Labels: Blanco Y Negro, Def American
Peak chart position: UK 13; US 98

Personnel:
Jim Reid – vocals (tracks 1–4, 6, 8, 10, 13–15), guitar, bass, production/William Reid – vocals (tracks 5, 7, 9–14, 16–17), guitar, production/Ben Lurie – guitar, harmonica, organ, bass/Steve Monti – drums, percussion

Additional personnel:
Hope Sandoval – vocals (track 3)/Shane MacGowan – vocals (track 12)/

Alan Moulder – engineer (tracks 1–2, 9, 11, 14), mixing (tracks 1–2, 7, 9, 13–14)/Dick Meaney – engineer (tracks 3–8, 10, 12–13, 15–17), mixing (tracks 3–6, 8, 10–12, 15–17)/Stylorouge – design/Sophie Muller – photography

Track listing (all written by William Reid unless otherwise stated): 'Dirty Water'/'Bullet Lovers'/'Sometimes Always'/'Come On' (Jim Reid)/'Between Us'/'Hole' (Jim Reid)/'Never Saw It Coming'/'She' (Jim Reid)/'Wish I Could'/'Save Me' (Jim Reid/William Reid)/'Till It Shines'/ 'God Help Me'/'Girlfriend'/'Everybody I Know'/'You've Been A Friend' (Jim Reid)/'These Days'/'Feeling Lucky'

Munki
Released: 9 June 1998
Labels: Creation, Sub Pop
Peak chart position: UK 47; US did not chart

Personnel:
Jim Reid – vocals (tracks 1–4, 6, 8, 10, 13–15), guitar, production/ William Reid – vocals (tracks 1–3, 5, 7, 9–14, 16–17), guitar, production/Ben Lurie – guitar, bass/Nick Sanderson – drums

Additional personnel:
Sister Vanilla – vocals (track 5)/Sean Lebon – vocals (track 5)/Hope Sandoval – vocals (track 6)/Terry Edwards – horns/Dick Meaney – mixing (tracks 1–7, 9–12, 14, 16–17)/Alan Moulder – mixing (tracks 8, 13, 15)/Nick Addison – additional mixing (track 6)

Track listing:
'I Love Rock'n'Roll' (Jim Reid)/'Birthday' (William Reid)/'Stardust Remedy' (Jim Reid)/'Fizzy' (William Reid)/'Moe Tucker' (Jim Reid)/ 'Perfume' (William Reid)/'Virtually Unreal' (Jim Reid)/ 'Degenerate' (William Reid)/'Cracking Up' (William Reid)/'Commercial' (William Reid)/'Supertramp' (Jim Reid)/'Never Understood' (William Reid)/'I Can't Find The Time For Times' (William Reid)/'Man On The Moon' (Jim Reid)/'Black' (William Reid)/'Dream Lover' (Jim Reid)/'I Hate Rock'n'Roll' (William Reid)

LIVE ALBUMS

Live In Concert
Released: 25 May 2003
Label: Strange Fruit

Track listing:
'Catch Fire'/'Blues From A Gun'/'Head On'/'Reverence'/'Far Gone And Out'/'Half Way To Crazy'/'Sidewalking'/'Reverence'/'Snakedriver'/'Come On' (Jim Reid)/'Happy When It Rains'/'Teenage Lust'/'The Perfect Crime' (Jim Reid)/'Everybody I Know' (William Reid)/'Girlfriend' (William Reid)/'Hole' (Jim Reid)/'Head On'/'Sugar Ray'/'I Hate Rock'n'Roll' (William Reid)

COMPILATION ALBUMS

Barbed Wire Kisses
Released: April 1988
Labels: Blanco Y Negro, Warner Bros.
Peak chart position: UK 9; US 192
Certification: Gold (UK)

Personnel:
Jim Reid – vocals, guitar, production/William Reid – vocals, guitar, production

Additional personnel:
John Loder – production/Helen Backhouse – design/Andrew Catlin – photography

Track listing, LP:
'Kill Surf City'/'Head'/'Rider'/'Hit'/'Don't Ever Change'/'Just Out of Reach'/'Happy Place'/'Psychocandy'/'Sidewalking'/'Who Do You Love?' (Bo Diddley)/'Surfin' USA' (Chuck Berry/Brian Wilson)/'Everything's

Alright When You're Down'/'Upside Down'/'Taste Of Cindy (Acoustic)'/
'Swing'/'On The Wall (Demo)'

Extra tracks on CD:
'Cracked'/'Here It Comes Again'/'Mushroom (Live 1986)' (Can
[band])/'Bo Diddley Is Jesus'

The Sound Of Speed
Released: August 1993
Labels: Blanco Y Negro, Warner Bros.
Peak chart position: UK 15; US did not chart

Personnel:
Jim Reid – vocals, guitar, production/William Reid – vocals, guitar,
production, engineer (tracks 11–14, 16, 18–19)/Ben Lurie – bass (track
1), guitar (track 15)/Nick Sanderson – drums (tracks 1, 8)

Additional personnel:
Brad Davidson – bass (track 15)/Wiff – drums (track 15)/Dick Meaney
– engineer (tracks 1, 3, 5, 6, 8–10, 15)/Anjali Dutt – engineer (track 2)/
George Kaleve – engineer (track 4)/Alan Moulder – engineer (track 7)/
Flood – engineer (track 17)/John Loder – production (track 20)/Colin
Bell – photography

Track listing:
'Snakedriver'/'Reverence (Radio Mix)'/'Heat'/'Teenage Lust (acoustic
version)'/'Why'd You Want Me?'/'Don't Come Down'/'Guitarman'
(Jerry Reed/ Hubbard)/'Something I Can't Have'/'Sometimes'/'Write
Record Release Blues'/'Shimmer'/'Penetration'/'My Girl' (Smokey
Robinson)/'Tower Of Song' (Leonard Cohen)/'Little Red Rooster'
(Willie Dixon)/'Break Me Down'/'Lowlife'

Additional tracks on CD version:
'Deviant Slice'/'Reverberation' (Roky Erickson, Tommy Hall, Stacy
Sutherland)/'Sidewalking (Extended Version)'

The Jesus And Mary Chain Hate Rock'n'Roll
Released: September 1995
Label: Def American
Peak chart position: did not chart

Personnel:
Jim Reid – vocals, guitar, production/William Reid – vocals, guitar, production, engineer (track 7)/Ben Lurie – bass/Nick Sanderson – drums (tracks 1–6)/Steve Monti – drums (tracks 9–11)

Additional personnel:
Dick Meaney – engineer (tracks 1–6, 11)/Nick Addison – engineer (tracks 8–10)/Martin Schmeize – engineer (track 12)

Track listing:
'I Hate Rock'n'Roll' (William Reid)/'Snakedriver'/'Something I Can't Have'/'Bleed Me' (Jim Reid)/'33⅓' (Jim Reid)/'Lost Star' (William Reid)/ 'Penetration'/'New York City' (William Reid)/'Taking It Away' (Ben Lurie)/'I'm In With The Out Crowd' (Jim Reid)/'Little Stars' (William Reid)/'Teenage Lust (Desdemoana Mix)'/'Perfect Crime' (William Reid)

The Complete John Peel Sessions
Released: February 2000
Label: Strange Fruit
Peak chart position: did not chart

Personnel:
Jim Reid – vocals/William Reid – guitar/Douglas Hart – bass (tracks 1–7, 15–21)/Bobby Gillespie – drums (tracks 1–7)

Additional personnel:
Karen Parker – backing vocals (tracks 5–7)/Mark Radcliffe – production (tracks 1–4)/Dale 'Buffin' Griffin – production (tracks 5–14, 19–21)/Mike Robinson – production (tracks 15–18)/Mike Engels – engineer (tracks 5–7, 19–21)/Dave Dade – engineer (tracks 12–14)/ Mike Robinson – engineer (tracks 1–4, 15–18)/Simon Clifford – engineer (tracks 12–14)

Track listing:
'In A Hole'/'You Trip Me Up'/'Never Understand'/'Taste the Floor'/
'The Living End'/'Inside Me'/'Just Like Honey'/'Some Candy Talking'/
'Psychocandy'/'You Trip Me Up'/'Cut Dead'/'Fall'/'In The Rain'/
'Happy Place'/'Sidewalking'/'Coast To Coast'/'Take It'/'My Girl'
(Smokey Robinson/Ronald White)/'Far Gone And Out'/'Silverblade'/
'Here Comes Alice'

Tracks 1–4 recorded 23 October 1984
Tracks 5–7 recorded 3 February 1985
Tracks 8–11 recorded 29 October 1985
Tracks 12–14 recorded 25 November 1986
Tracks 15–18 recorded 31 May 1988
Tracks 19–21 recorded 26 November 1989

In 1985 John Peel's listeners voted The Jesus and Mary Chain 1st
('Never Understand'), 2nd ('Just Like Honey') and 12th ('You Trip Me
Up') in his annual Festive Fifty.

21 Singles
Released: July 2002
Label: Rhino
Peak chart position: UK 117; US did not chart

Track listing:
'Upside Down'/'Never Understand'/'You Trip Me Up'/'Just Like
Honey'/'Some Candy Talking'/'April Skies'/'Happy When It Rains'/
'Darklands'/'Sidewalking'/'Blues From A Gun'/'Head On'/
'Rollercoaster'/'Reverence'/'Far Gone And Out'/'Almost Gold'/
'Snakedriver'/'Sometimes Always' (William Reid)/'Come On' (Jim
Reid)/'I Hate Rock'n'Roll' (William Reid)/'Cracking Up' (William
Reid)/'I Love Rock'n'Roll' (Jim Reid)

The Power Of Negative Thinking: B-Sides & Rarities
Released: September 2008
Labels: WEA, Rhino
Peak chart position: did not chart

Track listings:

Disc 1

'Up Too High' (Demo '83) (William Reid)/'Upside Down' (Jim Reid/William Reid)/'Vegetable Man' (Syd Barrett)/'Suck' (Jim Reid/William Reid)/'Ambition' (Vic Godard)/'Just Out Of Reach' (Jim Reid/William Reid)/'Boyfriend's Dead' (Jim Reid/William Reid)/'Head' (Jim Reid/William Reid)/'Just Like Honey' (Demo October '84) (Jim Reid/William Reid)/'Cracked' (Jim Reid/William Reid)/'Taste Of Cindy' (Acoustic version) (Jim Reid/William Reid)/'The Hardest Walk' (Jim Reid/William Reid)/'Never Understand' (Alternate take) (Jim Reid/William Reid)/'My Little Underground' (Demo version) (Jim Reid/William Reid)/'The Living End' (Demo version) (Jim Reid/William Reid)/'Some Candy Talking' (Jim Reid/William Reid)/'Psychocandy' (Jim Reid/William Reid)/'Hit' (Jim Reid/William Reid)/'Cut Dead' (Acoustic version) (Jim Reid/William Reid)/'You Trip Me Up' (Acoustic version) (Jim Reid/William Reid)/'Walk and Crawl' (Jim Reid/William Reid)

Disc 2

'Kill Surf City' (Jim Reid/William Reid)/'Bo Diddley Is Jesus' (Jim Reid/William Reid)/'Who Do You Love?' (Ellas McDaniel ['Bo Diddley'])/'Everything's Alright When You're Down' (Jim Reid/William Reid)/'Shake' (Jim Reid/William Reid)/'Happy When It Rains' (Demo version) (Jim Reid/William Reid)/'Happy Place' (Jim Reid/William Reid)/'F. Hole' (Jim Reid/William Reid)/'Rider' (Jim Reid/William Reid)/'On The Wall' (Portastudio demo) (Jim Reid/William Reid)/'Surfin' USA' (Chuck Berry/Brian Wilson)/'Here It Comes Again' (Jim Reid/William Reid)/'Don't Ever Change' (Jim Reid/William Reid)/'Swing' (Jim Reid/William Reid)/'Sidewalking' (Jim Reid/William Reid)/'Surfin' USA' (Summer Mix) (Berry/Wilson)/'Shimmer' (Jim Reid/William Reid)/'Penetration' (Jim Reid/William Reid)/'Break Me Down' (Jim Reid/William Reid)/'Subway' (Jim Reid/William Reid)/'My Girl' (Smokey Robinson/Ronald White)

Disc 3

'In The Black' (Jim Reid/William Reid)/'Terminal Beach' (Jim Reid/William Reid)/'Deviant Slice' (Jim Reid/William Reid)/'I'm Glad I

Never' (Lee Hazlewood)/'Drop' (Acoustic remix) (Jim Reid/William Reid)/'Rollercoaster' (Jim Reid/William Reid)/'Silverblade' (Jim Reid/William Reid)/'Lowlife' (Jim Reid/William Reid)/'Tower Of Song' Leonard Cohen/'Heat' (Jim Reid/William Reid)/'Guitarman' (Hubbard/Jerry Reed)/'Why'd You Want Me' (Jim Reid/William Reid)/'Sometimes' (Jim Reid/William Reid)/'Teenage Lust' (Acoustic version) (Jim Reid/William Reid)/'Reverberation (Doubt)' (Roky Erickson/Tommy Hall/Stacy Sutherland)/'Don't Come Down' (Jim Reid/William Reid)/'Snakedriver' (Jim Reid/William Reid)/'Something I Can't Have' (Jim Reid/William Reid)/'Write Record Release Blues' (Jim Reid/William Reid)/'Little Red Rooster' (Chester Arthur Burnett/Willie Dixon)

Disc 4
'The Perfect Crime' (Jim Reid)/'Little Stars' (William Reid)/'Drop' (Re-recorded) (William Reid)/'I'm In With The Out Crowd' (Jim Reid)/'New York City' (William Reid)/'Taking It Away' (Ben Lurie)/'Ghost Of A Smile' (Shane MacGowan)/'Alphabet Street' (Prince)/'Coast To Coast' (Alternate, William vox) (Jim Reid/William Reid)/'Dirty Water' (Demo, William vox) (William Reid)/'Till I Found You' (Jim Reid/William Reid)/'Bleed Me' (Jim Reid)/'33⅓' (Jim Reid)/'Lost Star' (William Reid)/'Hide Myself' (Jim Reid)/'Rocket' (Ben Lurie)/'Easylife, Easylove' (Jim Reid)/'40,000k' (Jim Reid)/'Nineteen 666' (Dick Meaney/William Reid)/'Some Candy Talking' (Acoustic version; iTunes US bonus track) (Jim Reid/William Reid)

Upside Down: The Best Of The Jesus And Mary Chain
Released: September 2010
Labels: Music Club Deluxe
Peak chart position: did not chart

Track listing, disc one:
'Just Like Honey'/'April Skies'/'Blues From A Gun'/'Far Gone And Out'/'Some Candy Talking'/'Come On'/'Head On'/'I Love Rock'n'Roll'/'All Things Must Pass'/'Reverence'/'Sidewalking'/'Cracking Up'/'Upside Down'/'Never Understand'/'The Hardest Walk'/'Happy When It Rains'/'The Perfect Crime'/'Sometimes Always'/'Almost Gold'/'Darklands'/'45 RPM'/'Head'

Disc two:
'Half Way To Crazy'/'You Trip Me Up'/'Rollercoaster'/'Birthday'/
'Happy Place'/'Something I Can't Have'/'I Hate Rock'n'Roll'/'Tower
Of Song'/'Vegetable Man'/'In A Hole'/'Kill Surf City'/'33⅓'/'Cherry
Came Too'/'Between Planets'/'Moe Tucker'/'Little Stars'/'God Help
Me'/'New York City'/'Nine Million Rainy Days'/'Drop'/'Black'/
'Psychocandy'

EPS

'Some Candy Talking'
Released: July 1986
Label: Blanco Y Negro
Peak chart position: UK 13; Ireland 11

Personnel:
Jim Reid – vocals, producer/William Reid – guitar, producer/Douglas
Hart – bass/Bobby Gillespie – drums

Additional personnel:
Flood – engineer ('Some Candy Talking')/John Loder – engineer
('Psychocandy', 'Hit', 'Taste of Cindy')/Alan Moulder – assistant engi-
neer ('Some Candy Talking')/Phil Ward-Large – producer ('Cut Dead
(Acoustic)', 'Psychocandy (Acoustic)', 'You Trip Me Up (Acoustic)',
'Some Candy Talking (Acoustic)')

Track listing, 7-inch:
'Some Candy Talking'/'Psychocandy'/'Hit'

2×7-inch:
'Some Candy Talking'/'Psychocandy'/'Hit'/'Cut Dead (Acoustic)'/
'Psychocandy (Acoustic)'/'You Trip Me Up (Acoustic)'/'Some Candy
Talking (Acoustic)'

12-inch:
'Some Candy Talking'/'Taste Of Cindy'/'Hit'/'Psychocandy'

'Happy When It Rains'
Released: August 1987
Label: Blanco Y Negro
Peak chart position: UK 25; Ireland 25

Personnel:
Jim Reid – vocals, guitar/William Reid – guitar, producer

Additional personnel:
Bill Price – producer ('Happy When It Rains')/John Loder – producer ('Shake', 'Everything's Alright When You're Down'), backing vocals ('Everything's Alright When You're Down')/Linda Reid – design/Helen Backhouse – design

Track listing, 7-inch:
'Happy When It Rains'/'Everything's Alright When You're Down'

7-inch limited box with postcards:
'Happy When It Rains'/'Everything's Alright When You're Down'/ 'Shake'

10-inch:
'Happy When It Rains'/'Shake'/'Everything's Alright When You're Down'/'Happy When It Rains (Demo)'

12-inch:
'Happy When It Rains'/'Shake'/'Happy Place'/'F-Hole'

'Darklands'
Released: October 1987
Label: Blanco Y Negro
Peak chart position: UK 33; Ireland 23

Personnel:
Jim Reid – vocals, guitar/William Reid – vocals, guitar, producer

Additional personnel:
Bill Price – producer ('Darklands')/John Loder – producer ('Rider', 'Here It Comes Again')/Linda Reid – design/Helen Backhouse – design

Track listing, 7-inch:
'Darklands'/'Rider'/'On The Wall (Portastudio Demo)'

10-inch:
'Darklands'/'Rider'/'Here It Comes Again'/'On The Wall (Portastudio Demo)'

12-inch:
'Darklands'/'Rider'/'Surfin' USA' (Chuck Berry/Brian Wilson)/'On The Wall (Portastudio Demo)'

'Rollercoaster'
Released: September 1990
Label: Blanco Y Negro
Peak chart position: UK 46; Ireland 25

Personnel:
Jim Reid – vocals, guitar, producer/William Reid – guitar, producer, engineer (track 4)

Additional personnel:
Flood – engineer (tracks 1–3)/Ian Cooper – mastering

Track listing, 7-inch, 12-inch, CD and cassette:
'Rollercoaster'/'Silverblade'/'Lowlife'/'Tower Of Song' (Leonard Cohen)

'The Peel Sessions'
Released: September 1991
Label: Strange Fruit
Peak chart position: did not chart

Personnel:
The Jesus and Mary Chain

Additional personnel:
Dale 'Buffin' Griffin – producer (tracks 1–3)/Mike Engels – engineer (tracks 1–3)/Dave Dade – producer (tracks 4–6)/Simon Clifford – engineer (tracks 4–6)/Don Walker – mastering

Track listing, 12-inch and CD:
'Inside Me'/'The Living End'/'Just Like Honey'/'Fall'/'Happy Place'/'In The Rain (About You)'

Tracks 1–3 recorded 3 February 1985
Tracks 4–5 recorded 25 November 1986

'Sound Of Speed'
Released: July 1993
Label: Blanco Y Negro
Peak chart position: UK 30; Ireland did not chart

Personnel:
Jim Reid – vocals, guitar, producer/William Reid – vocal, guitar, producer

Additional personnel
Dick Meaney – engineer

Track listing, 7-inch, 10-inch and CD:
'Snakedriver'/'Something I Can't Have'/'Write Record Release Blues'/'Little Red Rooster' (Willie Dixon)

SINGLES

'Upside Down'
(non-album single) (Jim Reid/William Reid)
Released: November 1984
Label: Creation Records
Peak chart position: did not chart

Personnel:
Jim Reid – vocals, producer/William Reid – guitar, producer/Douglas Hart – bass/Murray Dalglish – drums

Additional personnel:
Alan McGee – producer (track 1)/Joe Foster – producer (track 2)/Pat Collier – engineer

B-side: 'Vegetable Man' (Syd Barrett)

'Never Understand'
(Jim Reid/William Reid)
From *Psychocandy*
Released: February 1985
Label: Blanco Y Negro
Peak chart position: UK 47

Personnel:
Jim Reid – vocals, producer/William Reid – guitar, producer/Douglas Hart – bass, producer/Bobby Gillespie – drums, producer

John Loder – engineer

Track listing, 7-inch:
'Never Understand'/'Suck'

12-inch:
'Never Understand'/'Suck'/'Ambition' (Vic Godard)

'You Trip Me Up'
(Jim Reid/William Reid)
From *Psychocandy*
Released: May 1985
Label: Blanco Y Negro
Peak chart position: UK 55

Personnel:
Jim Reid – vocals, producer/William Reid – guitar, producer/Douglas
Hart – bass, producer/Bobby Gillespie – drums, producer

Additional personnel:
John Loder – engineer/Pat Collier – mixing

Track listing, 7-inch:
'You Trip Me Up'/'Just Out of Reach'

12-inch:
'You Trip Me Up'/'Just Out Of Reach'/'Boyfriend's Dead'

'Just Like Honey'
(Jim Reid/William Reid)
From *Psychocandy*
Released: September 1985
Label: Blanco Y Negro
Peak chart position: UK 45

Personnel:
Jim Reid – vocals, producer/William Reid – guitar, producer/Douglas
Hart – bass, producer/Bobby Gillespie – drums, producer

Additional personnel:
Karen Parker – backing vocals/John Loder – engineer

Track listing, 7-inch:
'Just Like Honey'/'Head'

2 x 7-inch gatefold:
'Just Like Honey'/'Head'/'Inside Me'/'Just Like Honey (Demo)'

12-inch:
'Just Like Honey'/'Head'/'Cracked'/'Just Like Honey (Demo)'

'April Skies'
(Jim Reid/William Reid)
From *Darklands*
Released: April 1987
Peak chart position: UK 8; Ireland 6

Personnel:
Jim Reid – vocals, guitar/William Reid – guitar, producer

Additional personnel:
Bill Price – producer (track 1)/John Loder – producer (tracks 2–4)/
Linda Reid – design/Helen Backhouse – design

Track listing, 7-inch:
'April Skies'/'Kill Surf City'

2 x 7-inch gatefold:
'April Skies'/'Kill Surf City'/'Mushroom (Live)' (Can [band])/'Bo
Diddley Is Jesus'

12-inch:
'April Skies'/'Kill Surf City'/'Who Do You Love?' (Bo Diddley)

'Happy When It Rains'
(Jim Reid/William Reid)
From *Darklands*
Released: August 1987
Peak chart position: UK 25; Ireland 15

Personnel:
Jim Reid – vocals, guitar/William Reid – guitar, producer

Additional personnel:
Bill Price – producer ('Happy When It Rains')/John Loder – producer
('Shake', 'Everything's Alright When You're Down'), backing vocals
('Everything's Alright When You're Down')/Linda Reid – design/Helen
Backhouse – design

Track listing, 7-inch:
'Happy When It Rains'/'Everything's Alright When You're Down'

7-inch limited box with postcards:
'Happy When It Rains'/'Everything's Alright When You're Down'/
'Shake'

10-inch, 'Happy When It Rains E.P.':
'Happy When It Rains'/'Shake'/'Everything's Alright When You're
Down'/'Happy When It Rains (Demo)'

12-inch:
'Happy When It Rains'/'Shake'/'Happy Place'/'F-Hole'

'Darklands'
(Jim Reid/William Reid)
From *Darklands*
Released: October 1987
Peak chart position: UK 33; Ireland 23

Personnel:
Jim Reid – vocals, guitar/William Reid – vocals, guitar, producer

Additional personnel:
Bill Price – producer ('Darklands')/John Loder – producer ('Rider',
'Here It Comes Again')/Linda Reid – design/Helen Backhouse – design

Track listing, 7-inch:
'Darklands'/'Rider'/'On The Wall (Portastudio Demo)'

10-inch and CD single, 'Darklands E.P.':
'Darklands'/'Rider'/'Here It Comes Again'/'On The Wall (Portastudio
Demo)'

12-inch:
'Darklands'/'Rider'/'Surfin' U.S.A.' (Chuck Berry/Brian Wilson)/'On
The Wall (Portastudio Demo)'

'Sidewalking'
(Jim Reid/William Reid)
Released: March 1988
Peak chart position: UK 30; Ireland 20

Personnel:
Jim Reid – vocals, guitar, producer/William Reid – guitar, producer

Additional personnel:
John Loder – producer/Westwood One – engineer (live tracks)/Helen Backhouse – design/Andrew Catlin – photography

Track listing, 7-inch:
'Sidewalking'/'Taste Of Cindy (Live)'

12-inch:
'Sidewalking (Extended)'/'Sidewalking (Short)'/'Taste Of Cindy (Recorded Live in Detroit)'/'April Skies (Recorded Live in Detroit)'

CD:
'Sidewalking (Short)'/'Sidewalking (Extended)'/'Taste Of Cindy (Recorded Live in Detroit)'/'Sidewalking (Chilled To The Bone)'

'Blues From A Gun'
(Jim Reid/William Reid)
From *Automatic*
Released: September 1989
Peak chart position: UK 32; Ireland 15; US Modern Rock Tracks 1

Personnel:
Jim Reid – guitar, synthesizer, drum programming, producer/William Reid – vocals, guitar, synthesizer, drum programming, producer

Additional personnel:
Alan Moulder – engineer (track 1)/Andrew Catlin – photography

Track listing, 7-inch:
'Blues From A Gun'/'Shimmer'

10-inch gatefold:
'Blues From A Gun'/'Shimmer'/'Penetration'/'Break Me Down'

12-inch:
'Blues From A Gun'/'Shimmer'/'Penetration'/'Subway'

CD:
'Blues From A Gun'/'Shimmer'/'Penetration'/'My Girl' (Smokey Robinson/Ronald White)

'Head On'
(Jim Reid/William Reid)
From *Automatic*
Released: November 1990 in seven different formats over a period of weeks, one of which included a box to contain the full set.
Peak chart position: UK 57; US Modern Rock Tracks 2

Personnel:
Jim Reid – vocals, guitar, synthesizer, drum programming, producer/
William Reid – guitar, synthesizer, drum programming, producer

Additional personnel:
Alan Moulder – engineer ('Head On', 'Drop')

Track listing, 7-inch:
'Head On'/'In The Black'

7-inch:
'Head On'/'Terminal Beach'

7-inch:
'Head On'/'Deviant Slice'

7-inch:
'Head On'/'I'm Glad I Never' (Lee Hazlewood)

12-inch:
'Head On'/'In The Black'/'Terminal Beach'

CD:
'Head On'/'In The Black'/'Drop (Acoustic Remix)'/'Break Me
Down'

Cassette:
'Head On'/'In The Black'

'Reverence'
(Jim Reid, William Reid)
From *Honey's Dead*
Released: February 1992
Peak chart position: UK 10

Personnel:
Jim Reid – vocals, guitar, producer/William Reid – guitar, producer

Additional personnel:
Alan Moulder – engineering ('Reverence', 'Guitarman')/Dick Meaney
– engineering ('Heat')/Anjali Dutt – engineering ('Reverence (Radio
Mix)')/Al Jourgensen – remixing ('Reverence (Al Jourgensen Mix)')/
Mark Stent – remixing ('Reverence (Mark Stent Mix)')

Track listing, 7-inch and cassette:
'Reverence'/'Heat'

12-inch and CD single:
'Reverence'/'Heat'/'Reverence (Radio Mix)'/'Guitarman' (Jerry Reed/
Hubbard)

Def American CD single:
'Reverence (Album Version)'/'Reverence (Jim and William Reid Mix)'/

'Reverence (Al Jourgensen Mix)'/'Reverence (Mark Stent Mix)'/
'Guitarman' (Jerry Reed/ Hubbard)

'Far Gone And Out'
(Jim Reid/William Reid)
From *Honey's Dead*
Released: April 1992
Peak chart position: UK 23; US Modern Rock Tracks 3

Personnel:
Jim Reid – vocals, guitar, producer/William Reid – guitar, producer

Additional personnel:
Alan Moulder – engineering ('Far Gone And Out')/Dick Meaney –
engineering ('Sometimes', 'Why'd You Want Me?')/Al Jourgensen
– remixing ('Reverence (Al Jourgensen Mix)')/George Drakoulias –
remixing ('Far Gone And Out (Arc Weld Mix)')

Track listing, 7-inch:
'Far Gone And Out'/'Why'd You Want Me?'

12-inch:
'Far Gone And Out'/'Sometimes'/'Why'd You Want Me?'

12-inch box with insert and postcards:
'Far Gone And Out'/'Reverence (Al Jourgensen Mix)'/'Sometimes'/
'Why'd You Want Me?'

CD-s holographic disc:
'Far Gone And Out'/'Far Gone And Out (Arc Weld Mix)'/'Sometimes'/
'Why'd You Want Me?'

'Almost Gold'
(Jim Reid/William Reid)
From *Honey's Dead*
Released: June 1992
Peak chart position: UK 41; US Modern Rock Tracks 13

Personnel:
Jim Reid – vocals, guitar, producer/William Reid – vocals, guitar, producer

Additional personnel:
Alan Moulder – engineer ('Almost Gold')/Georg Kaleve – engineer ('Teenage Lust (Acoustic Version)')/Dick Meaney – engineer ('Don't Come Down')/Mark Radcliffe – producer (live tracks)/Greg Jakobek – design

Track listing, 7-inch:
'Almost Gold'/'Teenage Lust (Acoustic Version)'

10-inch:
'Almost Gold'/'Catchfire (Live)'/'Blues From A Gun (Live)'/'Head On (Live)'

12-inch and CD-s:
'Almost Gold'/'Teenage Lust (Acoustic Version)'/'Reverberation (Doubt)' (Roky Erickson/Tommy Hall/Stacy Sutherland)/'Don't Come Down'
Live tracks recorded by the BBC at the Sheffield Arena on 14 May 1992.

'Sometimes Always'
(William Reid)
From *Stoned & Dethroned*
Released: July 1994
Peak chart position: UK 22; US Hot 100 96; US Modern Rock Tracks 4

Personnel:
Jim Reid – vocals, guitar, producer/William Reid – guitar, producer

Additional personnel
Hope Sandoval – vocals/Dick Meaney – engineer

Track listing, 7-inch:
'Sometimes Always' (William Reid)/'The Perfect Crime' (Jim Reid)

10-inch, 12-inch and CD-s:
'Sometimes Always' (William Reid)/'The Perfect Crime' (Jim Reid)/
'Little Stars' (William Reid)/'Drop Re-Recorded' (William Reid)

'Come On'
(Jim Reid)
From *Stoned & Dethroned*
Released: October 1994
Peak chart position: UK 52

Personnel:
Jim Reid – vocals, guitar, production/William Reid – guitar,
production

Additional personnel:
Dick Meaney – engineer/Nick Addison – engineer ('I'm In With The
Out Crowd')

Track listing, 7-inch:
'Come On'/'I'm In With The Out Crowd'

12-inch and CD:
'Come On'/'New York City' (William Reid)/'Taking It Away' (Ben
Lurie)/'I'm In With The Out Crowd'

CD:
'Come On'/'Ghost Of A Smile' (Shane MacGowan)/'Alphabet Street'
(Prince)/'A New Kind Of Kick (Live)' (Lux Interior/Ivy Rorschach)
Live track recorded at UC San Diego, California, USA, on 11 November
1992.

'I Hate Rock'n'Roll'
(William Reid)
From *I Hate Rock'n'Roll*
Released: May 1995
Peak chart position: UK 61

Personnel:
Jim Reid – vocals, guitar, production/William Reid – guitar, production/
Ben Lurie – bass, guitar/Nick Sanderson – drums

Additional personnel:
Dick Meaney – engineer

Track listing, numbered 10-inch and CD:
'I Hate Rock'n'Roll' (William Reid)/'Bleed Me' (Jim Reid)/'33⅓' (Jim
Reid)/'Lost Star' (William Reid)

'Cracking Up'
(William Reid)
From *Munki*
Released: April 1998
Peak chart position: UK 35

Personnel:
Jim Reid – vocals, guitar, production/William Reid – guitar, production/
Ben Lurie – bass, guitar/Nick Sanderson – drums

Additional personnel:
Dick Meaney – engineer

Track listing, 7-inch:
'Cracking Up'/'Rocket' (Ben Lurie)

CD:
'Cracking Up'/'Hide Myself' (Jim Reid)/'Rocket' (Lurie)/'Commercial'

'I Love Rock'n'Roll'
(Jim Reid)
From *Munki*
Released: May 1998
Peak chart position: UK 38

Personnel:
Jim Reid – vocals, guitar, production/William Reid – guitar, production/
Ben Lurie – bass, guitar/Nick Sanderson – drums

Additional personnel:
Dick Meaney – engineer

Track listing, 7-inch:
'I Love Rock'n'Roll'/'Nineteen666' (Dick Meaney/William Reid)

CD:
'I Love Rock'n'Roll'/'Easylife, Easylove'/'40,000K'/'Nineteen666'

VIDEO ALBUMS

The Jesus And Mary Chain
Released 1988
Label: Warner Music Vision

Videos: 198 –1989
Released: 1990
Label: Warner Music Japan

Credits

'At the volume Jesus and sons play at, anything is enervating and psychologically disorienting', live review by Ralph Traitor, December 1984, *Sounds*.

Sounds interview with Sandy Robertson, 9 February 1985.

'Like A Virgin', interview with John Robb for *ZigZag*, 1985.

'Don't you think it's quite funny that sound men don't understand the word treble?', William Reid interview conducted by Biba Kopf for *NME*, 16 February 1985.

'Jesus Wept', Max Bell for *The Face*, June 1985.

Interview with Jim and Douglas, *Picture Disc*, 1985.

'The Jaz and Maz boys continue to attach delightful thumbnail sketches . . .', 'You Trip Me Up' reviewed as *NME* Single of the Week, 1 June 1985.

'Sweet Things', Richard Lowe, *The Hit*, 26 October 1985.

'("Jesus Fuck") was just downright repulsion at how sacred the name Jesus was . . .', Jim Reid to *NME*'s Mat Snow, July 1986.

Jim: 'We took some time off because we were getting really pissed off with it. Just couldn't stand it . . .', *Smash Hits*, April 1987.

'Ch-Ch-Ch-Ch-Change-Jeez', Steve Sutherland for *RAM*, 18 May 1988.

'*Automatic* chops out all the crap bits of rock . . .', David Quantick, review of *Automatic* in *NME*, 1989.

Tokyo press conference with Jim and William Reid, 8 July 1992, interpreter: Steve Harris.

Alan Jackson, *Vox*, March 1992.

Miranda Sawyer, *Q* magazine, March 1992.

'Welcome To The Drugstore', David Cavanagh, *Select*, May 1992.

'So All Is Well With The Unholy Family . . .', *Honey's Dead* review, Stuart Maconie, *NME*, 21 March 1992.

'Stoned And Dethroned', *Melody Maker*, 16 July 1994.

Bradley Bardin, *Interview* magazine, December 1994.

Nina Malkin, *Raygun* magazine, September 1994.

Kevin Westerberg, *Melody Maker*, 1994.

'It Could Be Iggy Pop's Country Album . . .', David Quantick, review of *Stoned & Dethroned*, NME, August 1994.

'The Jesus and Mazzy Chain', Matt Hendrickson, *Rolling Stone*, 6 October 1994.

'Single Of The Moment – "I Hate Rock'n'Roll"', Jon Wiederhorn, *Rolling Stone*, 2 November 1995.

Rockin' On, Japan, August 1995.

'Reid All About It', David Belcher, *The Herald*, 3 April 1998

'Feedback to the Future', James Oldham, *NME*, 4 April 1998.

'Remember Indie? It's His Fault', James Duerden, *Q*, May 1998.

'On The Couch', Kitty Empire, *NME*, 23 May 1998.

'Backtalk With The Jesus And Mary Chain', Neva Chonin, *Option*, July 1998.

'It All Makes Sense', John Fortunato, *The Aquarian Weekly*, 8 July 1998.

Jason Jophes, *The Rocket*, 10 June 1998.

'Crash And Burn', Nick Hasted's interview with William Reid for *Uncut*, August 2000.

'I Thought You Were Dead', Simon Goddard, *Uncut*, December 2001.

John Moore 'In Search Of The Jesus And Mary Chain', John Moore, *The Guardian*, 2007.

'Scarlett Johansson Joined My Old Band', John Moore, *The Guardian*, 2008.

'Heaven And Hell', Jonathan Garrett's interview with Jim and William Reid, *Pitchfork*, 8 March 2009.

Dimitri Coats, *Goldmine* magazine, April 2010.

Jim Reid speaks to Thomas H Green, *The Arts Desk,* November 2010

Psychocandy 2012 reissue (Demon Music Group) liner notes.

Creation Stories, Alan McGee (Sidgwick & Jackson, 2013).

Index

and William's move to LA 211
and 'You Trip Me Up' video 92
Reid, Julie 216
Reid, Linda ('Sister Vanilla') 199,
    201–2, 203, 214–15
Reid, William
  accent of 119–20
  age of 41, 42, 44
  and alcohol 25, 29, 66, 79, 98,
    101, 106, 161–2, 185–6
  ambition of 64
  arguments with Jim 165–6, 207–8,
    217–18
  arrest of 205
  and artwork for *Munki* 200
  and *Automatic* recording session
    158
  and B-sides 148
  birth of 2
  and Blanco Y Negro deal 64
  breakdowns of 106, 185–6
  broken fuzz pedal 17
  buys first guitar 5
  closeness with Jim 2, 8–9
  clothes customisation 32
  confidence in Mary Chain 17, 91
  and Daisy Chain 16–18
  and Dalglish quitting 44
  and *Darklands* recording session
    131–4
  and *David Letterman Show* 175–6
  dead-end jobs of 5
  and death of Sanderson 221–2
  dole 'anniversary' 72
  domesticity of 214
  drug-taking of 33, 61, 91, 132,
    162, 175
  and Drugstore Studio 169–70

and drummer audition 24
education of 22
and Electric Ballroom gig 101, 102
and Estonia trip 154
fight with Lurie 207–8
and flight to Philadelphia 182–3
and Fulham flats 72–3
and grunge 185
guitar playing of 82, 168, 172
and guitarist auditions 159
and House of Blues gig 208–9
humour of 161–2
and ICA Rock Week gig 70
and Ice Cube 181
and Iggy Pop 157
insularity of 3, 10, 24, 42, 94
interviews
  Goldmine 93
  Interview 173
  Melody Maker 188, 190, 191
  NME 172
  Raygun 180
  Rolling Stone 196
  Select 109
  style of 59, 84
  Uncut 179, 186
  VOX 169–70
  ZigZag 42
and Jaffe 160
and Japan tour 165
and Jim's closeness with Lurie 182
and 'Just Like Honey' 93
and 'Kill Surf City' 149
and *Later . . . With Jools Holland*
    189–90
letter writing to local radio station
    31
and line-up choices 151–2